Guide to SPANISH Suffixes

Dorothy M. Devney

PASSPORT BOOKS
a division of NTC/CONTEMPORARY PUBLISHING COMPANY
Lincolnwood, Illinois USA

ABOUT THE AUTHOR

Dorothy M. Devney is a private Spanish instructor and the director of the Devney Spanish Group, a service which provides Spanish instructors, translators and interpreters to businesses and individuals in the Minneapolis-St. Paul area.

Ms. Devney holds degrees in Linguistics, Philosophy and Educational Administration. She has studied and lived in Colombia and has traveled widely throughout South America.

In addition to *Guide to Spanish Suffixes,* Ms. Devney has written *No-Fail Spanish,* a textbook/workbook for adults, and in the late 1980s she was commissioned to write two books, *Mi Primer Libro de Español* and *Mi Segundo Libro de Español,* for children studying Spanish.

Published by Passport Books
An imprint of NTC/Contemporary Publishing Company
4255 West Touhy Avenue, Lincolnwood (Chicago), Illinois 60646-1975 U.S.A.
Printed in the United States of America
International Standard Book Number: 0-8442-7323-6

7 8 9 0 VP 9 8 7 6 5 4

Dedication

To my parents,
Raymond and Verona Devney

ACKNOWLEDGMENTS

I would like to thank several people for their contributions to this book. Dr. Carol A. Klee, Associate Professor of Spanish at the University of Minnesota, gave me the encouragement needed to take on the endeavor of compiling this book and the assurance that such a text would be helpful to students and instructors. Dr. James M. May, Professor of Classics at St. Olaf College in Northfield, Minnesota, gave thoughtful attention to the Latin and Greek terms used. Dr. May's help went well beyond prevailing standards of academic generosity. Mitchell E. Blatt, M.D., reviewed the medical terms used and offered succinct definitions when needed. Joe Thurston set up the computer program for this book and stayed with the project through its final stage. Joe's patience and humor saved me from many technological crises and panics, and brought me into the twentieth century in the nick of time. Michael Ross, National Textbook Company's Editorial Director for Foreign Languages, was very supportive of this project, and his ideas for developing the book helped greatly. Finally, I wish to thank especially Lola Lorenzo, a native of Madrid, who considered every Spanish term in this book and whose suggestions and help vastly improved the work I had originally done. I reserve for myself sole responsibility for any errors. The contributions of these highly skilled people made the work involved in preparing this book a joy and I am honored to be associated with each of them.

CONTENTS

viii   Contents

INTRODUCTION

Far more than most modern languages, Spanish relies on suffixes to denote parts of speech, modify the word root, or even convey subtle nuances of meaning. This *Guide to Spanish Suffixes* will help expand your vocabulary and comprehension through mastery of the most common Spanish word endings.

Vocabulary building never ends, even in one's native language, but the task in a foreign language can overwhelm. Familiarity with the logic of Spanish word endings, however, promotes a geometric increase in vocabulary for each new term learned.

For example, most students learn *el papel* (paper) during the first weeks of study, but learning the suffixes resulting in such terms as *la papelería (stationery shop), la papelera* (waste basket; paper case), *el papelero* (paper-maker; stationer), *el papeleo* (paper work; red-tape) and e*l papelito* (small piece of paper), often comes much later. The suffixes involved -- *-ería, -era, -ero, -eo and -ito* -- will often be helpful in expanding the use of other basic terms as you learn them.

The dictionary too often has been the tool of necessity in vocabulary building, and everyone finds, at least from time to time, that its use can be tedious or frustrating. I compiled this book in order to make the job of building your vocabulary easier and more interesting, as well as to encourage the confident use of familiar word roots in new and adventurous ways.

You will find that armed with a basic knowledge of Spanish terms—those covered in most first-year courses—and an awareness of Spanish suffixes, you will be able both to recognize and create new terms: you will become more self-reliant and less threatened by Spanish literature and conversation. I'm not suggesting that you can put your dictionary out of easy reach, but you can give it a rest.

As far as I have been able to determine, this book is unique. Information on Spanish suffixes can be found here and there in various texts; but typically only a handful of endings are given, with few examples and little or no analysis.

This book contains well over 100 Spanish suffixes, which I chose on the basis of their frequent recurrence throughout the language. Some endings are far more common than others, but all are found in words you will encounter in everyday usage.

The suffixes are arranged alphabetically and appear at the top of cach page, along with the important features of each particular ending: (1) its meaning; (2) its English equivalent (when one exists); and (3) the part(s) of speech of the words formed.

This basic information is followed by a short paragraph which discusses the meaning of the particular suffix, how words employing it are formed, and interesting features and/or unusual constructions characteristic of that particular ending. Where appropriate, idiomatic or vernacular applications also are discussed.

Next, you will find an illustrative list of words taking the suffix. Along with this list you are given the English equivalent of each term and the stem to which it is related (many of which you probably already know), as well as that stem's English equivalent. When a term refers to a person I give only the masculine form in order to emphasize the word; however, formation of its feminine counterpart always is discussed in the paragraph preceding the list.

Most of the formed terms given in this book are related to other Spanish terms; however, some words come directly from Latin or Greek. When this is the case, these terms are noted accordingly. In addition, when a term appears that is used only in a specific context, e.g., technically or colloquially, this also is noted. Please consult the listing of abbreviations for these notations.

You will also find on the bottom of nearly every page examples of Spanish idiomatic expressions which employ several terms found on that page. These expressions, many of which are earthy or colorful, indicate the context in which to use these terms.

At the end of this book is an index that allows you to find a specific suffix according to its part of speech, most often nouns and adjectives.

I sincerely hope that this book will enable you to read, write and speak Spanish with greater confidence and enjoyment.

Dorothy M. Devney

ABBREVIATIONS

(adj.)	adjective	*(gram.)*	grammatical
(adv.)	adverb	*(Gr.)*	Greek
(aer.)	aeronautical	*(hort.)*	horticulture
(anat.)	anatomy	*(ichth.)*	ichthyology
(arch.)	architecture	*(interj.)*	interjection
(astron.)	astronomy	*(joc.)*	jocular
(Bib.)	Bible	*(Lat.)*	Latin
(biol.)	biology	*(lit.)*	literally
(bot.)	botany	*(m.)*	masculine
(build.)	building	*(math.)*	mathematics
(chem.)	chemistry	*(med.)*	medicine
(coll.)	colloquial	*(mus.)*	music
(com.)	commerce	*(n.)*	noun
(contempt.)	contemptuous	*(naut.)*	nautical
(dent.)	dentistry	*(obs.)*	obsolete
(eccles.)	ecclesiastic	*(orn.)*	ornithological
(ent.)	entymology	*(polit.)*	politics
(elec.)	electrical	*(prov.)*	provincial
(f.)	feminine	*(sl.)*	slang
(fam.)	familiar	*(v.)*	verb
(fig.)	figuratively	*(vet.)*	veterinarian
(geog.)	geography	*(zool.)*	zoology
(geom.)	geometry		

-a

Meaning: *resulting object; resulting action*
English equivalent: none
Found in: nouns

There are thousands of Spanish words that end in -a; but what makes these words distinctive is that they all are derived from -ar verbs: -er and -ir verbs use different suffixes to indicate resulting actions or nouns. Also, while it may appear that these terms simply end in -a, upon closer inspection, you will see that such nouns not only are derived from -ar verbs, but that when that verb is a stem-changing verb, the stem change is made in the resulting noun: *la prueba* (proof; quiz), from *probar* (to prove, test); *la rueda* (wheel), from *rodar* (to roll). All such nouns are feminine.

Formed Word	English Equivalent	Related to	English Equivalent
la ayuda[1]	help; aid; assistance	ayudar	to aid, help, assist
la burla[2]	scoff(ing); mockery; hoax	burlar	to mock, laugh at, hoax
la busca	search; hunt; pursuit	buscar	to seek, search, look for
la caricia	caress; stroke	acariciar	to caress, stroke, fondle, cherish
la causa[3]	cause; (law) case; trial	causar	to cause
la cena[4]	supper; dinner	cenar	to dine, eat supper or dinner
la cocina[5]	kitchen; cooking; cookery	cocinar	to cook
la compra[6]	purchase; buy; buying	comprar	to buy, purchase
la copia	copy; duplicate	copiar	to copy, duplicate
la cuenta[7]	bill; account; tab	contar	to count, charge
la disciplina	discipline; scourge; whip	disciplinar	to discipline, scourge, whip

Formed Word	English Equivalent	Related to	English Equivalent
la ducha	shower	duchar(se)	to (take a) shower
la escucha	listening; listening-place	escuchar	to listen (to), hear
la espera[8]	wait(ing); expectation	esperar	to wait; await, expect
la fecha[9]	date	fechar	to date
la guarda	guard; care; safekeeping	guardar	to keep, guard, protect
la hipoteca	mortgage	hipotecar	to mortgage
la lágrima	tear; teardrop	lagrimar	to weep, cry, shed tears
la mira[10]	sight; watch-tower; aim; view	mirar	to look (at), watch, gaze
la muestra[11]	signboard; sample; specimen	mostrar	to show
la noticia	news; news item; piece of news	noticiar	to give notice of, notify, make known
la obra	work; piece of work; task	obrar	to work, carry out, perform
la pausa	pause; break; stop	pausar	to pause, slow down
la pinta[12]	spot; mark; look	pintar	to paint, scribble, depict, draw
la plancha	iron; ironing	planchar	to iron, press

Formed Word	English Equivalent	Related to	English Equivalent
la planta	plant	plantar	to plant
la práctica	practice; training	practicar	to practice
la pregunta[13]	question; query; inquiry	preguntar	to ask, inquire
la prueba[14]	proof; (piece of) evidence; test	probar	to prove, test, try out
la renta	rent; income; taxes	rentar	to rent, tax
la resulta	result; outcome	resultar	to result, turn out, prove to be
la rueda	wheel; caster; roller	rodar	to roll, roll along
la ruina[15]	ruin; fall; downfall; wreck	ruinar	to ruin, destroy
la subasta	auction; auction sale	subastar	to auction, sell at auction
la tizna	blackening; lampblack	tiznar	to smut, smudge, blacken
la toma	taking; dose; capture	tomar	to take, have, get, gather
la vela	watch; vigil; wakefulness	velar	to watch (over), keep vigil, stay awake
la visita[16]	visit; visitor(s); social call	visitar	to visit, call upon, search, inspect

---

[1]ayuda de costa = financial aid
[2]de burla = in jest
[3]a causa de = owing to; on account of; because of
[4]la Ultima Cena = the Last Supper
[5]libro de cocina = cookbook
[6]ir de compras = to go shopping

[7](lit., fig.) ajustar cuentas = to settle accounts
[8]sala de espera = waiting room
[9]hasta la fecha = to date
[10]estar a la mira = to be on the lookout
[11]dar muestras de = to show signs of
[12]tener buena pinta = to look good
[13]hacer una pregunta = to ask a question
[14]prueba de indicios or indiciaria = circumstantial evidence
[15]estar hecho una ruina = to be a wreck
[16]derecho de visita = right of search

-able

Meaning: *able to; capable of*
English equivalent: *-able*
Found in: adjectives

The Spanish suffix *-able* is identical to its English counterpart both in spelling and in meaning: both mean exactly what they imply, namely, *able to* or *capable of*. Note below that all words taking the suffix *-able* are derived from *-ar* verbs. Another suffix, *-ible*, which performs the same function, is found in words derived from *-er* and *-ir* verbs.

Formed Word	English Equivalent	Related to	English Equivalent
acabable	that can be finished; achievable	acabar	to finish (off), conclude
adorable	adorable	adorar	to adore
aplacable	appeasable	aplacar	to appease, pacify
besable	kissable	besar	to kiss
calculable	calculable	calcular	to calculate
compensable	able to be compensated	compensar[1]	to compensate
conciliable	reconcilable	conciliar[2]	to reconcile, conciliate, win
condenable	worthy of condemnation	condenar[3]	to condemn
conservable	preservable	conservar	to preserve, conserve
criticable	open to criticism; criticizable	criticar	to criticize
cultivable	cultivatable	cultivar	to cultivate

Formed Word	English Equivalent	Related to	English Equivalent
dudable	doubtful; doubtable	dudar[4]	to doubt
evitable	avoidable	evitar	to avoid
falseable	falsifiable	falsear[5]	to falsify, forge, counterfeit
imputable	imputable	imputar	to impute, ascribe
mudable	changeable; fickle	mudar	to change, move
narrable	capable of being narrated	narrar	to narrate
navegable	navigable	navegar	to navigate, sail
negable	deniable	negar	to deny, refuse
negociable	negotiable	negociar	to negotiate
notable	notable; remarkable	notar[6]	to note, notice, mark
opinable	questionable; debatable	opinar	to think, have or express opinions
organizable	organizable	organizar	to organize
palpable	palpable; clear; obvious	palpar	to touch, feel, see as self-evident
pasable	passable	pasar[7]	to pass
penable	punishable	penar	to punish, chastise
penetrable	penetrable	penetrar	to penetrate
soportable	tolerable; supportable; bearable	soportar	to tolerate, bear, endure
vulnerable	vulnerable	vulnerar	to injure

---

[1] no compensa = it's not worth it
[2] conciliar el sueño = to woo or induce sleep

[3]condenar a trabajos forzados = to sentence to penal servitude or hard labor
[4]lo dudo = I doubt it
[5]falsear el cuerpo = to duck out of the way
[6]se nota que = it's obvious that
[7]pasar las de Caín = to go through hell; pasar por agua (un huevo) = to boil (an egg)

-aco (-aca)

Meaning: deprecative
English equivalent: none
Found in: nouns; adjectives

The ending -aco is an uncommon but powerful deprecative ending. When added to the base word, it brings strong, negative connotations. When added to a noun, it remains a noun; when added to an adjective, it remains an adjective. As an adjective, the ending is -aca when the term describes a feminine noun.

Formed Word	English Equivalent	Related to	English Equivalent
bellaco	cunning; sly; wicked	bello[1]	beautiful; fair
el bicharraco	revolting creature	el bicho[2]	creature
currutaco	foppish	curro	cute; nice; showy
el libraco	(coll.) wretched book; tedious tome	el libro[3]	book
el pajarraco	great, ugly bird	el pájaro[4]	bird

[1]Bella Durmiente = Sleeping Beauty
[2](coll.) bicho raro = funny guy; peculiar individual
[3]ahorcar los libros = to give up one's studies
[4]tener la cabeza a pájaros = to be a birdbrain

-acho; -acha

Meaning: augmentative; deprecative
English equivalent: none
Found in: nouns; adjectives (rarely)

Spanish words ending with -acho or -acha generally denote an exaggeration of the root word, and often carry deprecative connotations. For example, el rico is simply a rich man, while el ricacho is someone who is filthy rich, a "moneybags." (The filthy rich woman is la ricacha.) This is not a common ending, but it is a powerful one, and because of this many words ending with -acho or -acha should be used with discretion. The suffix -acho or -acha almost always is a noun ending: the only exception below is vivaracho (vivaracha when describing a feminine noun), which is an adjective. All words ending in -acho are masculine, while those ending with -acha are feminine.

Formed Word	English Equivalent	Related to	English Equivalent
la aguacha	foul water	el agua (f.)[1]	water
el amigacho	chum; crony; pal	el amigo	friend
el barbicacho	ribbon tied under the chin	la barba	chin
la bocacha	great hideous mouth	la boca	mouth
el cocacho	rap on the head	la coca	(coll.) head
el dicharacho	crude, vulgar expression	el dicho[2]	saying; saw
la hilacha	shred; fraying	el hilo	thread
el hornacho	furnace (for casting statues)	el horno[3]	oven; kiln
el mamarracho	sissy	la mamá	mother; mom
el mancebacho	youth; adolescent; teenager	el mancebo	lad; bachelor
el marimacho	mannish woman	(Lat.) maritus	husband
el poblacho	old, run-down town	el pueblo	town
el populacho	mob; rabble	(Lat.) populus	people
el riacho	small, dirty river	el río[4]	river
el ricacho	(coll.) "moneybags"	el rico[5]	rich individual
el tabernacho	run-down bar; "dive"	la taberna	tavern; bar
el terminacho	(coll.) crude, vulgar expression	el término	term
el tiranacho	wretched tyrant	el tirano	tyrant
el verdacho	green earth	el verde	green (color)
vivaracho	(coll.) lively; spirited; frisky	vivir[6]	to live
el vulgacho	mob; rabble	el vulgo	common people

[1] agua corriente = running water
[2] del dicho al hecho, hay gran trecho = talk and action are two very different things
[3] alto horno = blast furnace
[4] río revuelto = troubled waters
[5] nuevo rico = nouveau riche; upstart
[6] vivir de = to live on

-ada

Meaning: *group; collection; amount; flock; drove,* etc.
English equivalent: none
Found in: nouns

The suffix *-ada* can indicate a collective use or large number of its root word. It is a common ending for groups of animals as well as other goods. This ending can also denote a span of time *(la década)*, approximations *(la millonada)*, and groups of people *(la indiada)*. All such words are feminine.

Formed Word	English Equivalent	Related to	English Equivalent
la animalada	great amount; "hell of a lot"	el animal	animal
la arañada	collection of spiders	la araña	spider
la armada	navy; fleet; squadron	el arma *(f.)*	weapon; arm; force
la borregada	large flock of lambs	el borrego	young lamb
la boyada	drove of oxen	el buey	ox
la burrada	drove of asses	el burro	ass; donkey
la caballada	group of horses	el caballo	horse
la carnerada	flock of sheep	el carnero	sheep
la centenada	hundred	cien	one hundred
la cerdada	herd of swine	el cerdo	*(lit.,fig.)* pig; hog
la cotonada	cotton goods	el cotón	printed cotton
la década	decade; ten years	*(Gr.)* deca	*ten*
la endécada	eleven years	*(Gr.)* endeca	*eleven*
la gatada	litter of cats	el gato[1]	cat
la invernada	winter season	el invierno	winter
la mesada	monthly pay; wages	el mes[2]	month
la millonada	huge sum of money	el millón	million
la mulada	drove of mules	el mulo	mule
la novillada	drove of young bulls	el novillo[3]	young bull
la obrada	day's work	la obra[4]	work; piece of work; task
la otoñada	autumn season	el otoño	autumn
la palabrada	verbiage	la palabra[5]	word

Formed Word	English Equivalent	Related to	English Equivalent
la pavada	flock of turkeys	el pavo	turkey
la peonada	gang of laborers	el peón	laborer
la perrada	pack of dogs	el perro[6]	dog
la riñonada	dish of kidneys	el riñón[7]	kidney
la torada	drove of bulls	el toro[8]	bull
la uvada	glut of grapes	la uva	grape
la vacada	herd of cattle	la vaca	cow
la veranada	summer season	el verano	summer

[1]llevar el gato al agua = to accomplish a difficult task
[2]meses mayores = last months of pregnancy
[3]hacer novillos = to play truant
[4]estar en obras = to be under repair
[5]de palabra = by word of mouth
[6]perro de aguas = spaniel; perro de lanas = poodle
[7]tener riñones = to have guts
[8]toro bravo *or* toro de lidia = fighting bull

-ada

Meaning: *blow or strike with or from; resulting action*
English equivalent: none
Found in: nouns

In this group of words ending with *-ada,* we find many words similar to those ending in *-azo* (blow or strike with or from), in which the root noun indicates the object used for hitting. A good example is *la puñada* (punch or blow with the fist) from *el puño* (fist). Also listed are several words that designate result or resulting action, generally from the root noun, e.g., *la ojeada* (glance; look) from *el ojo* (eye). When the root is a verb, the ending *-ada* indicates the result of that verb, e.g., *la tirada* (throw) from *tirar* (to throw). All nouns ending in *-ada* are feminine.

Formed Word	English Equivalent	Related to	English Equivalent
la azadada	blow with a spade or hoe	la azada	spade; hoe
la badajada	stroke of the clapper	el badajo	clapper (of a bell)
la cabezada[1]	shake of the head	la cabeza[2]	head
la coleada	swish of a tail	la cola[3]	tail
la corazonada	hunch; presentiment	el corazón	heart
la cuchillada	gash from a knife	el cuchillo	knife

Formed Word	English Equivalent	Related to	English Equivalent
la fumada	puff/whiff of smoke	fumar[4]	to smoke
la galopada	race at a gallop	el galope	gallop
la gargantada	liquid or blood ejected from throat	la garganta	throat
la gatada	cat trick; catlike act	el gato	cat
la gaznatada	violent blow on windpipe	el gaznate	gullet; windpipe
la hombrada	manly action	el hombre	man
la lengüetada	lick; licking	la lengua	tongue
la limonada	lemonade	el limón	lemon
la llamada	call; knock; ring (telephone)	llamar[5]	to call, call upon
la llegada[6]	arrival	llegar[7]	to arrive
la mangonada	punch with the arm	la manga[8]	sleeve
la mazada	blow with mace or club	la maza	mace; war club
la morrada	butting with the head	la morra	crown; top of the head
la muchachada	childish prank	el muchacho	boy; lad
la nalgada	slap on or with the buttocks	la nalga	buttock
la naranjada	orange juice; orangeade	la naranja	orange (fruit)
la ojeada	glance; look	el ojo	eye
la palmada	slap	la palma	palm of the hand
la palotada	stroke with a drumstick	el palote	drumstick
la panderada	stroke with a tambourine	la pandereta	tambourine
la patada	kick	la pata	foot; paw
la pernada	kick with the leg	la pierna	leg
la puñada	punch; blow with the fist	el puño	fist
la puñalada	stab	el puñal	dagger

Formed Word	English Equivalent	Related to	English Equivalent
la rodillada	push with the knee	la rodilla	knee
la tijeretada	clip; cut with a scissors	tijeretear	to cut with a scissors
la tirada	throw	tirar	to throw
la tomada	taking; capture	tomar	to take
la uñada	scratch with a fingernail	la uña	fingernail
la zancada[9]	long stride	la zanca[10]	shank; long leg

---

[1]echar una cabezada = to have a snooze
[2]cabeza de turco = scapegoat
[3]cola de milano *or* cola de pato = dovetail; swallowtail; fantail
[4]fumarse una clase = to skip a class
[5]llamar la atención = to attract attention
[6]a la llegada = on arrival
[7]llegar a ser = to become
[8]en mangas de camisa = in shirtsleeves
[9]en dos zancadas = in two shakes
[10]por zancas o por barrancas = by hook or by crook

-ada; -ado

Meaning: denotes fullness of a measure or vessel
English equivalent: *-ful; -load*
Found in: nouns

The suffix *-ada* (in rare cases *-ado*) indicates fullness of the root noun, which generally is a vessel of some sort. Usually, the fullness is literal, as in *la cucharada* (spoonful); however, sometimes the meaning can be stretched a bit and done so humorously, as in *la narigada* (portion of snuff; "noseful"). All words ending with *-ada* are feminine, while those ending with *-ado* are masculine.

Formed Word	English Equivalent	Related to	English Equivalent
la barcada	boatload	el barco	boat
el bocado[1]	mouthful	la boca[2]	mouth
la bofada	lungful	el bofe	lung
la botelada	boatload	el bote	boat
la brazada	armful	el brazo[3]	arm
la calderada	cauldronful	la caldera	cauldron; boiler

Formed Word	English Equivalent	Related to	English Equivalent
la canastada	basketful	la canasta	basket; hamper
la capada	capeful; cloakful	la capa	cape; cloak
la carretada	wagonload	la carreta	wagon
la carretillada	wheelbarrow-load	la carretilla	wheelbarrow
la carretonada	truckload	el carretón	truck; cart
la cazolada	panful	el cazo	pan
la cestada	basketful	la cesta	basket
la cucharada	spoonful	la cuchara	spoon
la dedada[4]	small portion; "fingerful"	el dedo[5]	finger
la esquifada	boatload	el esquife	skiff
la hornada	batch; "ovenful"	el horno	oven
la lagarada	pressful	el lagar	winepress
la lanchada	lighterload	la lancha[6]	lighter; barge
la narigada	portion of snuff; "noseful"	la nariz	nose
la palada	shovelful	la pala	shovel
la paletada	trowelful	la paleta	trowel
la panzada	bellyful	la panza	belly
la ponchada	bowlful of punch	el ponche	punch
la pulgada	inch; "thumbful"	el pulgar	thumb
el puñado[7]	handful; fistful	el puño	fist
la sartenada	frying-panful	la sartén	frying pan
la tonelada	ton; "barrelful"	el tonel	barrel
la vagonada	truckful; carload	el vagón[8]	truck; boxcar
la zurronada	bagful	el zurrón	shepherd's pouch; leather bag

[1] en un bocado = in one gulp
[2] boca de riego = hydrant
[3] ser el brazo derecho de alguien = to be someone's right-hand man
[4] (coll.) dedada de miel = taste of honey

⁵dedo anular = ring or third finger
⁶lancha salvavidas = lifeboat
⁷a puñados = by the fistful; galore
⁸vagón restaurante = dining car

-ado (-ada)
Meaning: *like; relating to*
English equivalent: none
Found in: adjectives

The suffix *-ado* is one of several adjectival endings meaning *like, relating to*. The examples given below all are derived from nouns. The formation of this suffix is easy: generally speaking, if the root noun ends in a vowel, drop that vowel and add *-ado;* if the root noun ends in a consonant, simply add *-ado*. As this is an adjectival ending, when describing nouns of the feminine gender, these words will end with *-ada*.

Formed Word	English Equivalent	Related to	English Equivalent
anisado	mixed with aniseed; aniselike	el anís	anise; aniseed; anisette
arrojado	bold; fearless	el arrojo	boldness; intrepidity
avergonzado	ashamed; embarrassed	avergonzar	to shame, embarrass
azafranado	saffronlike; saffron-colored	el azafrán	saffron
colorado	colored	el color[1]	color
cruzado[2]	crossbred; crossed	la cruz	cross
cuadrado	square; square-shaped	el cuadro	square
enojado	angry; mad	el enojo	anger
estrellado	starry	la estrella	star
ferrado	plated with iron	el fierro	iron
hadado[3]	fateful; magic	el hado	fate; destiny
halconado	falconlike; hawklike	el halcón	falcon; hawk
irisado	rainbow-hued	el iris	rainbow
jironado	shredded; tattered	el jirón	shred; tatter
jorobado	hump- or hunch-backed	la joroba	hump

Formed Word	English Equivalent	Related to	English Equivalent
lanzado	at full tilt; rushing	la lanza[4]	lance
leonado	lion-colored; tawny	el león[5]	lion
letrado	learned; lettered	la letra[6]	letter
limonado	lemony; lemon-colored	el limón	lemon
logrado	successful; well executed	el logro	gain; profit
naranjado	orange-colored	la naranja	orange (fruit)
nevado	snow-covered; snowy	la nieve	snow
nublado	cloudy; overcast	la nube[7]	cloud
ovalado	egg-shaped; oval-shaped	el óvalo	oval
patronado	having a patron	el patrón	patron; protector
pesado	heavy	el peso	weight
pintado[8]	spotted; mottled; speckled	la pinta	spot; mark
playado	beach-lined	la playa	beach
rayado	striped; streaked	la raya	stripe
recortado	*(bot.)* incised	el recorte[9]	cutting; clipping
rosado	rose-colored; pink	la rosa	rose; rose-color
sargado	sergelike	la sarga	serge
triangulado	triangular; triangle-shaped	el triángulo	triangle
vomitado	*(coll.)* palefaced; thin	el vómito	vomit; vomiting

[1]color vivo = bright color
[2]traje cruzado = double-breasted suit
[3]bien hadado = lucky
[4]correr lanzas = to joust
[5]parte del león = lion's share
[6]letra mayúscula = capital letter; letra minúscula = small letter
[7]estar por las nubes = to be sky-high (in price)
[8]papel pintado = wallpaper
[9]álbum de recortes = scrapbook

-ado (-ada)

Meaning: *one who; result of action*
English equivalent: none
Found in: nouns

The noun ending -*ado* can denote a person doing something or the result of an action. In either case, whether the reference is to the performer or to the action performed, such nouns ending in -*ado* all are derived from -*ar* verbs. Thus, the formation is simple: drop the -*ar* from the infinitive and add -*ado*. While all the examples listed are in the masculine form, if the resulting noun is a person, and that person is female, the suffix is -*ada (el empleado; la empleada)*. Otherwise, all nouns ending with -*ado* are masculine.

Formed Word	English Equivalent	Related to	English Equivalent
el abogado[1]	lawyer; advocate	abogar	to advocate, plea
el adobado	pickled meat (esp. pork)	adobar	to pickle (meat)
el adoptado	adopted person	adoptar	to adopt
el ahijado	godchild; protégé	ahijar	to adopt, espouse
el cercado	enclosure; fenced-in garden	cercar	to enclose, fence in
el constipado	cold; chill	constipar[2]	to give a cold to
el convidado	guest; person invited	convidar	to invite
la criada	maid; servant	criar	to rear, bring up
el chalado	*(coll.)* crazy person; nut-case	chalar	to drive crazy
el decorado	decoration; décor	decorar	to decorate, adorn
el delegado	delegate; commissioner	delegar	to delegate
el desagrado	displeasure; reluctance	desagradar	to displease
el emigrado	emigré	emigrar	to emigrate
el empleado	employee	emplear	to employ, use
el enamorado	lover	enamorar[3]	to enamor, cause to fall in love

Formed Word	English Equivalent	Related to	English Equivalent
el encargado	person in charge	encargar	to entrust, put in charge
el enlistonado	lath-work	enlistonar	to lath
el enterrado	buried person	enterrar	to bury, inter
el enviado	messenger; envoy	enviar	to send
el estado[4]	state; commonwealth; condition	estar	to be (in place or condition)
el granizado	iced drink	granizar	to hail down (upon)
el guisado	stew; ragout; fricassee	guisar	to cook, stew, (fig.) cook up
el helado	ice cream	helar	to freeze, turn to ice
el hilado	spinning; yarn; thread	hilar	to spin
el invitado	person invited; guest	invitar	to invite
el licenciado	university graduate; lawyer	licenciar	to confer a degree upon, license
el peinado	hairdo; hairstyle	peinar[5]	to comb, do the hair of
el rizado	curl	rizar	to curl
el sobrado	attic; loft	sobrar	to be left over
el teclado	keyboard (piano, typewriter, etc.)	teclear	to touch upon, play chords
el tornado	tornado	tornar[6]	to turn, return, change

---

[1]abogado del diablo = devil's advocate
[2]constiparse = to catch a cold

³enamorarse (de) = to fall in love (with)
⁴en estado = expecting a baby
⁵peinar canas = to be getting old
⁶tornar a = to do again

-aje
Meaning: *collection; set;* forms abstract noun
English equivalent: *-age*
Found in: nouns

When added to a root noun, the suffix *-aje* enlarges upon it: from the single *la vela* (sail), we get *el velaje* (set of sails); or from *el ancla* (anchor), we get *el anclaje* (anchorage). In the case of the sails, we go from the specific to the collection; whereas in the case of the anchor, we go from the specific to the abstraction, idea, or purpose of the root noun. All words ending with *-aje* are masculine.

Formed Word	English Equivalent	Related to	English Equivalent
el alambraje	wiring	el alambre	wire
el almacenaje	storage	el almacén	store; warehouse
el anclaje	anchorage	el ancla *(f.)*[1]	anchor
el andamiaje	scaffolding	el andamio	scaffold; platform
el camionaje	trucking; truckage	el camión	truck
el caudillaje	leadership; tyranny	el caudillo	chief; leader; *(mil.)* commander
el correaje	straps; belting	la correa	leather strap; thong
el hembraje	females in flock; "womenfolk"	la hembra	female
el herbaje	herbage	la hierba	grass; herb
el herraje	hardware; ironwork	el hierro[2]	iron
el lenguaje	language	la lengua	tongue
el linaje	lineage	la línea	line
el maderaje	woodwork	la madera	wood
el marinaje	sailors; seamanship	el marino	sailor
el monedaje	coins; coinage	la moneda	coin

Formed Word	English Equivalent	Related to	English Equivalent
el mueblaje	furniture (in general)	el mueble	(piece of) furniture
el obraje	manufacture; handiwork	la obra[3]	work; piece of work
el paisanaje	civilian population; civilians	el paisano	civilian; peasant
el peonaje	gang of laborers	el peón	laborer
el plantaje	collection of plants	la planta	plant
el plumaje	plumage; feathers	la pluma	feather
el porcentaje	percentage	por ciento	percent
el pupilaje	pupilage; wardship; boarding	la pupila	pupil; ward; boarder
el ramaje	mass of branches	la rama[4]	branch
el rendaje	set of reins and bridles	la rienda	rein
el rodaje	set of wheels	la rueda[5]	wheel
el ropaje	clothing (in general)	la ropa[6]	clothes; dry goods
el ultraje	outrage; affront	*(Lat.)* ultra	beyond
el varillaje	ribs; ribbing (of umbrella)	la varilla	rib (of a fan or umbrella)
el vasallaje	vassalage; servitude	el vasallo	vassal; subject
el vatiaje	wattage	el vatio	watt
el velaje	set of sails	la vela[7]	sail
el vendaje	bandage; bandaging	la venda	band; blindfold
el ventanaje	row of windows	la ventana	window

[1] estar sobre el ancla = to be anchored
[2] ser de hierro = to be as hard as iron or steel, tireless
[3] obra maestra = masterpiece
[4] andarse por las ramas = to beat around the bush
[5] silla de ruedas *or* sillón de ruedas = wheelchair
[6] ropa interior = underwear
[7] alzar velas = to hoist sails

-aje

Meaning: *fee; toll; rent; dues*
English equivalent: none
Found in: nouns

Spanish words ending in *-aje* can denote the fee, toll, rent, or dues for a service rendered. The suffix *-aje* is attached to the root noun that denotes the object or service acquired. All words ending with *-aje* are masculine.

Formed Word	English Equivalent	Related to	English Equivalent
el agiotaje	agiotage; money exchange	el agio	agio
el almacenaje	warehouse rent	el almacén[1]	warehouse; store; shop
el barcaje	boat fare	el barco	boat
el bodegaje	warehouse dues	la bodega	warehouse
el caballaje	stud service	el caballo[2]	horse
el cabestraje	fee paid to a drover	el cabestro	halter; bell-ox
el cabotaje	coasting trade	el cabo[3]	cape; coast
el carneraje	tax or duty on sheep	el carnero	sheep
el carretaje	carting fee	la carreta	wagon
el castillaje	castle-toll	el castillo[4]	castle
el herbaje	pasturage fee	la hierba	grass; herb
el hornaje	fee for baking bread	el horno	oven for baking bread
el hospedaje	lodging; board	el huésped[5]	guest
el muellaje	dues paid on entering a port	el muelle	pier; dock; wharf
el pasaje	ticket; fare	el paso[6]	passage; walk; situation
el pasturaje	duty for grazing cattle	la pastura	pasture; fodder
el pedaje	toll	(Lat.) pes	foot
el pontaje	bridge-toll	el puente	bridge

Formed Word	English Equivalent	Related to	English Equivalent
el recuaje	duty for the passing of cattle	la recua	drove; string (of mules, etc.)
el terraje	rent paid for land	la tierra	land
el vareaje	retail trade; selling by the yard	la vara	yard; yardstick
el vasallaje	vassalage; liege money	el vasallo	vassal; subject

[1]tener en almacén = to have in storage
[2]a caballo = on horseback
[3]de cabo a cabo *or* de cabo a rabo = from head to tail, top to bottom, end to end
[4]castillo de naipes = house of cards; flimsy structure
[5]casa de huéspedes = boardinghouse
[6]cerrar el paso = to bar or block the way

-aje

Meaning: *landing*
English equivalent: none
Found in: nouns

Another use of *-aje* is to denote a particular type of landing. This is not a common use of the widely used ending *-aje*. All such terms are masculine.

Formed Word	English Equivalent	Related to	English Equivalent
el alunizaje	moon landing	alunizar	to land on the moon
el amarraje	landing on water	amarrar	to land a boat, moor
el arribaje	*(naut.)* arrival; landing	arribar	to arrive, put into harbor
el aterraje	*(naut.)* landfall; *(aer.)* landing	aterrar	to land
el aterrizaje[1]	*(aer.)* landing	aterrizar	*(aer.)* to land

[1]aterrizaje forzoso = rough landing

-ajo

Meaning: pejorative; diminutive; result of action
English equivalent: none
Found in: nouns

The suffix -ajo often holds pejorative connotations with regard to the root word. Words ending in -ajo are derived from either nouns or verbs: when derived from a verb, the word generally carries a specific meaning resulting from that verb's broader meaning, e.g., espantajo (scarecrow) from espantar (to scare). Note below that several words ending in -ajo are colloquial in their usage. All nouns ending with -ajo are masculine.

Formed Word	English Equivalent	Related to	English Equivalent
el arrendajo	(orn.) mockingbird	arrendar	to imitate
el bebistrajo	(coll.) rotten drink; concoction	la bebida	drink; beverage
el borrajo	embers; cinders	borrar	(fig.) to expunge, obliterate
el camistrajo	(fam.) pallet; poor bed	la cama	bed
el cintajo	rotten or tawdry old ribbon	la cinta[1]	ribbon; tape; band
el colgajo	hanging/flapping rag or tatter	colgar	to hang, suspend
el comistrajo	(coll.) hodgepodge; concoction	la comistión	mixture (of food)
el escobajo	old broom	la escoba[2]	broom
el escupitajo	(coll.) spit; spittle	escupir	to spit, spit at
el espantajo	scarecrow	espantar	to scare, frighten
el espumarajo	ugly foam or froth	la espuma	foam; lather; froth
el estropajo	(dish) scourer; piece of rubbish	estropajear	to rub, scour
el guanajo	(coll.) simpleton	el guano	guano
el hatajo	small herd or flock	el hato	herd (of cattle)
el lagunajo	puddle; pool	la laguna	small lake; lagoon

Formed Word	English Equivalent	Related to	English Equivalent
el latinajo	*(coll.)* pig latin	el latín	Latin; Latin language
el lavajo	water hole	lavar	to wash
el pingajo	rag; tatter	el pingo[3]	rag
el sombrajo	shadow cast by another person; hut	la sombra[4]	shade; shadow; shelter
el tendajo	small, tumbledown shop	la tienda	shop; store
el terminajo	*(coll.)* coarse or crude expression	el término	term
el tiznajo	*(coll.)* smudge; stain	la tizna	blackening; lampblack
el trapajo	old rag; tatter	el trapo	rag; cleaning rag
el zancajo	heel; heel of a shoe	el zanco[5]	stilt

[1]cinta de sombrero = hat band
[2]escoba nueva barre bien = new brooms sweep clean
[3]los pingos = cheap clothes; "duds"
[4]tener mala sombra = to be dull or a drag; to be tactless
[5]en zancos = high up

-al

Meaning: augmentative; *outgrowth; place*
English equivalent: none
Found in: nouns

The noun ending -al often signifies an enlargement of the root noun. Usually it simply indicates that something is big, as in the case of *el ventanal* (large window). However, -al also can mean an extension, outgrowth, or collection of the root noun, as in *el santal* (choir book; book of saints' lives). Finally, this augmentative ending can enlarge the root so greatly as to denote an entire place, as seen in *el riscal* (cliffy, craggy place), which is derived from *el risco* (cliff; crag). All nouns ending in -al are masculine.

Formed Word	English Equivalent	Related to	English Equivalent
el bancal	bench cover	el banco	bench; pew
el cabezal	small pillow	la cabeza[1]	head
el dedal	thimble	el dedo	finger

Formed Word	English Equivalent	Related to	English Equivalent
el dineral	fortune	el dinero	money
el festival	festival	la fiesta[2]	party; feast; holiday
el lodazal	quagmire	el lodo	mud; mire
el matorral	thicket; underbrush	la mata	bush; shrub
el misal	missal; mass-book	la misa[3]	mass
el nidal	(coll.) hangout	el nido	nest
el ojal	buttonhole	el ojo	eye
el ostral	oyster bed	la ostra	oyster
el parral	large earthen jar	la parra	honey jar
el pecinal	slimy pool	la pecina	slime
el peñascal	rocky place	la peña	rock; crag; boulder
el platal	great wealth; riches	la plata	silver; silverware; money
el portal	doorway	la puerta	door
el pozal	covering for a well	el pozo[4]	well; pit; deep hole
el ramal	branch line	la rama	branch
el rectoral	rectory	el rector	rector
el riscal	cliffy, craggy place	el risco	cliff; crag
el ritual	ritual	el rito	rite
el santoral	choir book; book of saints' lives	el santo[5]	saint
el secadal	barren ground	la seca	dry season; dry sand bank
el semental	stud horse; breeding animal	el semen	semen; sperm; seed
el soportal	portico; arcade	el soporte	support; stand; rest
el tribunal	tribunal; court (of justice)	el tribuno	tribune; political orator

Formed Word	English Equivalent	Related to	English Equivalent
el varal	long pole	la vara	pole; rod; staff
el varganal	enclosure; stockade	el várgano	railing or stake (of a fence)
el ventanal	large window	la ventana	window
el vitral	stained-glass window	*(Lat.)* vitrum	glass

[1]cabeza de chorlito = scatterbrain
[2]sala de fiestas = nightclub
[3]misa mayor = high mass; misa rezada = low mass
[4]pozo negro = cesspool
[5]santo titular = patron saint

-al

Meaning: *like; relating to*
English equivalent: *-al*
Found in: adjectives

The adjectival suffix *-al* is a common one both in Spanish and in English. Very broadly, it means *like* or *relating to,* and is used in almost any context, including references to time periods *(semanal),* to shape *(codal),* to color *(negral).* Many Spanish adjectives ending in *-al* are cognates of their English counterparts, as you will see below.

Formed Word	English Equivalent	Related to	English Equivalent
añal	annual	el año[1]	year
arsenical	arsenical	el arsénico	arsenic
asnal	asinine	el asno	ass
astral	astral	el astro	heavenly body; *(fig.)* star
central	central	el centro[2]	center; middle
cincuentañal	relating to or lasting 50 years	cincuenta	fifty
codal	elbow-shaped	el codo	elbow
colonial	colonial	la colonia	colony
cuaresmal	relating to Lent; Lenten	la Cuaresma	Lent

Formed Word	English Equivalent	Related to	English Equivalent
disciplinal	disciplinary	la disciplina	discipline
elemental	elemental	el elemento	element
experimental	experimental	el experimento	experiment
final[3]	final	el fin[4]	end; ending; aim; limit
grupal	relating to a group	el grupo	group
horizontal	horizontal	el horizonte	horizon
intelectual	intellectual	el intelecto	intellect; understanding
labial[5]	labial; of the lips	el labio	lip; labium
marzal	relating to the month of March	marzo	March
mental	mental	la mente	mind
mundial	worldwide; world	el mundo[6]	world; (coll.) crowd; mob
negral	blackish	el negro	black (color)
oriental	oriental	el oriente	orient; east
ornamental	ornamental	el ornamento	ornament
otoñal	autumnal	el otoño	autumn; fall
papal	papal	el Papa	the Pope
parroquial	parochial	la parroquia	parish
personal	personal; characteristic	la persona[7]	person; human being
poligonal	polygonal	el polígono	polygon
procesal	belonging to a lawsuit	el proceso	criminal case or suit; trial
sacerdotal	of the priesthood; priestly	el sacerdote	priest; clergyman
semanal	weekly	la semana[8]	week

Formed Word	English Equivalent	Related to	English Equivalent
suplemental	supplemental	el suplemento	supplement
terrenal	earthly; mundane; worldly	la tierra	earth; land
uval	grapelike	la uva[9]	grape
vecinal	belonging to a neighborhood	el vecino	neighbor
veinteñal	relating to or lasting 20 years	veinte	twenty

[1]año escolar or año lectivo = school or academic year
[2]centro de mesa = centerpiece (for a table)
[3]al final = at or in the end
[4]en fin = in short; to sum up
[5]lápiz labial = lipstick
[6]todo el mundo = everybody
[7]buena persona = decent person
[8]Semana Santa = Holy Week
[9]*(fig.)* uvas verdes = sour grapes

-al; -ar
Meaning: *field; orchard; patch; plantation; plant; tree;* etc.
English equivalent: none
Found in: nouns

This pair of suffixes is interesting in that one might first assume the unfamiliar word to be either an adjective (as are many Spanish words ending in *-al*) or an infinitive (as are most words ending in *-ar*). Nonetheless, this is a suffix with a specific chore, that of naming the type of field, orchard, etc., of the plant name to which it is attached. Note that in some cases, the root can take either suffix, and there is no change in meaning (e.g., *el manzanal; el manzanar*). All such words are masculine.

Formed Word	English Equivalent	Related to	English Equivalent
el alcachofal	artichoke field	la alcachofa	artichoke
el alcornocal	plantation of cork trees	el alcornoque	*(bot.)* cork oak; *(fig.)* blockhead
el alfalfar	alfalfa field	la alfalfa	alfalfa
el almendral	almond grove	la almendra[1]	almond
el arrozal	rice field	el arroz	rice
el avenal	oat field	la avena	oat

Formed Word	English Equivalent	Related to	English Equivalent
el bananal	banana plantation	la banana	banana
el berenjenal	eggplant plantation	la berenjena	eggplant
el berzal	cabbage patch	la berza[2]	cabbage
el cafetal	coffee plantation	el café	coffee
el calabazar	pumpkin patch	la calabaza	pumpkin
el cauchal	rubber plantation	el caucho	rubber
el cebollar	onion patch	la cebolla	onion
el cerezal	cherry orchard	la cereza	cherry
el ciruelar	plum orchard	la ciruela	plum
el fresal	strawberry patch	la fresa	strawberry
el frutal	fruit tree	el fruto[3]	fruit
el guisantal	pea field	el guisante[4]	pea
el henar	hay field	el heno	hay
el limonar	lemon grove	el limón	lemon
el maizal	maize field	el maíz[5]	maize
el majolar	white hawthorn grove	el majuelo	white hawthorn
el manzanal/ar	apple orchard	la manzana	apple
el melonar	melon patch	el melón	melon
el naranjal	orange grove	la naranja	orange
el olivar	olive grove	la oliva	olive
el patatal	potato field	la patata[6]	potato
el pepinar	cucumber field	el pepino	cucumber
el peral	pear tree	la pera	pear
el pimental	pepper plantation	el pimiento	pepper
el pinar	pine grove; pine forest	el pino	pine; pine tree
el platanal/ar	banana tree plantation	el plátano	banana
el rabanal	radish patch	el rábano[7]	radish
el robledal	oak grove	el roble	oak
el rosal	rosebush	la rosa	rose
el sandiar	watermelon patch	la sandía	watermelon

Formed Word	English Equivalent	Related to	English Equivalent
el tomatal	tomato field	el tomate	tomato
el trigal	wheat field	el trigo[8]	wheat

[1]almendras garrapiñadas = sugared almonds
[2]el berza = country bumpkin; yokel; *(fam.)* clod
[3]dar fruto = to yield fruit
[4]guisante de olor = sweet pea
[5]harina de maíz = cornmeal
[6]no saber ni una patata (de) = not to know the first thing (about)
[7]rábano picante = horseradish
[8]trigo chamorro = winter wheat

-ancia
Meaning: *act; state of being; result of action*
English equivalent: *-ance; -ancy*
Found in: nouns

The Spanish suffix *-ancia,* found nearly always in cognates of their English counterparts, denotes the state, act, or result of a root verb. Note that words ending in *-ancia* are feminine, and that they are derived from *-ar* verbs. To form these words, remove the *-ar* from the infinitive and add *-ancia.*

Formed Word	English Equivalent	Related to	English Equivalent
la abundancia[1]	abundance; plenty; opulence	abundar[2]	to abound
la ambulancia[3]	ambulance	ambular	to wander about, ambulate
la asonancia	assonance	asonar	to be assonant
la consonancia	consonance	consonar	to harmonize, rhyme, agree
la constancia[4]	constancy; proof; record	constar	to be certain, be on record
la discrepancia	discrepancy	discrepar	to differ, disagree
la disonancia	dissonance	disonar	to be dissonant

Formed Word	English Equivalent	Related to	English Equivalent
la distancia[5]	distance	distar	to be distant, far, remote
la escancia	pouring or serving of wine	escanciar	to pour or serve wine
la estancia	stay; day in a hospital	estar	to be (in a place, state, condition)
la exuberancia	exuberance	exuberar *(obs.)*	to be exuberant
la importancia	importance	importar	to be important, matter
la infancia[6]	infancy; childhood	*(Lat.)* in + fari	to not speak
la instancia	instance	instar	to press, urge, be urgent
la intolerancia	intolerance	*(Lat.)* in + tolerar	to not tolerate, be intolerant
la militancia	militancy	militar	to serve in the army, militate
la observancia	observance	observar	to observe
la perseverancia	perseverance	perseverar	to persevere
la redundancia	redundance	redundar	to redound, overflow
la relevancia	relevance	relevar	to emboss, make stand out
la repugnancia	repugnance	repugnar	to disgust, nauseate
la resonancia[7]	resonance; repercussion	resonar	to resound, echo
la tolerancia	tolerance	tolerar	to tolerate

Formed Word	English Equivalent	Related to	English Equivalent
la vacancia	vacancy	vacar[8]	to resign from a job, leave, take a vacation
la vagancia	vagrancy	vagar	to wander, roam about
la vigilancia	vigilance	vigilar[9]	to watch, keep guard over

---

[1]cuerno de la abundancia = horn of plenty
[2]abundar en riquezas = to abound in wealth
[3]ambulancia de correos = mail truck
[4]dejar constancia de una cosa = to leave something on record
[5]control *or* mando a distancia = remote control
[6]jardín de infancia = kindergarten
[7]tener resonancia = to cause a stir
[8]vacar de = to lack
[9]vigilar de cerca = to keep a close watch upon

-ano (-ana)

Meaning: *native; native of; adherent to (a system of beliefs); like; relating to*
English equivalent: *-an*
Found in: nouns; adjectives

The suffix *-ano* denotes origin of birth or thought. Words taking this suffix are both nouns and adjectives: *La americana sirve el café colombiano* (The American woman serves the Colombian coffee). Note that these words are not capitalized as they are in English. The ending *-ano* changes to *-ana* when denoting or describing a feminine noun.

Formed Word	English Equivalent	Related to	English Equivalent
(el) aldeano	villager; relating to a village	la aldea	small village; hamlet
(el) alsaciano	Alsatian (native)	Alsacia	Alsace
(el) americano	American (native)	América	America
(el) australiano	Australian (native)	Australia	Australia
(el) boliviano	Bolivian (native)	Bolivia	Bolivia
(el) californiano	Californian (native)	California	California

Formed Word	English Equivalent	Related to	English Equivalent
(el) camboyano	Cambodian (native)	Camboya	Cambodia
(el) castellano	Castilian (native)	Castilla	Castile
(el) centroamericano	Central American (native)	Centroamérica	Central America
(el) colombiano	Colombian (native)	Colombia	Colombia
(el) cristiano	Christian (member)	Cristo	Christ
(el) cubano	Cuban (native)	Cuba	Cuba
(el) jerosolimitano	(native) of Jerusalem	Jerusalén	Jerusalem
(el) luterano	Lutheran (member)	Lutero	Luther
(el) mendeliano	Mendelian (theorist)	Mendel	Mendel
(el) mexicano/ mejicano	Mexican (native)	México/Méjico	Mexico
(el) neomejicano	New Mexican (native)	Nuevo Méjico	New Mexico
(el) norcoreano	North Korean (native)	Corea del Norte	North Korea
(el) norteamericano	North American (native)	Norteamérica	North America
(el) paraguayano	Paraguayan (native)	Paraguay	Paraguay
(el) peruano	Peruvian (native)	Perú	Peru
(el) presbiteriano	Presbyterian (member)	el presbítero	presbyter; priest
(el) republicano	Republican; republican	la república	republic
(el) siberiano	Siberian (native)	Siberia	Siberia
(el) siciliano	Sicilian (native)	Sicilia	Sicily
(el) sudamericano	South American (native)	Sudamérica	South America
(el) surcoreano	South Korean (native)	Corea del Sur	South Korea
(el) vegetariano	vegetarian	el vegetal	vegetable
(el) veneciano	Venetian (native)	Venecia	Venice
(el) venezolano	Venezuelan (native)	Venezuela	Venezuela

-ante

Meaning: *like; relating to; doing*
English equivalent: *-ing*
Found in: adjectives

The following words ending in *-ante* all are adjectives formed from verbs and, in describing a noun, indicate that that person, place, or thing exhibits qualities relating directly to the root verb. Since the English equivalent almost always is *-ing*, be careful not to confuse the English translations with the English present progressive (which ends in *-ing* as in "I am study<u>ing</u>"). The classic ambiguous English sentence, "They are entertaining women," becomes two very different sentences in Spanish.[1] Note that these words all come from *-ar* verbs (this suffix's counterpart is *-ente,* whose adjectives are derived from *-er* and *-ir* verbs).

Formed Word	English Equivalent	Related to	English Equivalent
abundante	abundant; plentiful; copious	abundar	to abound
agravante	aggravating	agravar	to aggravate
alarmante	alarming	alarmar	to alarm
ambulante	walking; ambulatory	ambular	to wander about
anticipante	anticipating	anticipar	to anticipate
aplastante	crushing	aplastar	to crush, flatten
brillante	brilliant; bright; sparkling	brillar[2]	to shine, sparkle, glisten
colgante[3]	hanging	colgar	to hang, hang up
espumante	flaming; sparkling (wine)	espumar	to foam, sparkle
fascinante	fascinating	fascinar	to fascinate
fecundante	fertilizing	fecundar	to fertilize
festejante	entertaining	festejar	to entertain, feast
flagrante[4]	flagrant; resplendent	flagrar	*(poet.)* to flame, blaze
flamante	flaming	flamear	to flame, blaze
instante	instant; urgent; pressing	instar	to press, urge

Formed Word	English Equivalent	Related to	English Equivalent
interesante[5]	interesting	interesar	to interest, concern
jadeante	panting; out of breath	jadear	to pant
juzgante	judging	juzgar	to judge
madurante	maturing; ripening	madurar	to ripen, mature, mellow
mandante	commanding	mandar	to command
parlante	talking; chatting	parlar	to chatter, babble
participante	participating	participar	to participate
peleante	fighting	pelear(se)[6]	to fight
penetrante	penetrating	penetrar	to penetrate
plasmante	molding; shaping	plasmar	to mold, shape
rotante	revolving	rotar	to revolve
saltante	jumping	saltar	to jump
santificante	blessing; sanctifying	santificar[7]	to sanctify, hallow
silbante	sibilant; hissing	silbar	to whistle
sobrante	remaining; left over	sobrar	to remain, be left over
sonante[8]	sounding	sonar	to sound
sudante	sweating	sudar	to sweat
susurrante	whispering	susurrar	to whisper
tronante	thundering	tronar	to thunder
vacilante	vacillating	vacilar	to vacillate

[1]*Ellas son mujeres festejantes* or *Ellos están festejando a las mujeres.*
[2]brillar por su ausencia = to be conspicuous by one's absence
[3]puente colgante = suspension bridge
[4]en flagrante = in the very act; red-handed
[5]*(coll.)* estado interesante = pregnancy
[6]pelearse con alguien = to fight with somebody
[7]santificar las fiestas = to keep holy days
[8]dinero contante y sonante = ready cash

-ante

Meaning: *one who;* denotes profession
English equivalent: *-ant; -er; -or*
Found in: nouns

The suffix *-ante* is one of several Spanish suffixes that mean *one who.* A unique feature of words taking this ending is that they all are derived from *-ar* verbs. This ending remains *-ante* whether the referent is male or female: *el danzante; la danzante.*

Formed Word	English Equivalent	Related to	English Equivalent
el amante	lover	amar[1]	to love
el anunciante	advertiser; announcer	anunciar	to advertise, announce
el caminante	passerby; walker	caminar	to walk, go, travel
el cantante	singer	cantar[2]	to sing
el celebrante	celebrant (priest)	celebrar	to celebrate, say mass
el comandante[3]	commander	comandar	to command
el comerciante	businessman; merchant	comerciar	to trade, deal, do business
el confesante	confessor	confesar	to confess
el copiante	copier; copyist	copiar[4]	to copy, copy down
el danzante	dancer	danzar	to dance
el debutante	beginner; debutante	debutar	to begin, make one's first appearance
el delineante	draftsman	delinear	to delineate, outline, draft
el dibujante	drawer	dibujar	to draw
el donante[5]	donor	donar	to donate, give
el emigrante	emigrant	emigrar	to emigrate
el estudiante	student	estudiar	to study

Formed Word	English Equivalent	Related to	English Equivalent
el gobernante	ruler	gobernar	to govern, rule
el habitante	inhabitant; dweller	habitar	to inhabit, live in
el ignorante	ignoramus	ignorar	to not know, be ignorant of
el litigante	litigant	litigar	to litigate
el maleante	crook	malear	to damage, spoil, pervert, corrupt
el mendigante/el mendicante	beggar; mendicant	mendigar	to beg
el navegante	navigator	navegar	to navigate, sail
el negociante	businessman; dealer; trader	negociar	to negotiate, deal, trade
el opinante	one who gives his views	opinar	to express an opinion
el participante	participant	participar	to participate
el protestante	protestant; Protestant	protestar	to protest
el solicitante	applicant	solicitar	to solicit, apply for
el traficante	dealer; merchant	traficar	to deal, trade, traffic
el veraneante	summer resident	veranear	to summer, spend the summer
el viajante	traveler	viajar	to travel
el visitante	visitor	visitar	to visit
el votante	voter	votar	to vote

[1]amar de corazón = to love wholeheartedly; amar con locura = to love madly
[2]el gallo canta = the cock crows

³comandante en jefe = commander-in-chief
⁴copiar al pie de la letra = to copy word for word
⁵donante de sangre = blood donor

-anza

Meaning: *quality; state of being; condition; process*
English equivalent: *-ance*
Found in: nouns

The following words ending in *-anza* all are derived from *-ar* verbs, and denote the quality, state of being, condition, or process of those verbs. More simply put, a word taking the suffix *-anza* indicates the result of the action of the verb from which it is derived: from *probar* (to prove, test) we get *probanza* (proof; evidence—the result of proving or testing something). All nouns ending in *-anza* are feminine.

Formed Word	English Equivalent	Related to	English Equivalent
la acechanza	spying; watching; stalking	acechar	to spy on, lurk, lie in wait for
la adivinanza	*(coll.)* prophecy; prediction; guess	adivinar	to guess, divine, solve
la alabanza¹	praise; commendation; glory	alabar	to praise, extol
la alianza	alliance; wedding ring	aliar	to ally
la(s) andanza(s)²	wandering(s); travel(s); doings	andar	to walk, travel, go
la añoranza	longing; sorrow; homesickness	añorar	to long, yearn for
la balanza³	balance; scales; judgment	balancear	to balance
la cobranza	collection; receiving; recovery	cobrar	to collect, receive
la comparanza	comparison	comparar	to compare
la confianza	confidence; trust; reliance	confiar	to confide, entrust
la crianza	raising; rearing; nursing	criar	to raise, rear, bring up

Formed Word	English Equivalent	Related to	English Equivalent
la desalabanza	disparagement	desalabar	to disparage, criticize
la desconfianza	distrust; mistrust; suspicion	desconfiar	to distrust, mistrust, be suspicious of
la desemejanza	dissimilitude; dissimilarity	desemejar	to change the look of
la desesperanza	despair	desesperar	to despair, lose hope (of)
la destemplanza	inclemency (of weather)	destemplar	to disturb, upset the harmony of
la enseñanza[4]	teaching; instruction; education	enseñar	to teach, train, instruct
la esperanza[5]	hope; expectance	esperar	to hope, expect, wait (for)
la fianza[6]	surety; bond; bail; guarantee	fiar	to guarantee, warrant
las finanzas	finances	financiar	to finance
la holganza	rest; leisure; idleness	holgar[7]	to rest, be idle
la labranza	cultivation; farming	labrar	to work, labor, cultivate
la malandanza	misfortune	mal + andar	bad + to walk, travel, go
la matanza	killing; slaughter; butchery	matar	to kill

Formed Word	English Equivalent	Related to	English Equivalent
la mudanza	removal; change	mudar	to change, move, remove
la ordenanza	ordinance; method; order	ordenar	to put into order, arrange
la privanza	private life	privar	to deprive, forbid
la probanza	proof; evidence	probar	to prove, test
la pujanza	strength; force; drive	pujar	to push, bid up
la semejanza[8]	resemblance	semejar	to resemble
la sobrepujanza	great strength; exceeding vigor	sobrepujar	to surpass, excel
la tardanza	delay	tardar	to take a long time
la templanza	temperance	templar	to temper
la usanza	use; usage; custom	usar	to use, wear
la venganza	vengeance; revenge	vengar	to avenge
la venturanza	happiness	aventurar	to venture, risk

[1]cantar las alabanzas de uno = to sing someone's praises
[2]buena (mala) andanza = good (bad) fortune
[3]balanza de comercio = balance of trade
[4]segunda enseñanza = secondary education
[5]llenar la esperanza = to fulfil one's hopes
[6]bajo fianza = on bail
[7]huelga decir = needless to say
[8]a semejanza de = in the likeness of

-arca

Meaning: *ruler*
English equivalent: *-arch*
Found in: nouns

Spanish words ending with *-arca* denote a specific sort of ruler. Such words generally are easy to figure out, for their English counterparts often have the same base. The ending *-arca* nearly always is *-arch* in English, e.g., *el monarca* (monarch); *la matriarca*(matriarch), etc. The ending *-arca* does not change with regard to a male or female referent: *el monarca; la monarca.*

Formed Word	English Equivalent	Related to	English Equivalent
el biarca	biarch; one of two	*(Lat.)* bis	twice
el jerarca[1]	*(eccles.)* hierarch; leader	*(Gr.)* hieros	sacred
la matriarca	matriarch	*(Lat.)* mater	mother
el monarca[2]	monarch	*(Gr.)* monos	alone
el oligarca[3]	oligarch	*(Gr.)* oligos	few; little
el patriarca	patriarch	*(Lat.)* pater	father
el pentarca[4]	pentarch; one of five	*(Gr.)* pente	five

[1]jerarquía = hierarchy
[2]monarquía = monarchy
[3]oligarquía = oligarchy
[4]pentarquía = pentarchy; government by five people

-ario

Meaning: *book; bound collection; printed matter*
English equivalent: none
Found in: nouns

This use of the ending -*ario* is highly specific. The examples given all refer to a book or something printed with a particular function. One word, *el diario* (diary), is unusual insofar as it is a noun in this milieu, while in the following entry of words ending with -*ario,* one finds the adjective *diario* (daily). The meaning of this term thus depends upon context. All nouns ending with -*ario* are masculine.

Formed Word	English Equivalent	Related to	English Equivalent
el abecedario	alphabet or spelling book; primer	abecé	(the letters) a b c
el anuario	yearbook; yearly report	*(Lat.)* annus	year
el calendario[1]	calendar	las calendas	calends: refer to first day of the month on the Roman calendar
el confesionario	treatise with rules for confession	la confesión	confession

Formed Word	English Equivalent	Related to	English Equivalent
el cuestionario	questionnaire	la cuestión[2]	question; issue; matter; subject
el devocionario	prayer book	la devoción	devotion; piety
el diario[3]	diary	el día[4]	day
el diccionario	dictionary	la dicción	diction
el epistolario	epistolary; collection of letters	la epístola	Epistle; epistle; letter
el glosario	glossary	la glosa	gloss; comment; footnote
el himnario	hymnal	el himno	hymn; anthem
el horario	timetable; schedule	la hora[5]	hour; time
el inventario	inventory; catalogue of property	inventariar	to inventory, list
el maitinario	book containing matins	los maitines	matins
el noticiario	newsreel; newscast	la noticia[6]	news; news item; piece of news
el vocabulario	vocabulary; compendium of words	el vocablo	word; term

[1]hacer calendarios = to forecast hastily
[2]cuestión candente = burning question
[3]diario de navegación = logbook
[4]días caniculares = dog days
[5]hora punta = rush hour
[6]noticia bomba = bombshell (news); sensational news

-ario (-aria)
Meaning: *like; relating to; one who*
English equivalent: *-ary*
Found in: adjectives; nouns

The suffix -ario usually is an adjectival ending meaning *like* or *relating to,* as do several other Spanish suffixes. In this capacity, adjectives ending in -ario can be related to nouns, verbs, or other adjectives. Some words ending with -ario can act either as a noun or an adjective, as noted below. Nouns ending in -ario are masculine; however, when the reference is to a person, e.g., *el millonario,* the ending changes to -aria when the person is female *(la millonaria).* Similarly, adjectives ending with -ario take the feminine form -aria when the term is used to describe a feminine noun.

Formed Word	English Equivalent	Related to	English Equivalent
el adversario[1]	adversary; opponent; antagonist	adverso	adverse; calamitous
arbitrario	arbitrary	arbitrar	to arbitrate
bancario	relating to banking	el banco	bank
(el) beneficiario	beneficiary (*n. & adj.*)	beneficiar	to benefit, do good to, improve
canario	of the Canary Islands	las Canarias	the Canary Islands
centenario	centenary	ciento[2]	one hundred
(el) contrario[3]	contrary; opposite; contradictory	contra	opposite; opposite sense
coronario	coronary; relating to the heart	el corazón[4]	heart
diario	daily	el día[5]	day
el dignatario	dignitary	digno	worthy; fitting; decent; honest
estacionario	stationary	la estación	station
hereditario	hereditary	heredar	to inherit, leave property to
(el) honorario	honorarium (*n.*); honorary (*adj.*)	el honor	honor
literario	literary	la letra[6]	letter
lunario	lunar; relating to the moon	la luna[7]	moon

Formed Word	English Equivalent	Related to	English Equivalent
(el) millonario	millionaire (n. & adj.)	millón	million
el misionario	missionary	misionar	to preach missions, reprimand
nonagenario	nonagenarian	*(Lat.)* nonaginta	ninety
el notario	notary; notary public	notar[8]	to note, notice, mark
(el) ordinario[9]	ordinary; ecclesiastical judge	el orden[10]	order
planetario	planetary; relating to the planets	el planeta	planet
plenario	plenary	pleno[11]	full; complete
primario	primary	primo	first; prime
quincenario	fortnightly; every two weeks	quince	fifteen
rutinario	routine	la rutina[12]	routine; rut
el salario	salary; wage; wages; pay	la sal[13]	salt
sanitario	sanitary; of health	sano[14]	sound; healthy; fit
secundario	secondary	segundo	second
sedentario	sedentary	sedente	sitting; seated
el seminario	seminary; seminar	el semen	semen; sperm; seed
suplementario	supplementary	el suplemento	supplement
terciario	tertiary	el tercio	third
(el) visionario	visionary (*n. & adj.*)	la visión	vision
voluntario	voluntary	la voluntad[15]	will; willingness; willpower

[1]los adversarios = reference notes
[2]por ciento = per cente; ciento por ciento = (a) hundred percent; el diez por ciento = ten percent

[3]tiempo contrario = adverse weather
[4]blando de corazón = softhearted; llevar el corazón en la mano = to wear one's heart on one's sleeve
[5]día de fiesta = holiday
[6]a la letra = to the letter; literally; strictly
[7]media luna = half moon; tener lunas = to be moody
[8]se nota que = it's obvious that
[9]de ordinario = usually
[10]hombre (mujer) de orden = law-abiding man (woman)
[11]en pleno día = in broad daylight; in the middle of the day
[12]por rutina = from (mere) force of habit; unthinkingly
[13]sal de la Higuera = Epsom salts
[14]sano y salvo = safe and sound
[15]de voluntad = willingly

-asma; -asmo

Meaning: *result of action; being; condition*
English equivalent: *-asm*
Found in: nouns

Spanish terms ending with *-asma* or *-asmo* all are derived from Greek and are masculine nouns whether they end with *-asma* or with *-asmo*. Spanish words ending with the letters *-ma* are masculine when the direct derivation is Greek instead of Latin.

Formed Word	English Equivalent	Related to	English Equivalent
el entusiasmo	enthusiasm	*(Gr.)* enthousiazein	to be inspired or possessed by the god
el espasmo	spasm	*(Gr.)* spasmos	convulsion; spasm
el fantasma	ghost; phantom; *(fig.)* scarecrow	*(Gr.)* phantasma	appearance; vision
el marasmo	*(med.)* marasmus; stagnation	*(Gr.)* marainein	to waste away
el miasma	miasma	*(Gr.)* miasma	defilement
el orgasmo	orgasm	*(Gr.)* organ	to swell
el plasma	*(biol.)* plasma	*(Gr.)* plasma	anything molded or modeled
el sarcasmo	sarcasm	*(Gr.)* sarkazein	to tear flesh like dogs

-astro; -astra
Meaning: denotes step-relations; diminutive in status
English equivalent: often the prefix *step-*
Found in: nouns

The endings *-astro* and *-astra* perform two functions. The first and more common is to denote step-relations in the family, e.g., *el padrastro* (stepfather), from *el padre* (father). A less frequent function is to diminish the status of the base word, e.g., *el medicastro* (third-rate doctor), from *el médico* (doctor). Words ending with *-astro* are masculine, while those ending with *-astra* are feminine.

Formed Word	English Equivalent	Related to	English Equivalent
el camastro	rickety old bed	la cama[1]	bed
el cochastro	young sucking-boar	el cocho	(prov.) pig
la hermanastra	stepsister	la hermana	sister
el hermanastro	stepbrother	el hermano[2]	brother
la hijastra	stepdaughter	la hija[3]	daughter
el hijastro	stepson	el hijo[4]	son
la madrastra	stepmother; bad mother	la madre[5]	mother
el medicastro	third-rate doctor; "quack"	el médico[6]	doctor; physician
la nietastra	stepgranddaughter	la nieta	granddaughter
el nietastro	stepgrandson	el nieto	grandson
el padrastro	stepfather	el padre[7]	father
el pillastro	roguish fellow; rascal	el pillo	rogue; scamp; rascal
el pinastro	wild pine	el pino	pine; pine tree
la pollastra	pullet	el pollo	chicken
el pollastro	cockerel	el pollo	chicken

[1] cama camera *or* cama sencilla = single bed
[2] hermano de leche = foster brother
[3] hija política = daughter-in-law
[4] hijo de familia = minor
[5] madre de leche = wet nurse
[6] médico de cabecera = family doctor
[7] padre de familia = head of a family

-ato; -ado

Meaning: *office; position; system; duty; domain*
English equivalent: *-ship; -ate*
Found in: nouns

The noun suffix *-ato* or, less commonly, *-ado* denotes the office or domain belonging to the root term (almost always a person) to which it is attached: *el canciller* (chancellor) finds his position/domain in *el cancillerato* (the chancellorship). The ending *-ato* or *-ado* implies high station, rank, or office. All words ending with either of these suffixes are masculine.

Formed Word	English Equivalent	Related to	English Equivalent
el bachillerato	baccalaureate	el bachiller	holder of a degree
el campeonato	championship	el campeón	champion
el cancelariato	chancellorship (of a university)	el cancelario	chancellor (of a university)
el cancillerato	chancellorship	el canciller	chancellor
el canonicato	canonry; *(coll.)* sinecure	el canon[1]	canon
el cardenalato	cardinalship	el cardenal	cardinal
el celibato	bachelorhood; celibacy	el célibe	bachelor; celibate
el clericato	clergy; priesthood	el clérigo[2]	clergyman; cleric
el colonato	system of colonial land settlement	la colonia[3]	colony
el concubinato	concubinage	la concubina	concubine
el consulado	consulate; consulship	el cónsul[4]	consul
el diaconato	deaconship	el diácono	deacon
el doctorado[5]	doctorate	el doctor	doctor
el economato	guardianship; trusteeship	el ecónomo	guardian; trustee
el generalato	generalship	el general[6]	general
el liderato	leadership	el líder	leader
el notariato/ado	notary's title, practice, profession	el notario	notary; notary public

Formed Word	English Equivalent	Related to	English Equivalent
el noviciado	novitiate; apprenticeship	el novicio	novice; beginner
el orfanato	orphanage	el huérfano	orphan
el procerato	high station or rank	el prócer	nobleman; grandee
el profesorado	professorship; professorate	el profesor	professor
el reinado	reign; kingship	el rey[7]	king
el sultanato	sultanate	el sultán	sultan
el superiorato	office of a superior	el superior	superior

[1]los cánones = canons; canon law
[2]clérigo de misa = priest
[3](agua de) colonia = eau-de-Cologne
[4]cónsul general = consul-general
[5](fig.) tener doctorado en = to know all about, be an expert in
[6]general de brigada = brigadier general
[7]los Reyes Magos = the Magi; the Three Wise Men

-avo (-ava)

Meaning: *denominator of a fraction*
English equivalent: *-th*
Found in: nouns

The suffix *-avo* is used to denote the denominator of a fraction (the denominator is the term below the line). Thus, one would say, *Yo leí un seisavo del libro* (I read one-sixth of the book); or *Yo comí una octava de la torta* (I ate one-eighth of the cake). When *-avo* refers to a feminine noun, e.g., *la torta,* the ending changes to *-ava.*

Formed Word	English Equivalent	Related to	English Equivalent
seisavo	sixth	seis	six
octavo	eighth	(Lat.) octo	eight
onceavo	eleventh	once	eleven
doceavo	twelfth	doce	twelve
treceavo	thirteenth	trece	thirteen
catorceavo	fourteenth	catorce	fourteen
quinceavo	fifteenth	quince	fifteen
dieciseisavo	sixteenth	dieciseis	sixteen

Formed Word	English Equivalent	Related to	English Equivalent
diecisieteavo	seventeenth	diecisiete	seventeen
decimoctavo	eighteenth	*(Lat.)* decem + octo	eighteen
diecinueveavo	nineteenth	diecinueve	nineteen
veintavo	twentieth	veinte	twenty
veintiunavo	twenty-first	veintiuno	twenty-one
veintidosavo	twenty-second	veintidós	twenty-two
veintitresavo	twenty-third	veintitrés	twenty-three
veinticuatroavo	twenty-fourth	veinticuatro	twenty-four
veinticincoavo	twenty-fifth	veinticinco	twenty-five
veintiseisavo	twenty-sixth	veintiséis	twenty-six
veintisieteavo	twenty-seventh	veintisiete	twenty-seven
veintioctavo	twenty-eighth	veinte + octo	twenty-eight
veintinueveavo	twenty-ninth	veintinueve	twenty-nine
treintavo	thirtieth	treinta	thirty
cuarentavo	fortieth	cuarenta	forty
cincuentavo	fiftieth	cincuenta	fifty
sesentavo	sixtieth	sesenta	sixty
setentavo	seventieth	setenta	seventy
ochentavo	eightieth	ochenta	eighty
noventavo	ninetieth	noventa	ninety
centavo	hundredth	cien; ciento	one hundred

-az; -oz
Meaning: *full of*
English equivalent: *-cious*
Found in: adjectives

Spanish words ending in *-az* or *-oz* generally have English cognates ending with *-cious*. In both languages, the ending indicates that the person or thing described strongly holds the attributes referred to in the base term. These formed words relate to Spanish nouns or, at times, come directly from Latin. A good spelling aid you will find is that the suffix *-az* translates to *-acious* (audaz; audacious), while *-oz* generally is found in English words ending with *-ocious* (precoz; precocious).

Formed Word	English Equivalent	Related to	English Equivalent
atroz	atrocious	(Lat.) ater	black; dark
audaz	audacious	la audacia	audacity; boldness
capaz	capable	la capacidad (fig.)	capacity; ability; capability
contumaz	contumacious; stubborn	la contumacia	obstinacy; obduracy; stubbornness
eficaz	efficacious	la eficacia	efficacy; efficiency
falaz	fallacious	la falacia	fallacy
feraz	fertile	la feracidad	fecundity; fertility; fruitfulness
feroz	ferocious	la ferocidad	ferocity; wildness; fierceness
incapaz	incapable	la incapacidad	incapacity; incompetence; incapability
lenguaz	loquacious; garrulous; talkative	la lengua[1]	tongue
locuaz	loquacious; talkative	la locuacidad	loquacity; talkativeness
mendaz	mendacious; given to lying	la mendacidad	mendacity
montaraz	wild	el monte[2]	mountain; mount; woodland
mordaz	mordant; biting	la mordacidad	mordacity; mordant or biting nature
perspicaz	perspicacious	la perspicacia	perspicacity; clear-sightedness

Formed Word	English Equivalent	Related to	English Equivalent
pertinaz	pertinacious	la pertinacia	pertinacity; doggedness; stubbornness
precoz	precocious	la precocidad	precocity
pugnaz	pugnacious; quarrelsome; scrappy	la pugnacidad	pugnacity; quarrelsomeness
rapaz[3]	rapacious; of prey; (fig.) thievish	la rapacidad	rapacity; greed
sagaz	sagacious	la sagacidad	sagacity
salaz	salacious; wanton	(Lat.) salire	to spring, leap, jump, bound
suspicaz	suspicious	la suspicacia	suspiciousness; mistrust
tenaz	tenacious	la tenacidad	tenacity; tenaciousness
veloz	swift	la velocidad[4]	velocity; speed
veraz	veracious; truthful	la veracidad	veracity; truthfulness
vivaz	vivacious	la vivacidad	vivacity; liveliness; energy; vigor
voraz	voracious	la voracidad	voracity; voraciousness

[1] andar en lenguas = to be much talked about, be the subject of gossip
[2] echarse al monte = to take to the hills
[3] las rapaces = (orn.) birds of prey
[4] en gran velocidad = express; by passenger train

-aza
Meaning: augmentative; forms abstract noun
English equivalent: none
Found in: nouns

The ending -aza (like its more commonly found sister suffix -azo) indicates enlargement or exaggeration of the root term. At times this enlargement is no more than a physical increase in size, e.g., *la pernaza* (thick or big leg), from *la pierna* (leg); however, the ending -aza often also carries negative connotations, e.g., *la bocaza* (big ugly mouth), from *la boca* (mouth). All terms ending with -aza are feminine.

Formed Word	English Equivalent	Related to	English Equivalent
la barbaza	great shaggy beard	la barba	beard
la barcaza	barge	la barca	boat
la bocaza	big ugly mouth	la boca[1]	mouth
la carnaza	fleshiness	la carne[2]	flesh; meat
la hilaza	yarn; fiber	el hilo	thread
la madraza	doting mother	la madre	mother
la manaza	hefty hand; paw	la mano	hand
la matronaza	plump, respectable woman	la matrona	matron
la pajaza	stalks of horses' fodder left uneaten	la paja[3]	straw; chaff; trash
la pernaza	thick or big leg	la pierna[4]	leg
la sangraza	thick, heavy blood	la sangre[5]	blood
la terraza	terrace	la tierra	land; earth
la trapaza	fraud; trick	trapacear	to cheat, swindle

[1] boca del estómago = pit of the stomach
[2] ser carne y sangre = to be kith and kin
[3] no dormirse en las pajas = not to let the grass grow under one's feet
[4] estirar las piernas = to stretch one's legs
[5] a sangre fría = in cold blood

-azgo
Meaning: *office; post; dignity; relationship; tariff*
English equivalent: *-ship*
Found in: nouns

Added to a noun, the suffix -azgo usually denotes high position, office, post, or territory. In this capacity, -azgo is similar in meaning and function to the endings -ato and -ado (office; position; system, etc.). It also can indicate a particular relationship, e.g., *el comadrazgo* (relationship between the mother and godmother), or specific tariffs or fees, e.g., *el terrazgo* (land rent). All words ending with -azgo are masculine.

Formed Word	English Equivalent	Related to	English Equivalent
el alaminazgo	office of a surveyor/ clerk	el alamín	surveyor; clerk
el alarifazgo	office of a builder	el alarife	architect; builder
el albaceazgo	executorship	el albacea	executor
el alferazgo	dignity of an ensign; ensigncy	el alférez	ensign
el alguacilazgo	office of a constable	el alguacil	constable
el almirantazgo	admiralship	el almirante	admiral
el almotacenazgo	inspector's office and duty	el almotacén	inspector (of weights and measures)
el cacicazgo	dignity/territory of a political boss	el cacique	political boss; Indian chief
el cillazgo	storehouse fees	la cilla	granary
el comadrazgo	relationship between mother and godmother	la comadre[1]	reciprocal name of mother and godmother
el compadrazgo	relationship between child's parents and godfather	el compadre	father or godfather *(with respect to each other);* mate; pal; chum
el liderazgo	leadership	el líder	leader (political)
el mayorazgo	primogeniture	el mayor[2]	the eldest (male)
el mecenazgo	patronage	el mecenas	patron (of art or literature)

Formed Word	English Equivalent	Related to	English Equivalent
el noviazgo	engagement; courtship	el novio	bridegroom; groom-to-be
el padrinazgo	(baptismal) sponsorship; patronage	el padrino	godfather; patron
el papazgo	papacy; pontificate	el Papa	the Pope
el pontazgo	bridge-toll	el puente[3]	bridge
el primazgo	cousinhood	el primo	cousin
el sobrinazgo	relationship of a nephew or niece	el sobrino	nephew
el tenientazgo	lieutenantship; deputy's office	el teniente	lieutenant; deputy
el terrazgo	arable land; land-rent	la tierra[4]	land
el vicealmirantazgo	vice-admiralship	el vicealmirante	vice-admiral
el villazgo	charter of a town	la villa[5]	town; villa; municipal council

[1]las Alegres Comadres de Windsor = the Merry Wives of Windsor
[2]mayor de edad = of age
[3]puente giratorio = swing bridge; puente colgante = suspension bridge
[4]tierra firme = continent
[5]casa de la villa = town hall

-azo

Meaning: augmentative
English equivalent: none
Found in: nouns

In this group of words, the addition of -azo (like its sister suffix -aza) indicates enlargement of the base term. Usually the augmentation is physical, as in el gatazo (big cat). However, it can be somewhat deprecative, as in el padrazo (doting father). While this suffix is considered a noun ending, note that in one instance it works outside this milieu (see antañazo). Note as well that el copo and la copa each yield el copazo, but with entirely different meanings. All terms ending with -azo are masculine.

Formed Word	English Equivalent	Related to	English Equivalent
el aceitazo	thick oil	el aceite	oil
el animalazo	large hulking animal	el animal	animal
antañazo *(adv.)*	*(coll.)* way back in time	antaño *(adv.)*	in days of yore
el bigotazo	large mustache	el bigote	mustache
el bombazo	great big bomb	la bomba[1]	bomb
el boyazo	large ox	el buey	ox
el copazo	large snowflake	el copo	snowflake
el copazo	large wine glass; goblet	la copa	wine glass
el exitazo	terrific success; "smash hit"	el éxito[2]	success
el gatazo	large cat	el gato	cat
el gustazo	great pleasure; relish	el gusto[3]	pleasure
el hombrazo	great hefty fellow	el hombre	man
el humazo	dense smoke	el humo[4]	smoke
el maretazo	heavy surge; swell	la marea[5]	tide; gentle sea breeze
el maridazo	doting husband	el marido	husband
el padrazo	doting father	el padre	father
el perrazo	great hefty dog or hound	el perro	dog
el platazo	platter; large helping of food	el plato[6]	plate; dish
el playazo	long, wide beach	la playa	beach
el plumazo	feather mattress or pillow	la pluma	feather
el terrazo	landscape	la tierra	land; earth
el vejazo	very old man	el viejo	old man
el vinazo	strong, heavy wine	el vino	wine
el zapatazo	large shoe	el zapato	shoe

[1]bomba fétida = stink bomb
[2]tener mucho éxito = to be very successful
[3]estar a gusto = to feel at home, comfortable
[4]irse todo en humo = to go up in smoke
[5]marea menguante = ebb tide; marea muerta = neap tide
[6]plato fuerte = main dish

-azo

Meaning: *blow or strike with or from; resulting action*
English equivalent: none
Found in: nouns

The following list of words offers a wonderful example of Spanish at its most simple and logical, and English at its least. The suffix *-azo* is commonly used in Spanish to signify a blow given by or with the root noun. As there is no English equivalent, we have to add the words "blow," "strike," "hit," and so on to convey the meaning found simply in the Spanish ending *-azo*. All words ending with *-azo* are masculine.

Formed Word	English Equivalent	Related to	English Equivalent
el balazo	shot; gunshot; bullet wound	la bala[1]	bullet
el botellazo	blow with a bottle	la botella	bottle
el botonazo	thrust with fencing-foil	el botón	tip (of a foil in fencing)
el calabazazo	blow from a pumpkin	la calabaza	pumpkin
el codazo	shove with an elbow	el codo	elbow
el culatazo	kick of a gun	la culata	butt of a gun
el chinelazo	blow with a slipper	la chinela	slipper
el escopetazo	gunshot wound; *(fig.)* thunderbolt	la escopeta	shotgun
el espaldarazo	back slap	la espalda	back *(anat.)*
el estacazo	blow with a stake	la estaca	stake; stick; bludgeon
el gatillazo	click of a trigger	el gatillo	trigger (of a gun)
el golpazo	violent blow	el golpe[2]	blow; hit
el guantazo	slap with the open hand	el guante[3]	glove
el latigazo	whiplash	el látigo	whip
el librazo	blow with a book	el libro	book
el martillazo	hammer-stroke	el martillo	hammer
el palazo	blow with a shovel	la pala	shovel
el pelotazo	shot with a ball	la pelota	ball
el picazo	jab; peck	el pico	beak; bill
el pistoletazo	pistol shot	la pistola	pistol

Formed Word	English Equivalent	Related to	English Equivalent
el plumazo	stroke of a pen	la pluma	pen
el porrazo	blow; knock; fall	la porra	stick; nightstick
el portazo	door slam	la puerta	door
el pretinazo	swipe with a belt; belting	la pretina	belt; girdle; waistband
el puñetazo	blow with a fist; punch	el puño	fist
el rodillazo	shove with the knee	la rodilla[4]	knee
el tablazo	stroke with a board	la tabla[5]	board
el tacazo	stroke with a billiard cue	el taco	billiard cue
el tijeretazo	cut with a scissors	la tijera[6]	scissors
el timbrazo	sharp ring of a bell	el timbre	bell
el varazo	swipe with a pole, stick	la vara	pole; rod; staff
el ventanazo	slamming of a window	la ventana	window
el zapatazo	blow with a shoe	el zapato	shoe

[1]como una bala = like a shot
[2]golpe de estado = coup d'état
[3]guantes de cabritilla = kid gloves
[4]de rodillas = on one's knees; kneeling
[5]hacer tabla rasa = to make a clean sweep
[6]catre de tijera = folding cot; silla de tijera = folding chair; deck chair

-cial

Meaning: *like; relating to*
English equivalent: *-cial; -tial*
Found in: adjectives

Spanish words ending with *-cial* generally are cognates of their English counterparts, making them easy to recognize and learn. The ending *-cial* is found in adjectives, and indicates that someone or something holds characteristics of the base noun.

Formed Word	English Equivalent	Related to	English Equivalent
artificial[1]	artificial; manmade	el artificio	workmanship; artifice; craft

Formed Word	English Equivalent	Related to	English Equivalent
comercial	commercial; relating to trade	el comercio[3]	trade; commerce
consecuencial	consequential; resulting	el consecuente	consequence
crucial	crucial; cross-shaped	la cruz[4]	cross
esencial	essential	la esencia[5]	essence; scent
especial[6]	special; particular	la especia[7]	species; kind; class; sort
existencial	existential	la existencia	existence
exponencial	(math.) exponential	el exponente	exponent
judicial	judicial; judiciary	el juicio[8]	judgment; sense; opinion
palacial	palatial	el palacio	palace
parcial	partial; biased	la parte[9]	part
penitencial	penitential	la penitencia	penance; penitence
perjudicial	harmful; hurtful	el perjuicio	detriment; damage; harm
policial	(of the) police	la policía	police (department)
prejudicial	(law) requiring judicial decision	el prejuicio	prejudice; bias; prejudgment
presencial[10]	relating to actual presence	la presencia	presence
providencial	providential	la providencia	providence; foresight
provincial	provincial	la provincia	province
racial	racial	la raza[11]	race; breed; stock
residencial	residential	la residencia	residence; domicile

Formed Word	English Equivalent	Related to	English Equivalent
social[12]	social	el socio[13]	partner; member; fellow
superficial	superficial; shallow	la superficie	surface; area
sustancial	substantial; solid; having body	la sustancia	substance; solidness; body
tangencial	tangential	la tangente	tangent
torrencial	torrential; overpowering	el torrente	torrent; avalanche; rush

[1]fuegos artificiales = fireworks
[2]beneficio bruto = gross profit; beneficio neto = net profit
[3]comercio exterior = foreign trade
[4]en cruz = crosswise; with arms extended
[5]por esencia = essentially
[6]en especial = specially
[7]la especie humana = mankind
[8]juicio temerario = rash or hasty judgment
[9]ir a la parte = to share, go halves, go Dutch
[10]testigo presencial = eyewitness
[11]de raza = thoroughbred
[12]trabajador social = social worker
[13]socio capitalista = financial partner

-ción

Meaning: *result of action; state of being; act*
English equivalent: *-tion*
Found in: nouns

The Spanish suffix *-ción* corresponds to the English *-tion:* in both languages the suffix refers to a result of action, state of being, or act. Words taking this ending are related to verbs. Note below that with the exception of *la partición,* which is derived from *partir,* all examples are derived from *-ar* verbs. Infinitives that end in *-ctar* or *-ctuar* take a double *c* in the formed word (i.e., *actuar* gives us *acción*). All words ending in *-ción* are feminine, and drop the accent when made plural: *la opción; las opciones.*

Formed Word	English Equivalent	Related to	English Equivalent
la acción[1]	action	actuar	to act
la adoración[2]	adoration; worship	adorar	to adore, worship

Formed Word	English Equivalent	Related to	English Equivalent
la afiliación	affiliation	afiliar	to affiliate
la animación[3]	animation	animar	to animate
la aplicación	application; diligence	aplicar[4]	to apply
la asociación	association; fellowship	asociar	to associate
la aspiración	aspiration; inspiration	aspirar	to aspire
la celebración	celebration	celebrar	to celebrate
la colocación	placing; setting; arrangement	colocar[5]	to place, position
la condición[6]	condition; state; disposition	condicionar	to condition
la dicción	diction	dictar	to dictate
la difamación	defamation (of character)	difamar	to defame
la dominación	domination	dominar[7]	to dominate, master, command
la donación	donation; act of donating	donar	to donate, give
la embarcación	embarkation	embarcar	to embark
la explicación	explanation	explicar	to explain
la felicitación[8]	congratulation; greeting	felicitar	to congratulate
la formación	formation	formar	to form
la frustración	frustration	frustrar	to frustrate, thwart, foil
la infección	infection	infectar	to infect
la inyección	injection	inyectar	to inject
la limitación	limitation	limitar	to limit
la opción	option	optar[9]	to opt, choose
la operación	operation	operar	to operate

Formed Word	English Equivalent	Related to	English Equivalent
la oración[10]	oration; prayer	orar	to pray, make a speech
la organización	organization	organizar	to organize
la partición	partition	partir	to part
la plantación	plantation	plantar	to plant
la preparación	preparation	preparar	to prepare
la pronunciación	pronunciation	pronunciar	to pronounce, utter
la purificación	purification	purificar	to purify
la revolución	revolution	revolver	to stir, stir up, turn
la separación	separation	separar	to separate
la simulación	simulation	simular	to simulate
la situación[11]	situation; position; location	situar	to situate, locate, place
la subversión	subversion	subvertir	to subvert
la suplicación[12]	supplication; *(law)* appeal	suplicar	to entreat, supplicate; *(law)* appeal (against)
la suposición	supposition; assumption	suponer	to suppose, assume
la tentación	temptation	tentar	to tempt
la verificación	verification	verificar	to verify
la vindicación	vindication	vindicar	to vindicate
la violación	violation; rape	violar	to violate, rape
la visitación	visitation; visiting; visit	visitar	to visit

[1]día de la Acción de Gracias = Thanksgiving Day
[2]Adoración de los Reyes Magos = Epiphany
[3]las animaciones = entertainment; floor show
[4]aplicar el oído = to listen attentively
[5]colocar por orden = to place in order

[6]a condición de que *or* bajo la condición de que = on (the) condition that
[7]domina cuatro idiomas = he has a command of four languages
[8]¡Felicitaciones! = Congratulations!
[9]optar por = to choose to, decide on
[10]*(gram.)* partes de la oración = parts of speech
[11]situación activa = active service, position, or office
[12]a suplicación = on petition; by request

-culo; -cula; -ulo; -ula
Meaning: diminutive; resulting object or person
English equivalent: *-cule; -ule*
Found in: nouns; adjectives (rarely)

The suffix *-culo* and its less common variations *-cula, -ulo,* and *-ula* often denote something very small, e.g., *el gránulo* (granule). As you will see, many of these are taken directly from Latin. Within this group is *el minúsculo,* which is an adjective (small; tiny) as well as a noun (small letter); otherwise, words ending with *-culo, -cula , -ulo,* or *-ula* nearly always are nouns. Its second function is to denote result of action. These words are derived from verbs: *el obstáculo* (obstacle) is something that gets in the way, and comes from the verb *obstar* (to stand in the way). Note that the antepenultimate syllable is accented in words taking these endings.

Formed Word	English Equivalent	Related to	English Equivalent
el artículo[1]	article; item; joint	*(Lat.)* articulus	joint
el capítulo	chapter; heading; entry	*(Lat.)* capitulum	little head
la cápsula	capsule	*(Lat.)* capsula	little holder or container
el círculo[2]	circle; ring	*(Lat.)* circulus	circle
el cubículo	cubicle	el cubo	cube
el discípulo	disciple	*(Lat.)* discipulus	pupil
el edículo	small building; shrine; niche	*(Lat.)* aedicula	small building
el folículo	follicle	*(Lat.)* folliculus	small bag
el glóbulo	globule	el globo[3]	globe; ball; sphere
el gránulo	granule	el grano[4]	grain; seed; corn; pimple
(el) minúsculo	small letter; minuscule	*(Lat.)* minusculus	somewhat small; less

Formed Word	English Equivalent	Related to	English Equivalent
el módulo	module	el modo[5]	mode; manner; way
la molécula	molecule	(Lat.) moles	mass; bulk; pile
el montículo	mound; hillock	el monte	mountain; mount; woodland
el nódulo	nodule	cl nodo	node; knot
el obstáculo	obstacle	obstar	to stand in the way
el oráculo	oracle	orar	to pray
(el) párvulo	infant; very small	parvo	small; little; scanty
el pedículo	(bot.) pedicle; footstalk; little foot	(Lat.) pes	foot
la película	film; movie	(Lat.) pellicula	small skin
el péndulo[6]	pendulum	pender	to hang, dangle
el receptáculo	receptacle; repository; refuge	receptar	to receive, hide, shelter
(el) ridículo[7]	ridicule; ridiculous	(Lat.) ridiculus	exciting laughter
el signáculo	signet; seal	el signo[8]	sign; mark; symbol
el tabernáculo	tabernacle	la taberna	hut
el tentáculo	tentacle	tentar	to touch, feel
el testículo	testicle	(anat.) el teste	testis
la válvula[9]	valve; tube	(Lat.) valvae	folding doors
el vehículo	vehicle	(Lat.) vehiculum	vehicle
el ventrículo	ventricle	el vientre	abdomen
el versículo	small, short verse; Bible verse	el verso	verse

Formed Word	English Equivalent	Related to	English Equivalent
el vínculo	bond; tie	vincular	to tie, bind

---

[1](gram.) artículo definido or determinado (indefinido or indeterminado) = definite (indefinite) article
[2]círculo vicioso = vicious circle
[3]globo del ojo = eyeball
[4]ir al grano = to come or get to the point
[5]de otro modo = otherwise
[6](astron.) péndulo sidéreo = standard clock
[7]ponerse en ridículo = to make a fool of oneself
[8]signo externo = status symbol
[9]válvula de seguridad = safety valve

-dizo (-diza)

Meaning: *like; relating to; tending to*
English equivalent: none
Found in: adjectives

The adjectival suffix *-dizo* is used to describe what someone or something is like or tends to do. Adjectives ending in *-dizo* are derived from verbs. Note that the *-ar* verbs retain the *a* before the suffix, just as the *-er* verbs retain the letter *e*, and the *-ir* verbs retain the *i*. (From *olvidar* comes *olvidadizo*; from *llover, llovedizo*; from *escurrir, escurridizo*). As this is an adjectival ending, when you use these terms to describe feminine nouns, the suffix becomes *-diza*.

Formed Word	English Equivalent	Related to	English Equivalent
ablandadizo	soothing; easily persuaded	ablandar	to soften, mollify, mellow
acomodadizo	accommodating; obliging	acomodar	to accommodate
anegadizo	subject to flooding; easily flooded	anegar	to flood, inundate, submerge
apagadizo	tending to go out easily	apagar	to turn off, extinguish
apartadizo	antisocial; standoffish	apartar	to separate, turn aside
apretadizo	easily bound; compressed	apretar	to press, tighten
arrojadizo	made for throwing	arrojar	to throw, hurl

Formed Word	English Equivalent	Related to	English Equivalent
asustadizo	easily frightened or scared	asustar	to frighten, scare
bajadizo	descending; sloping gently	bajar	to lower, let down
bebedizo	drinkable	beber[1]	to drink
borneadizo	pliant; flexible	bornear	to bend, turn, twist
caedizo	ready to fall	caer[2]	to fall
caladizo	(fig.) smart; sharp	calar	to penetrate, soak through
cambiadizo	changeable; fickle	cambiar	to change, alter
clavadizo	nail-studded	clavar	to nail
cogedizo	which can be easily collected	coger	to pick up, collect
cosedizo	which can be stitched or sewed	coser	to stitch, sew
enojadizo	irritable; easily annoyed	enojar	to anger, vex, irritate
enviadizo	(regularly) sent	enviar	to send, remit, dispatch
erradizo	wandering	errar	to wander, miss
escurridizo	slippery; tricky	escurrir	to slip (away), sneak away
heladizo	easily congealed	helar	to freeze, turn to ice, chill
levadizo[3]	that can be lifted or raised	levantar	to lift, raise
llovedizo	leaky	llover[4]	to rain

Formed Word	English Equivalent	Related to	English Equivalent
manchadizo	easily stained or soiled	manchar	to stain, soil, spot
movedizo	movable	mover	to move
olvidadizo	forgetful	olvidar	to forget
rajadizo	fissile; easily split	rajar[5]	to split, rend, slash, slice
resbaladizo	slippery	resbalar	to slip, slide
saledizo	jutting; salient	salir[6]	to go out, leave
tornadizo	fickle; changeable	tornar	to turn, come back
traedizo	portable	traer	to carry, bring

[1]beber los vientos por = to sigh or long for
[2]dejar caer = to drop
[3]puente levadizo = drawbridge
[4]está lloviendo a cántaros = it's raining cats and dogs
[5]rajarse = *(coll.)* to back out
[6]salirse de madre = to lose control

-dor (-dora)

Meaning: *one who;* denotes profession
English equivalent: *-er; -or*
Found in: nouns

The following words that end in *-dor* denote persons who perform specific tasks. The task relates directly to the root verb. The formation of these terms is simple: remove the *r* from the infinitive, and add the suffix *-dor*. Thus, *matar* becomes *matador*; *morder* becomes *mordedor*; *exprimir* becomes *exprimidor* (one exception is *veedor* from *ver,* which adds an *e).* Several Spanish suffixes indicate *one who.* Note that words ending with *-dor* often refer to persons or professions possessing or requiring physical power and strength.

Formed Word	English Equivalent	Related to	English Equivalent
el aborrecedor	hater	aborrecer	to hate
el asaltador	assailant; assaulter	asaltar	to assault
el azotador	whipper	azotar	to whip

Formed Word	English Equivalent	Related to	English Equivalent
el batallador	battler; warrior; fencer	batallar	to battle, fight, fence
el bateador	batter	batear	to bat
el batidor	beater	batir	to beat
el boxeador	boxer	boxear	to box
el cazador[1]	hunter	cazar	to hunt
el conquistador	conqueror; *(coll.)* lady-killer	conquistar	to conquer; win (over)
el edificador	constructor; builder	edificar	to construct, build
el escupidor	spitter	escupir[2]	to spit, spit at or out
el exprimidor	squeezer	exprimir	to squeeze
el jaleador	cheerer	jalear	to cheer, encourage with shouts
el jugador[3]	player (game)	jugar	to play (a game)
el labrador	laborer	labrar	to labor
el luchador	fighter; struggler	luchar	to fight, struggle
el malgastador	squanderer; spendthrift; wastrel	malgastar	to misspend, squander, waste
el malversador	embezzler	malversar	to embezzle
el mamador	sucker; one who sucks	mamar	to suck
el matador	killer	matar[4]	to kill
el mordedor	biter	morder	to bite
el pateador	kicker	patear[5]	*(coll.)* to kick, stamp

Formed Word	English Equivalent	Related to	English Equivalent
el peleador	fighter	pelear	to fight
el pulverizador	pulverizer	pulverizar	to pulverize
el saltador	jumper	saltar[6]	to jump
el secuestrador[7]	kidnapper	secuestrar	to kidnap
el sitiador	besieger	sitiar	to besiege
el tirador	shooter	tirar[8]	to throw, shoot, fling, cast
el torcedor	twister	torcer	to twist
el toreador	bullfighter	torear	to fight bulls
el veedor	spy; prier	ver[9]	to see
el vencedor	conqueror	vencer	to conquer
el violador	violator; rapist	violar	to violate, rape

[1]cazador de dotes = fortune hunter; cazador furtivo = poacher
[2]escupir al cielo = to rail against Heaven
[3]jugador de manos = magician; prestidigitator
[4]matar de hambre = to starve to death
[5]se pateó todo Méjico = he traipsed all over Mexico
[6]saltar de alegría = to jump for or with joy
[7]secuestrador aéreo = airplane hijacker
[8]tirar un tiro = to fire a shot
[9]a ver = let's see

-dor; -dora
Meaning: *machine; appliance*
English equivalent: none
Found in: nouns

In the previous entry you find the ending -*dor* (or -*dora*), which indicates a person who performs a specific task. In this entry you will find a list of machines and appliances that perform specific chores, each directly derived from a verb. If the origin is an -*ar* verb, that *a* is retained, e.g., *el despertador* (alarm clock), from *despertar* (to wake up). If the origin is an -*er* or -*ir* verb, the *e* or *i* will be retained, respectively. Words ending with -*dor* are masculine, while those ending with -*dora* are feminine.

Formed Word	English Equivalent	Related to	English Equivalent
el abridor[1]	opener	abrir	to open
el acondicionador	air-conditioner	acondicionar	to air-condition

Formed Word	English Equivalent	Related to	English Equivalent
el asador	spit; rotisserie	asar[2]	to roast
la aspiradora	vacuum cleaner	aspirar	to breathe in, aspirate
el borrador	eraser	borrar	to erase, rub out
la calculadora	calculator	calcular	to calculate
la computadora	computer	computar	to compute, calculate
el congelador	freezer	congelar	to freeze, congeal
el contestador	(telephone) answering machine	contestar	to answer, reply
el copiador	duplicating or copying machine	copiar	to copy, duplicate
la cosechadora	harvester; reaping machine	cosechar	to reap, harvest
la cribadora	sifter	cribar	to sift
la cultivadora	cultivating machine; cultivator	cultivar	to cultivate, grow
el despertador	alarm clock	despertar	to awaken, rouse, wake up
el destornillador	screwdriver	destornillar	to unscrew
el destripador	(seam) ripper	destripar	to rip open
el estampador	stamper	estampar[3]	to stamp, print, imprint
la (máquina) expendedora	vending machine	expender	to spend, expend, lay out
la grabadora	tape recorder	grabar	to engrave, cut, tape
la grapadora	stapler; stapling machine	grapar	to staple
el humidificador	humidifier	humidificar	to humidify
el imprimador	(art) primer	imprimar	(art) to prime

Formed Word	English Equivalent	Related to	English Equivalent
el incinerador	incinerator	incinerar	to incinerate, cremate
la lavadora	washing machine	lavar	to wash
la mezcladora	blender; mixer	mezclar	to mix, blend
el ordeñador	milking machine	ordeñar	to milk
el perforador	drill	perforar	to drill or bore (through)
el purificador	purifier	purificar	to purify, cleanse
el radiador	radiator	radiar	to radiate
el rallador	grater (for cheese, etc.)	rallar	to grate, vex
el refrigerador	refrigerator; cooler	refrigerar	to cool, refrigerate
el rociador	sprinkler	rociar	to sprinkle
el secador	hair dryer	secar	to dry
la secadora	dryer (for laundry)	secar	to dry
la segadora[4]	mowing machine	segar	to mow, cut, or mow down
el tostador	toaster	tostar[5]	to toast
el transportador[6]	transporter; carrier	transportar	to transport, convey
la trilladora[7]	threshing machine	trillar	to thresh, beat
el vibrador	vibrator	vibrar	to vibrate
la voladora	fly wheel (of an engine)	volar[8]	to fly

---

[1]abridor de latas = can opener
[2]asar a la parrilla = to grill
[3]esto se le estampó en la memoria = this became fixed or engraved in (his) mind
[4]segadora de césped = lawn mower

[5]tostarse al sol = to bask in the sun
[6]correa transportadora = conveyor belt
[7]trilladora segadora = combine harvester
[8]volando = double quick

-dumbre; -umbre
Meaning: forms abstract noun
English equivalent: -ness
Found in: nouns

The addition of -dumbre or -umbre to a base word results in an abstraction of that term. Base words can be either nouns or adjectives. As you will see, -dumbre and -umbre are not common suffixes. Words taking these endings are feminine.

Formed Word	English Equivalent	Related to	English Equivalent
la certidumbre	certainty; certitude	cierto[1]	certain; sure
la dulcedumbre	sweetness	dulce[2]	sweet
la herrumbre	rust; irony taste	el hierro[3]	iron
la mansedumbre	gentleness; meekness; mildness	manso[4]	gentle; meek; mild; tame
la muchedumbre	multitude; crowd; (fig.) masses	mucho[5]	much; a great deal of
la pesadumbre	grief; sorrow; heaviness	el peso[6]	weight
la podredumbre	corruption; putrification	la podre	pus
la salsedumbre	saltiness	la sal[7]	salt
la techumbre	roofing	el techo	roof

[1]no, por cierto = no, by no means
[2]los dulces = candy
[3]hierro colado or hierro fundido = cast iron
[4]una mansa brisa = a gentle breeze
[5]ni mucho menos = far from it; not by a long shot
[6]peso muerto = dead weight
[7]sal gema = mineral salt

-dura
Meaning: *resulting action; resulting object*
English equivalent: *-ing*
Found in: nouns

The following words that end in *-dura* all are derived from verbs, and indicate either the act of the verb itself, e.g., *mascadura* (chewing) from *mascar* (to chew), or the physical object directly related to that verb, e.g., *vestidura* (clothing) from *vestir* (to dress). A spelling aid is built into these formed words: Those derived from *-ar* verbs retain the *a,* and thus end with *-adura;* those derived from *-er* verbs end in *-edura;* and those from *-ir* verbs end in *-idura.* (One exception is *tosidura,* which is derived from *toser*). Words ending with *-dura* are feminine.

Formed Word	English Equivalent	Related to	English Equivalent
la alisadura	planing; smoothing	alisar	to plane, smooth down
la anudadura	knotting; tying	anudar	to knot, tie
la añadidura[1]	addition; extra measure	añadir	to add, increase
la apañadura	fixing; arranging; mending	apañar	to fix, arrange, mend
la armadura	armor; armature	armar[2]	to arm
la arrodilladura	kneeling	arrodillar(se)	to kneel (down)
la bordadura	embroidery; embroidering	bordar	to embroider
la cabalgadura	mount; horse; beast of burden	cabalgar	to go horseback riding
la cerradura[3]	locking or shutting up; lock	cerrar[4]	to close, shut, lock
la escocedura	burning pain	escocer	to make smart or sting
la lamedura	lick; licking	lamer	to lick, lap
la ligadura	binding; tie	ligar	to bind, tie
la limpiadura	cleaning	limpiar	to clean, cleanse
la mascadura	chewing	mascar	to chew
la mecedura	rocking	mecer	to rock

Formed Word	English Equivalent	Related to	English Equivalent
la peladura	stripping; peeling	pelar	to strip, peel, skin
la perfiladura	profiling; outlining	perfilar	to profile, outline
la picadura	bite; prick; sting	picar	to prick, pierce
la quemadura	burn; scald	quemar[5]	to burn, scald, scorch
la rapadura	close haircut	rapar	to shave, crop the hair
la rasadura	leveling	rasar	to graze, skim, level
la raspadura	rasping; filing; scraping	raspar	to rasp, file, scrape
la retozadura	friskiness	retozar	to frolic, romp
la rifadura	brawl	rifar	to quarrel, dispute
la rociadura	sprinkling	rociar	to sprinkle
la rodadura	rolling	rodar	to roll
la rompedura	breakage; breaking	romper[6]	to break
la rozadura	friction; chafing; rubbing	rozar	to chafe, rub, scrape
la teñidura	dying; tinging	teñir	to dye, stain, tinge
la tosidura	coughing	toser	to cough
la tropezadura	stumbling	tropezar	to stumble, trip up
la vestidura	clothing; vestments; dress	vestir(se)	to dress (one's self)

[1]por añadidura = further; furthermore; in addition; besides; to boot
[2]armarse de valor = to pluck up courage
[3]cerradura de golpe = spring-lock
[4]cerrar el paso = to block or bar the way
[5]quemar la sangre a alguien = to needle or irritate someone
[6]romperse la cabeza = to rack one's brains

-eda; -edo

Meaning: *grove; orchard; place where something grows*
English equivalent: none
Found in: nouns

The suffix *-eda* or *-edo* generally denotes a large grouping of whatever kind of tree the root word denotes. Either ending can also indicate a place where something grows, i.e., *la cepeda* (land overgrown with heath), but nearly always refers to a collection of trees. The endings *-eda* and *-edo* are identical in the function they perform; the only difference is that *-eda* is always feminine, while *-edo* is masculine. Note that in some cases either ending is acceptable (with no change in meaning).

Formed Word	English Equivalent	Related to	English Equivalent
el ablanedo	hazelnut or filbert plantation	el ablano	hazelnut or filbert tree
el/la acebedo/a	holly tree plantation	el acebo	holly tree
la alameda	poplar grove	el álamo[1]	poplar
el alcornoquedo	grove of cork trees	el alcornoque	cork tree; *(fig.)* blockhead
el arandanedo	cranberry bog	el arándano	cranberry
el/la arboledo/a	grove; woodland	el árbol[2]	tree
el arcedo	maple grove	el arce	maple tree
el/la bujedo/a	boxwood grove	el boj	box tree
el carvalledo	oak grove	el carvallo	*(prov.)* oak
la castañeda	chestnut grove	el castaño	chestnut tree
la cepeda	land overgrown with heath	la cepa	vinestock
la cereceda	cherry orchard	el cerezo	cherry tree
la encineda	live oak or evergreen oak grove	la encina	live oak; evergreen oak; ilex
la fresneda	ash grove	el fresno[3]	ash tree
el hayedo	beech forest	la haya	beech tree
el/la madroñedo/a	strawberry grove	el madroño	strawberry plant; strawberry fruit
la moreda	grove of mulberry trees	el moral	mulberry tree

Formed Word	English Equivalent	Related to	English Equivalent
el olmedo	elm grove	el olmo	elm tree
la peraleda	pear orchard	el peral	pear tree
la robleda	oak grove	el roble	oak tree
la rosaleda	rose garden	el rosal[4]	rose bush
la sauceda	willow grove	el sauce[5]	willow tree

[1]álamo temblón = aspen
[2]árbol de pie = seedling
[3]fresno americano = white ash
[4]rosal castellano = red rose
[5]sauce llorón = weeping willow

-edad; -dad

Meaning: *state of being;* forms abstract noun
English equivalent: *-ness; -hood*
Found in: nouns

As most of the words following demonstrate, the addition of *-edad* or *-dad* to an adjective creates an abstract noun that relates to the qualities of that adjective. Either suffix also can be attached to a noun, denoting then the abstract collection of that noun. The more common form is *-edad;* but generally, if the final consonant of the root word is an *l* or an *n,* the suffix is simply *-dad.* All words ending in *-edad* or *-dad* are feminine.

Formed Word	English Equivalent	Related to	English Equivalent
la beldad	beauty; belle	bello	beautiful; fair
la brevedad	briefness; brevity	breve	brief; short
la ceguedad	blindness	ciego	blind
la contrariedad	opposition; annoyance; irritation	contrario[1]	contrary; contradictory; opposite
la cortedad	smallness; *(fig.)* shyness	corto[2]	short; brief; shy
la crueldad	cruelty	cruel[3]	cruel
la chatedad	flatness; shallowness	chato	flat; flat-nosed
la ebriedad	drunkenness; intoxication	ebrio	drunk; intoxicated
la enfermedad	sickness; disease	enfermo	sick

Formed Word	English Equivalent	Related to	English Equivalent
la fidelidad	surety; guarantee; security	fiel[4]	faithful; loyal; true
la frialdad	coldness; coolness	frío	cold; cool
la hermandad	fraternity, brotherhood	(el) hermano	brother
la humedad	humidity; dampness	húmedo	humid; damp; moist
la humildad	humility; humbleness; lowliness	humilde	humble; lowly; meek; submissive
la igualdad	equality; evenness	igual[5]	equal
la impiedad	impiety; impiousness	impío	impious; irreligious
la levedad	lightness; slightness	leve	light; slight; trifling
la liviandad	lightness; fickleness	liviano	light; fickle; trivial
la mesmedad[6]	sameness; essential nature	mismo[7]	same; selfsame
la novedad	novelty; new thing	nuevo	new
la orfandad	orphanhood; neglect; dearth	el huérfano	orphan
la sequedad	dryness	seco[8]	dry; dried-up
la seriedad	seriousness; earnestness	serio	serious; earnest
la sobriedad	sobriety; frugality; moderation	sobrio	sober; frugal; moderate; sparing
la soledad	solitude; loneliness	solo	alone; lonely; solitary
la tochedad	rusticity; coarseness	tocho	rustic; uncouth; coarse

Formed Word	English Equivalent	Related to	English Equivalent
la tosquedad	coarseness; clumsiness	tosco	coarse; rude; clumsy
la turbiedad	turbidness	turbio	turbid; troubled; cloudy
la vastedad	vastness; huge expanse	vasto	vast; immense; huge
la vecindad	neighborhood	el vecino	neighbor
la viudedad	widowhood	la viuda	widow
la voluntariedad	voluntariness; willfulness	voluntario	voluntary
la zafiedad	boorishness; cloddishness	zafio	boorish; uncouth; cloddish

[1]ser contrario a = to be against or opposed to
[2]corto de vista = shortsighted
[3]cruel con or cruel para = cruel to
[4]en fiel = of equal weight; in equal balance
[5]por igual = evenly; without discrimination
[6]por su misma mesmedad = by itself; by the very fact
[7]lo mismo me da = it's all the same to me
[8]hojas secas = dead leaves

-ejo; -eja
Meaning: diminutive; pejorative
English equivalent: none
Found in: nouns

The ending -ejo or -eja generally indicates physical smallness of the base term. Either ending can, however, be pejorative and denote diminished status of that object: from el libro (book), we get el librejo, which is an old, worthless book. These two suffixes are identical in function; -ejo, however, is the more common. Words ending with -ejo are masculine, while those taking -eja are feminine.

Formed Word	English Equivalent	Related to	English Equivalent
el anillejo	small ring	el anillo	ring
el animalejo	wretched, ugly creature	el animal	animal; creature

Formed Word	English Equivalent	Related to	English Equivalent
el arbolejo	miserable little tree	el árbol	tree
el arenalejo	small sandy place	el arenal	sandy ground; stretch of sand
el atabalejo	small kettledrum	el atabal	kettledrum
el azoguejo	small marketplace	el azogue	marketplace
el barrilejo	small barrel	el barril	barrel
el batelejo	small boat	el batel	(naut.) small vessel
el bozalejo	small muzzle	el bozal	muzzle
el caballejo	wretched little horse	el caballo	horse
el cabezalejo	tiny pillow or bolster	el cabezal	small pillow
la calleja	small street; alley	la calle[1]	street
la canaleja	small canal	el canal	canal; channel; waterway
el castillejo	small castle	el castillo	castle
el collarejo	small collar or necklace	el collar	collar; necklace
la copleja	wretched little ballad	la copla	ballad; couplet
el cordelejo	miserable little cord	la cuerda[2]	cord; string; rope
la cuchilleja	small knife; paring knife	el cuchillo[3]	knife
el diablejo	scamp; little devil	el diablo	devil; demon; fiend
el librejo	old, worthless book	el libro	book
el lugarejo	wretched little village	el lugar[4]	place; spot; village
el marmolejo	small marble column	el mármol	marble
el martillejo	small hammer	el martillo	hammer
la palabreja	wretched or queer expression	la palabra	word

Formed Word	English Equivalent	Related to	English Equivalent
la pareja[5]	couple; team	el par[6]	pair; equal; peer
el puñalejo	small dagger	el puñal	dagger
el telarejo	small loom	el telar	loom
el vallejo	small valley	el valle[7]	valley; vale; glen
el zagalejo	young lad	el zagal	lad; youth; shepherd

[1]calle mayor = main street
[2]cuerdas vocales = vocal cords
[3]cuchillo de monte = hunter's knife
[4]fuera de lugar = out of place
[5]por parejas = in pairs; in twos
[6]sin par = matchless; peerless
[7]valle de lágrimas = vale of tears

-encia

Meaning: *act; state of being; result of action*
English equivalent: *-ence; -ency*
Found in: nouns

Spanish words that end in *-encia* nearly always are cognates of their English counterparts, and denote the state, act, or result of the verb from which they are derived. Usually, these words are derived from *-er* or *-ir* verbs; however, infinitives ending with *-enciar* often have resulting nouns that end with *-encia*. Some of these formed words are derived directly from Latin infinitives. All words ending with *-encia* are feminine.

Formed Word	English Equivalent	Related to	English Equivalent
la abstinencia[1]	abstinence; forbearance; fasting	abstenerse[2]	to abstain, forbear, refrain
la agencia[3]	agency; commission	agenciar	to bring about, engineer, get
la afluencia	affluence	afluir	to flow, flock in
la coexistencia	coexistence	coexistir	to coexist, live together

Formed Word	English Equivalent	Related to	English Equivalent
la coincidencia	coincidence	coincidir	to coincide
la competencia	competency; concern	competir	to belong, concern, appertain
la conciencia	conscience	concienciar	to create awareness in
la condescendencia	condescend-ence; condescension	condescender	to condescend
la conferencia	conference; lecture	conferenciar	to confer, lecture
la deferencia	deference	deferir	to defer, yield
la deficiencia	deficiency	(Lat.) deficere	to fail, disappoint, desert
la dependencia	dependency	depender	to depend on, be dependent on
la descendencia	descent	descender	to descend, come down
la diferencia	difference	diferir	to differ, be different
la divergencia	divergence	divergir	to diverge, dissent
la eficiencia	efficiency	(Lat.) efficere	to bring about, effect, accomplish
la eminencia	eminence	(Lat.) eminere	to stand out, be prominent
la evidencia	obviousness; certainty	evidenciar	to make evident, obvious, clear

Formed Word	English Equivalent	Related to	English Equivalent
la existencia[4]	existence	existir	to exist, live, have being
la incontinencia	incontinence	incontinente	incontinent
la independencia	independence; privacy	in + depender	not + to depend
la indulgencia	indulgence	(Lat.) indulgere	to grant, concede, make allowance
la influencia	influence	influir	to influence
la inocencia	innocence; guilelessness	inocente	innocent; guileless
la insistencia	insistence	insistir	to insist
la obediencia	obedience	obedecer	to obey
la opulencia	opulence	(Lat.) opulentare	to make rich, enrich
la penitencia[5]	penitence; penance	penitenciar	to impose a penance on
la preferencia	preference; priority	preferir	to prefer
la presencia[6]	presence	presenciar	to witness, be present at
la presidencia	presidency; chairmanship	presidir	to preside over
la residencia	residence	residir	to reside
la resistencia	resistance; reluctance	resistir	to resist, withstand
la reverencia	reverence	reverenciar	to revere, reverence
la tendencia	tendency; bent; leaning	(Lat.) tendere	to be inclined, aim at

---

[1] día de abstinencia = day of abstinence
[2] abstenerse de hacer algo = to refrain from doing something
[3] agencia de noticias = news agency

[4]*(com.)* en existencia = in stock
[5]*(coll.)* hacer penitencia = to take potluck
[6]presencia de ánimo = presence of mind

-engo (-enga)

Meaning: *like; relating to*
English equivalent: none
Found in: adjectives

This unusual suffix is one of several adjectival endings meaning *like* or *relating to*. The resulting adjective indicates that someone or something holds characteristics of the base term. When the adjective describes a feminine noun, *-engo* becomes *-enga*.

Formed Word	English Equivalent	Related to	English Equivalent
abadengo	pertaining to an abbot or an abbey	el abad	abbot
barbiluengo	long-bearded	la barba[1]	beard
frailengo	monkish	el fraile	friar; monk
luengo *(obs.)*	long; far	*(Lat.)* longus	long
mujerengo	effeminate	la mujer[2]	woman; wife
peciluengo	long-stalked (fruit)	el pezón	stalk; stem
realengo	royal; kingly	real	royal; real

[1]en sus barbas = to his face
[2]mujer fatal = femme fatale

-eno (-ena)

Meaning: denotes ordinal number
English equivalent: *-th*
Found in: adjectives; nouns

The ending *-eno* is a less common suffix denoting ordinal numbers (see *-ésimo; -imo*) or nouns (see *-avo*). As an adjective, you might say, *El noveno niño en la fila es mi primo* (The ninth boy in the row is my cousin). As a noun, you could say more simply, *El noveno en la fila es mi primo*. When used to describe or refer to feminine nouns, these formed adjectives or nouns take the ending *-ena*.

Formed Word	English Equivalent	Related to	English Equivalent
seiseno	sixth	seis	six

Formed Word	English Equivalent	Related to	English Equivalent
septeno	seventh	(Lat.) septem	seven
noveno	ninth	nueve	nine
deceno	tenth	(Lat.) decem	ten
onceno	eleventh	once	eleven
doceno	twelfth	doce	twelve
treceno	thirteenth	trece	thirteen
catorceno	fourteenth	catorce	fourteen
quinceno	fifteenth	quince	fifteen
dieciocheno	eighteenth	dieciocho	eighteen
veinteno	twentieth	veinte	twenty
treinteno	thirtieth	treinta	thirty
cuarenteno	fortieth	cuarenta	forty
cincuenteno	fiftieth	cincuenta	fifty
ochenteno	eightieth	ochenta	eighty
centeno	hundredth	cien	one hundred
mileno	thousandth	mil	thousand

-ense

Meaning: *native; native of; like; relating to*
English equivalent: none
Found in: nouns; adjectives

The suffix -ense is one of several endings that indicate origin. It is both a noun and an adjectival ending, with its part of speech borne out in the context of the sentence: *La nicaragüense lee el periódico nicaragüense* (The Nicaraguan [woman] reads the Nicaraguan newspaper). There is no change in this ending from masculine to feminine; again, context tells you whether the referent is a masculine or feminine noun (*el canadiense; la canadiense*). Unlike their English counterparts, these words are not capitalized. Some words ending with -ense are adjectives only (*hortense; pretoriense,* etc.).

Formed Word	English Equivalent	Related to	English Equivalent
(el) abulense	(native) of Avila	Avila	Avila
(el) ateniense	(native) of Athens	Atenas	Athens
(el) badajocense	(native) of Badajoz	Badajoz	Badajoz

Formed Word	English Equivalent	Related to	English Equivalent
(el) berlinense	(native) of Berlin	Berlín	Berlin
(el) bonaerense	(native) of Buenos Aires	Buenos Aires	Buenos Aires
(el) bracarense	(native) of Braga	Braga	Braga
(el) bruselense	(native) of Brussels	Bruselas	Brussels
(el) canadiense	(native) of Canada	Canadá	Canada
(el) cartaginense	(native) of Carthage	Cartago	Carthage
(el) costarricense	(native) of Costa Rica	Costa Rica	Costa Rica
(el) cretense	(native) of Crete	Creta	Crete
(el) escurialense	belonging to Escorial monastery	el Escorial	monastery in Spain
(el) estadounidense	(native) of the United States	Estados Unidos	United States
(el) gerundense	(native) of Gerona	Gerona	Gerona
hortense	pertaining to a garden or orchard	el huerto	orchard; garden
(el) lisbonense	(native) of Lisbon	Lisboa	Lisbon
(el) londinense	(native) of London	Londres	London
(el) manilense	(native) of Manila	Manila	Manila
(el) matritense	(native) of Madrid	Madrid	Madrid
(el) nicaragüense	(native) of Nicaragua	Nicaragua	Nicaragua
(el) parisiense	(native) of Paris	París	Paris
(el) peloponense	(native) Peloponnesian	Peloponeso	Peloponnesia

-ente

Meaning: *like; relating to; doing*
English equivalent: *-ing; -ent*
Found in: adjectives

The following formed words that end in *-ente* all are adjectives derived from *-er* and *-ir* verbs. These adjectives indicate that the persons, places, and/or things described exhibit qualities relating directly to the root verb. Since the English equivalent often is *-ing,* be careful not to confuse the English translations with the progressive mood (i.e., John is running down the street). This suffix closely relates to *-ante,* found in adjectives derived from *-ar* verbs. These adjectives do not change with regard to gender.

Formed Word	English Equivalent	Related to	English Equivalent
absorbente	absorbing; absorbent; engrossing	absorber	to absorb, drink in, engross
abstinente	abstinent	abstenerse	to abstain, forbear, restrain
atrayente	attractive; attracting	atraer	to attract
cedente	ceding; yielding	ceder	to cede, yield
correspondiente	corresponding	corresponder	to correspond
corriente[1]	running; current; common	correr[2]	to run
creyente	believing	creer	to believe
deprimente	depressing	deprimir	to depress, press down
diferente	different; differing	diferir	to differ, be different
durmiente[3]	sleeping; dormant	dormir[4]	to sleep
emergente	emergent; issuing	emerger	to emerge (from water)
existente	existent; existing	existir	to exist
influyente	influencing; influential	influir	to influence
leyente	reading	leer[5]	to read
luciente	shining; bright	lucir	to light, light up
mereciente	deserving	merecer	to deserve, merit
muriente	dying; faint	morir	to die
naciente	nascent; incipient	nacer	to be born
perteneciente	belonging; appertaining	pertenecer	to belong
poseyente	possessing; possessive	poseer	to possess, own

Formed Word	English Equivalent	Related to	English Equivalent
queriente	willing	querer[6]	to want, wish
referente	referring; relating	referir	to refer
reincidente	backsliding; relapsing	reincidir	to backslide, relapse
reluciente	shining; glittering	relucir	to shine, glitter
repelente	repellent; objectionable	repeler	to repel
residente	resident; residing	residir	to reside
resistente	resistant; resisting	resistir	to resist
riente	smiling; laughing	reír(se)	to laugh
rugiente	roaring	rugir	to roar
siguiente	following	seguir[7]	to follow, continue
sorprendente	surprising	sorprender	to surprise
sosteniente	sustaining; supporting	sostener	to support, hold up, sustain
sugerente	suggesting; thought-provoking	sugerir	to suggest, hint, imply
teniente	having; holding	tener	to have, hold
viviente	living; alive	vivir	to lie
yacente	lying	yacer[8]	to lie, be lying down

---

[1]corriente y moliente = run of the mill; el año (mes, semana) corriente = the present year (month, week)
[2]a todo correr = at full speed
[3]Bella Durmiente = Sleeping Beauty
[4]dormir como un leño = to sleep like a log
[5]leer entre líneas = to read between the lines
[6]querer más = to prefer
[7]seguir adelante = to go on or ahead, press on
[8]yacer con = to lie or sleep with

-ente; -enta

Meaning: *one who;* denotes profession
English equivalent: *-ent; -ant; -er; -or*
Found in: nouns

The suffix *-ente* or *-enta* is one of several Spanish endings that denote *one who*. As you will see below, all of the examples are derived from *-er* and *-ir* verbs (just as words ending with *-ante* are derived from *-ar* verbs). Most nouns ending with *-ente* are both masculine and feminine in form (e.g., *el creyente; la creyente*). Sometimes, however, the ending changes to *-enta* to denote a function typically performed by women: compare *la regenta* and *el regente*.

Formed Word	English Equivalent	Related to	English Equivalent
el adquirente	acquirer; purchaser	adquirir	to acquire, obtain, get
el arguyente	arguer	argüir	to argue; dispute
la asistenta	charwoman; daily help	asistir	to assist, attend
el asistente	assistant	asistir	to assist, attend
el compareciente	person appearing in court	comparecer	to appear in court
el contendiente	contender; litigant	contender	to contend, litigate
el contribuyente	contributor; taxpayer	contribuir	to contribute, pay taxes
el correspondiente	correspondent	corresponder	to correspond
el creyente	believer	creer[1]	to believe
el debiente	debtor	deber	to owe
la dependienta	shop assistant; saleswoman	depender	to be the responsibility of

Formed Word	English Equivalent	Related to	English Equivalent
el dependiente	shop assistant; salesman	depender	to be the responsibility of
el distribuyente	distributor	distribuir	to distribute
el doliente	sufferer; mourner; one in pain	doler[2]	to ache, hurt, give pain, grieve
el imponente	depositor	imponer	to deposit (money in the bank)
el influyente	influencer; person with power	influir	to influence
el maldiciente	curser; slanderer	maldecir[3]	to curse
el oyente	hearer; listener	oír	to hear, listen
la presidenta	president; president's wife	presidir	to preside over, govern
el presidente	president	presidir	to preside over, govern
el pretendiente	claimant; suitor; wooer; boyfriend	pretender	to try, attempt, claim; (coll.) to court
el recipiente	recipient	recibir	to receive
el regente	regent	regir	to rule, govern, manage, run
el residente	resident	residir	to reside
el respondiente	answerer; respondent	responder[4]	to answer, reply, respond

Formed Word	English Equivalent	Related to	English Equivalent
la sirvienta	servant-girl; maid	servir[5]	to serve
el sirviente	servant; server	servir	to serve
el sobreviviente	survivor	sobrevivir[6]	to survive

[1]ver y creer = seeing is believing
[2]dolerse de = to grieve at, feel sorrow for
[3]maldecir de = to speak ill of
[4]responder de or responder por alguien = to answer for someone
[5]servirse de = to make use of
[6]sobrevivir a alguien = to outlive someone

-eño (-eña)

Meaning: *like; relating to; native; native of*
English equivalent: *-y;* usually none
Found in: adjectives; nouns

Spanish words ending with *-eño* indicate a similarity to or derivation from the root noun. This suffix is often similar to several other endings that mean *like* or *relating to:* When this is the case, the formed word will be an adjective only, e.g., *roqueño* (rocky). However, when *-eño* is added to the name of a place, the formed word can act either as a noun or an adjective: *La brasileña lee el periódico brasileño* (The Brazilian [woman] reads the Brazilian newspaper). These referents to places and persons are not capitalized as they are in English. When these terms refer to a feminine noun, *-eño* becomes *-eña.*

Formed Word	English Equivalent	Related to	English Equivalent
borriqueño	asinine	el borrico	ass
(el) brasileño	Brazilian	Brasil	Brazil
caleño	containing lime	la cal	lime
costeño	coastal; coasting; sloping	la costa[1]	coast; shore
cuesteño	hilly	la cuesta[2]	hill; slope; incline
(el) cumbreño	(native) of the top of a mountain	la cumbre	summit; peak
galgueño	relating to greyhounds	el galgo	greyhound
(el) gibraltareño	(native) of Gibraltar	Gibraltar	Gibraltar
(el) guadalajareño	(native) of Guadalajara	Guadalajara	Guadalajara

Formed Word	English Equivalent	Related to	English Equivalent
(el) guayaquileño	(native) of Guayaquil	Guayaquil	Guayaquil
guijarreño	pebbly	el guijarro	(large) pebble
halagüeño	flattering	el halago	flattery
hogareño	home-loving	el hogar	home; hearth
(el) hondureño	Honduran	Honduras	Honduras
(el) isleño	(native) of an island	la isla[3]	island
(el) limeño	(native) of Lima	Lima	Lima
(el) lugareño	of a village; villager	el lugar[4]	place; spot; village
(el) madrileño	(native) of Madrid	Madrid	Madrid
marfileño	of ivory; like ivory	el marfil[5]	ivory
marmoleño	marbly; marblelike	el mármol	marble
mimbreño	willowy	el mimbre	willow; wicker
navideño	relating to Christmas	la Navidad	Christmas
(el) nicaragüeño	Nicaraguan	Nicaragua	Nicaragua
(el) norteño	northerner; of the north	el norte[6]	north; polestar; direction
(el) panameño	Panamanian	Panamá	Panama
(el) portorriqueño (el) puertorriqueño	Puerto Rican	Puerto Rico	Puerto Rico
ribereño	relating to a riverside	la ribera	riverside
risueño	smiling; pleasant	la risa	laugh; laughter
roqueño	rocky	la roca	rock
(el) salvadoreño	Salvadorean	El Salvador	El Salvador
sedeño	silken	la seda	silk
(el) sureño	southerner; of the south	el sur	south
(el) tarifeño	(native) of Tarifa	Tarifa	Tarifa (Cádiz)

Formed Word	English Equivalent	Related to	English Equivalent
trigueño	(of) wheat color	el trigo	wheat

[1]Costa de Marfil = Ivory Coast
[2]cuesta abajo = downhill; cuesta arriba = uphill
[3]Islas Malvinas = Falkland Islands
[4]tener lugar = to take place
[5]torre de marfil = ivory tower
[6]sin norte = aimless(ly)

-eo
Meaning: *resulting action*
English equivalent: *-ing*
Found in: nouns

This suffix, one of several that denote resulting action, is distinctive in that nouns that take the ending *-eo* are derived from verbs ending in *-ear*. Thus, when you encounter such a verb, you can most likely assume that its resulting action can be formed by replacing the *-ear* with *-eo*; and when you encounter such a noun, you can nearly always do the converse to figure out the infinitive. All nouns with the *-eo* suffix are masculine.

Formed Word	English Equivalent	Related to	English Equivalent
el barqueo	boating	barquear	to go about in a boat
el bazuqueo	shaking; stirring (of liquids)	bazuquear	to shake (liquids)
el besuqueo	slobbery kissing	besuquear	to kiss slobberingly, slobber over
el blanqueo	whitening; bleaching	blanquear	to whiten, bleach
el bloqueo	blockade	bloquear	to blockade, block
el cabeceo	nod; bob; shake of head	cabecear	to nod, bob, shake the head

Formed Word	English Equivalent	Related to	English Equivalent
el campaneo	bell-ringing; chime	campanear[1]	to ring bells
el careo	meeting; confrontation	carear[2]	to bring face to face
el ceceo	lisping	cecear	to lisp
el deletreo	spelling	deletrear	to spell
el devaneo	nonsense; loafing	devanear	to talk nonsense, loaf
el empleo	employment; use	emplear	to employ, use
el escopeteo	gunfire; shooting	escopetear	to shoot (at)
el fisgoneo	prying	fisgonear	to pry (into)
el lavoteo	hurried washing	lavotear(se)	to wash hurriedly
el paladeo	tasting; relish	paladear	to taste, relish, savor
el papeleo	paperwork; red tape	papelear	to search or rummage through papers
el paseo[3]	walk; stroll; ride	pasear[4]	to take a walk, stroll, ride
el pateo	(coll.) kicking; stamping	patear	(coll.) to kick, stamp
el recreo	recreation; recess; playtime	recrear	to divert, amuse
el repiqueteo	pealing; ringing	repiquetear	to chime, ring, peal
el revoloteo	fluttering	revolotear	to flutter about
el salteo	highway assault; robbery	saltear	to hold up, waylay, assault

Formed Word	English Equivalent	Related to	English Equivalent
el tartamudeo	stuttering; stammering	tartamudear	to stutter, stammer
el tecleo	fingering; touching (typewriter)	teclear	to touch, run over the keys
el tijereteo	clipping; snipping noise of scissors	tijeretear	to cut with scissors
el traqueteo	shake; rattle; chatter	traquetear	to shake, rattle
el voleo[5]	volley	volear	to volley
el volteo	whirling around	voltear	to whirl around
el zapateo	beating; tapping of foot	zapatear	to tap dance

[1]campanearse = to strut, swagger
[2]carearse con = to confront, face
[3]dar un paseo = to take a walk
[4]pasear la(s) calle(s) = to wander the streets, stroll around
[5]de un voleo = at one go or stroke

-eo (-ea)
Meaning: *like; relating to*
English equivalent: *-eous*
Found in: adjectives

Adjectives ending with *-eo* indicate that someone or something holds characteristics of the base noun. Note below that in all cases the *-eo* is preceded by a consonant (often *r, n,* or *c*), and that this consonant is always preceded by an accented vowel. Many of these words deal with things found in nature (plants, minerals, etc.). When describing a feminine noun, adjectives take the feminine form *-ea*.

Formed Word	English Equivalent	Related to	English Equivalent
aéreo	aerial; relating to air	*(Lat.)* aer	air
arbóreo	arboreal; arboraceous	el árbol	tree
arenáceo	arenaceous; sandy; gravelly	la arena	sand
aveníceo	oatlike; oaten	la avena	oat
bambusáceo	bamboolike	el bambú	bamboo

Formed Word	English Equivalent	Related to	English Equivalent
broncíneo	of bronze; bronzelike	el bronce[1]	bronze
ceráceo	cereous; waxy	la cera[2]	wax
cesáreo	Caesarean; like Caesar	César	Caesar
contemporáneo	contemporaneous; contemporary	con + el tiempo	with + time
coriáceo	pertaining to leather	el cuero[3]	leather
corpóreo	corporeal; corporal	el cuerpo[4]	body
etéreo	ethereal	el éter	ether
férreo	ferrous; made of iron	el fierro	iron
grisáceo	greyish	el gris	grey (color)
limitáneo	limitary; limitaneous; bounding	el límite	limit; bound; boundary
líneo	(bot.) linaceous; lined	la línea[5]	line
plúmeo	feathered; plumed	la pluma	feather; plume
purpúreo	purple colored	la púrpura	purple (color)
rosáceo	rosaceous	la rosa	rose
róseo	rosy; roseate	la rosa	rose
rúbeo	ruby; reddish; ruddy	el rubí	ruby
temporáneo	temporary; transient	el tiempo[6]	time
violáceo	violaceous; violet-colored	la violeta	(bot.) violet
virgíneo	virginal	la virgen	virgen
zafíreo	sapphire-like; sapphirine	el zafir/zafiro	sapphire

[1] edad de bronce = Bronze Age
[2] cera vieja = ends of wax candles
[3] cuero cabelludo = scalp
[4] tomar cuerpo = to take shape
[5] línea de puntos = dotted line
[6] el tiempo dirá = time will tell

-era

Meaning: *container; holder*
English equivalent: none
Found in: nouns

Several Spanish words for containers end in *-era*. This is a common and useful suffix, one that will enable you to learn many terms quickly and easily as most of the root words are everyday items. This ending has a sister suffix, *-ero,* which is a bit less common than *-era,* but which similarly denotes a container or holder for the root object. Words ending with *-era* are feminine.

Formed Word	English Equivalent	Related to	English Equivalent
la bañera	bathtub	el baño	bath
la budinera	pie plate	el budín	pie
la cafetera	coffeepot	el café	coffee
la cajonera	chest of drawers	el cajón	drawer
la caldera	soup kettle	el caldo	broth; clear soup
la carbonera	coal bin	el carbón	coal
la cartera	briefcase; pocketbook	la carta[1]	letter; card
la coctelera	cocktail shaker	el cóctel	cocktail
la cucarachera	nest of cockroaches; cockroach trap	la cucaracha	cockroach
la cuchillera	knife case; scabbard	el cuchillo	knife
la chocolatera	chocolate pot	el chocolate	chocolate
la ensaladera	salad bowl	la ensalada	salad
la escalera[2]	staircase; stairs	la escala	stepladder; ladder
la gasolinera	gas station	la gasolina	gasoline
la gorrinera	pigsty	el gorrín	(small) pig; hog; *(fig.)* filthy pig
la guantera	glove compartment	el guante[3]	glove
la jabonera	soap dish	el jabón	soap
la joyera	jewelry box	la joya	jewel
la lechera	milk pitcher	la leche[4]	milk
la leñera	woodshed; woodbin	la leña[5]	firewood; kindling

Formed Word	English Equivalent	Related to	English Equivalent
la licorera	liquor case; liquor cabinet	el licor	liquor; liquer
la panera	bread basket	el pan	bread
la papelera	wastebasket; paper case	el papel	paper
la pecera	fishbowl; aquarium	el pez[6]	fish
la perrera	dog kennel	el perro	dog
la pistolera	holster	la pistola	pistol
la polvera	powder case; compact	el polvo	powder; dust
la ponchera	punch bowl	el ponche	punch
la pulsera	bracelet	el pulso[7]	pulse; pulse-beat
la ratonera	mousetrap	el ratón	mouse
la regadera[8]	watering can	el riego	irrigation; watering
la relojera	clock-case; watch-case	el reloj[9]	clock; watch; timepiece
la salsera	gravy boat	la salsa	sauce; gravy
la sombrerera	hatbox	el sombrero	hat
la sopera	soup tureen	la sopa[10]	soup
la tabaquera	snuffbox	el tabaco	tobacco; snuff
la tetera	teapot	el té	tea
la tortera	baking pan; deep dish	la torta	cake; pancake; pie

---

[1]echar las cartas = to tell a person's fortune by cards
[2]escalera de caracol = winding staircase; escalera mecánica = escalator
[3]arrojar el guante = to throw down the gauntlet
[4]leche en polvo = powdered milk
[5]echar leña al fuego = to add fuel to the flames
[6]pez de color = goldfish
[7]tomar el pulso a alguien = to take the pulse of someone
[8]estar como una regadera = to be as crazy as a loon
[9]reloj de pulsera = wristwatch
[10]estar hecho una sopa = to be wet through, wet to the skin

-ería

Meaning: *shop; store*
English equivalent: none
Found in: nouns

The suffix *-ería* is commonly used in Spanish to denote a type of shop or store. The root noun to which this ending is attached is the main item being sold, dealt in, or manufactured. Remember that this suffix takes an accent over the *i,* and that all nouns ending with *-ería* are feminine.

Formed Word	English Equivalent	Related to	English Equivalent
la barbería	barbershop	la barba	beard
la botellería	bottle factory	la botella	bottle
la cafetería	coffee shop; cafeteria	el café	coffee
la carnicería	butcher shop	la carne	meat
la droguería	drugstore	la droga	drug
la dulcería	candy store	el dulce	candy
la especiería	spice shop	la especia	spice
la ferretería	hardware store	el fierro	iron
la floristería	florist's shop	la flor[1]	flower
la frutería	fruit shop	la fruta	fruit
la guantería	glover's shop	el guante	glove
la huevería	egg store	el huevo[2]	egg
la joyería	jewelry store	la joya	jewel
la juguetería	toy store	el juguete	toy
la lechería	milk store	la leche[3]	milk
la librería	bookstore	el libro	book
la licorería	liquor store	el licor	liquor
la mantequería	grocery store	la manteca	lard
la mueblería	furniture store	el mueble	furniture
la panadería	bakery	el pan[4]	bread
la papelería	stationery shop	el papel	paper
la pastelería	pastry shop; bakery	el pastel	pastry; cake
la peluquería	beauty shop	el pelo	hair
la pescadería	fish market	el pescado	fish
la platería	silversmith's shop	la plata	silver
la pollería	poultry shop	el pollo	chicken

Formed Word	English Equivalent	Related to	English Equivalent
la relojería[5]	watchmaker's shop	el reloj[6]	watch; clock
la ropería	clothing store	la ropa	clothing
la sombrerería	hat shop	el sombrero	hat
la tabaquería	tobacco shop	el tabaco	tobacco
la tortillería	tortilla shop	la tortilla	tortilla
la vaquería	dairy store	la vaca	cow
la vinatería	wine shop	el vino[7]	wine
la zapatería	shoe store	el zapato	shoe

[1]flor de la edad = prime or bloom of youth
[2]huevo escalfado = poached egg
[3]ama de leche = wet nurse
[4]pan ázimo = unleavened bread
[5]bomba de relojería = time bomb
[6]reloj de arena = hour-glass
[7]vino tinto = red wine

-ería; -ría; -ía
Meaning: forms abstract noun
English equivalent: -ry; -ness
Found in: nouns

This suffix forms an abstract noun when added to the root noun, adjective, or verb: from *el tubo* (tube), we get *la tubería* (tubing); *zalamear* (to flatter) becomes *la zalamería* (flattery). Most commonly we find *-ería;* however, at times the root term takes on *-ría* or *-ía*. All words ending with any of these endings are feminine.

Formed Word	English Equivalent	Related to	English Equivalent
la alegría	happiness	alegre[1]	happy; cheerful; sunny
la armería	armory; arsenal	el arma (f.)[2]	arm; weapon
la carcelería	imprisonment	la cárcel	jail; prison
la cobardía	cowardice	el cobarde	coward
la cohetería	rocketry	el cohete[3]	rocket
la chinería	Chinese object	el chino	Chinese

Formed Word	English Equivalent	Related to	English Equivalent
la españolería	that which is purely Spanish	España	Spain
la estantería	shelving	el estante	shelf
la feligresía	parish; congregation	el feligrés	parishioner
la galantería	gallantry	galante	gallant
la ganadería	cattle-raising	el ganado	cattle
la gitanería	gypsies; gypsydom	el gitano	gypsy
la golfería	loafing; hanging around	golfear	to loaf, hang around
la grosería	grossness; rudeness	grosero	gross; rude; coarse
la hombría	manliness	el hombre	man
la hotelería	hotel-keeping	el hotel	hotel
la palabrería	verbiage	la palabra[4]	word
la pobrería/ pobretería	poverty; beggars; wretched people	el pobre	poor person; pauper; beggar
la policía[5]	police	(Gr.) polis	city
la porrería	(coll.) stupidity; idiocy	porro	dull; thick; stupid
la ratería	petty thieving; pilfering	ratear	to pilfer, filch
la relojería[6]	(the art of) clock making	el reloj	clock; watch; timepiece
la roñería	stinginess	la roña	(coll.) stingy individual
la sabiduría	wisdom; learning; knowledge	(el) sabio	sage; wise; learned (person)
la supremacía	supremacy	supremo	supreme; final; last
la taponería	corks (in general)	el tapón	cork
la tesorería	treasury	el tesoro	treasure

Formed Word	English Equivalent	Related to	English Equivalent
la trapacería	fraud; deceit	trapacear	to deceive, cheat, swindle
la tubería	tubing; piping	el tubo[7]	tube
la tunantería	vagrancy; rascality	el tunante	loafer; rogue; rascal
la versería	compilation of poems	el verso[8]	verse
la vidriería	glassware	el vidrio	glass
la villanía	meanness; lowness of birth	villano	rustic; boorish; low-class
la vinatería	vintnery; wine trade	el vino	wine
la vocería	clamor; hallooing; outcry	vocear	to yell, bawl, cry out
la yesería	plasterwork	el yeso	plaster; gypsum
la zalamería	flattery; adulation	zalamear	to flatter
la zapatería	shoemaker's trade	el zapato	shoe

[1]un cielo alegre = a bright sky
[2]arma de fuego = firearm; gun
[3]cohete de salvamento = flare
[4]de palabra = by word of mouth
[5]policía municipal = city or town police
[6]bomba de relojería = time bomb
[7]tubo de ensayo = test tube
[8]verso blanco, libre, or suelto = blank verse

-erizo (-eriza)
Meaning: *herder*
English equivalent: *-herd*
Found in: nouns

The suffix *-erizo* is very specialized, and, as a result, there are few Spanish words that take this ending. The base term is the name of the particular animal being tended to or herded, and the formed word is the name for the person doing the tending or herding. When this person is female, the suffix becomes *-eriza*.

Formed Word	English Equivalent	Related to	English Equivalent
el boyerizo	ox-herd; ox driver	el buey[1]	ox
el caballerizo	head groom (of a stable)	el caballo[2]	horse
el cabrerizo	goatherd	la cabra[3]	goat
el porquerizo	swineherd	el puerco[4]	pig; hog
el vaquerizo	herdsman	la vaca[5]	cow
el yegüerizo	keeper of mares	la yegua	mare

[1]a paso de buey = at a snail's pace
[2]caballo de cargo = packhorse
[3]estar como una cabra = to be crazy as a loon
[4]puerco de mar = porpoise
[5]vaca lechera = dairy cow

-ero

Meaning: *container; holder*
English equivalent: none
Found in: nouns

The ending -ero is a handy suffix that will enable you to learn many new words quickly, as most of the root words are common items. This ending has a sister suffix, -era, which is somewhat more common than -ero, but which performs the same function, namely, to denote a container or holder for the root term. Words ending with -ero are masculine.

Formed Word	English Equivalent	Related to	English Equivalent
el alfiletero	pincushion; pin-case	el alfiler	pin
el arenillero	sandbox	la arena	sand
el azucarero	sugar bowl	el azúcar[1]	sugar
el basurero	garbage can; dump	la basura	refuse; rubbish; garbage; trash
el brasero	brazier; pan to hold coals	la brasa	live coal; red-hot coal or wood
el cenicero	ashtray	la ceniza[2]	ash
el cerillero	matchbox; matchbook	el cerillo	wax match

Formed Word	English Equivalent	Related to	English Equivalent
el cervecero	set of beer mugs	la cerveza	beer
el cochero	garage	el coche	car
el costurero	sewing room; sewing basket	la costura	sewing; stitching; seam
el cucharero	spoon rack	la cuchara	spoon
el florero	vase; flowerpot	la flor	flower
el frutero	fruit bowl or dish	la fruta[3]	fruit
el gatero	cat carrier	el gato	cat
el gavillero	place where sheaves are collected	la gavilla[4]	sheaf; (fig.) gang (of low people)
el harinero	flour bin	la harina[5]	flour
el helero	glacier	el hielo[6]	ice
el hormiguero	anthill	la hormiga[7]	ant
el lapicero	pencil-case; pencil holder	el lápiz[8]	pencil
el llavero	key ring	la llave[9]	key
el mantequero	butter dish	la manteca[10]	lard; grease; fat; pomade
el paragüero	umbrella stand	el paraguas	umbrella
el pastillero	pillbox	la pastilla	pill; tablet
el pimentero	pepper shaker	la pimienta	pepper
el ropero	wardrobe; locker	la ropa[11]	clothing
el salero	salt cellar	la sal	salt
el servilletero	napkin ring	la servilleta	napkin
el toallero	towel rack	la toalla	towel

[1]azúcar extrafino = powdered sugar
[2]Miércoles de Ceniza = Ash Wednesday
[3]fruta del tiempo = fruit in season
[4]gente de gavilla = low people
[5]harina de maíz = corn flour
[6]punto de hielo = freezing point
[7]ser una hormiga = to be very thrifty or a busy bee
[8]lápiz de color = crayon
[9]llave maestra = master key
[10]manteca de cacao = cocoa butter
[11]ropa sucia = laundry

-ero (-era)

Meaning: *like; relating to; able to*
English equivalent: *-y; -able*
Found in: adjectives

This use of the suffix *-ero* produces adjectives that refer to the properties of the root noun or verb. When derived from a noun, it means *like* or *relating to*, e.g. *suertero* (lucky), from *la suerte* (luck). When derived from a verb, it means *able to*, e.g., *bebedero* (drinkable), from *beber* (to drink). When the base term is a verb, a *d* is added between the infinitive stem and the suffix *-ero*. The ending *-ero* becomes *-era* when these formed words describe feminine nouns.

Formed Word	English Equivalent	Related to	English Equivalent
aduanero	relating to customs	la aduana	customs
aguadero	relating to water; aqueous	el agua (f.)	water
azucarero	relating to sugar	el azúcar	sugar
bananero	relating to bananas	la banana	banana
bebedero	drinkable	beber	to drink
bracero	relating to the arm	el brazo	arm
camero	relating to the bed	la cama	bed
caminero	relating to a road or highway	el camino	road; highway
campero	of the country; rustic	el campo	country
carbonero	relating to coal or charcoal	el carbón	coal; charcoal; carbon
casadero	marriageable	casar(se)	to marry
cucarachero	sneaky; sly	la cucaracha	cockroach
faldero[1]	of skirts or the lap	la falda[2]	skirt
guerrero	warlike	la guerra	war
hacendero	industrious and thrifty	hacer[3]	to make, do
harinero	of flour	la harina[4]	flour
hormiguero	pertaining to ants; feeding on ants	la hormiga	ant
lastimero	hurtful; injurious; pitiful	la lástima	pity; shame
llevadero	bearable; tolerable	llevar	to bear, carry

Formed Word	English Equivalent	Related to	English Equivalent
maderero	of wood or timber	la madera	wood; timber
mañanero	relating to morning	la mañana	morning
milagrero	miracle-working; superstitious	el milagro	miracle
noticiero	news-bearing; news-giving	la noticia	news; news item
novelero	fond of the latest fad or craze	novel	new; inexperienced
ovejero	relating to sheep	la oveja	ewe; female sheep
palabrero	wordy; windy	la palabra	word
pañero	of cloth	el paño	cloth
pendenciero	quarrelsome	la pendencia	quarrel; dispute
perecedero	perishable	perecer	to perish
pinturero	showy; flashy	la pintura	painting; picture
placero	pertaining to the marketplace	la plaza[5]	square; marketplace; market
playero	relating to the beach	la playa	beach
sensiblero	sentimental	sensible	sensitive; sentient
suertero	lucky; fortunate	la suerte[6]	luck
taquillero	relating to the box office	la taquilla	ticket window
terrero	earthly; of the earth	la tierra	earth; land
torero	relating to bullfighting	el toro	bull
traicionero	treacherous; deceptive	la traición	treason; treachery
verdadero	true; real; truthful	la verdad[7]	truth

---

[1] hombre faldero = ladies' man
[2] perrillo de falda = lapdog
[3] hacer por hacer = to do things for the sake of it
[4] donde no hay harina, todo es mohina = poverty brings discord

⁵plaza de toros = bullring
⁶probar suerte = to try one's luck
⁷de verdad = really; honestly

-ero (-era)

Meaning: *one who;* denotes profession
English equivalent: *-er; -man; -person*
Found in: nouns

In this group of words, the ending *-ero* combines with the root noun to name a person in a particular profession. The root noun can denote what the person works with: *el cartero* (mailman) works with *la carta* (letter); or the root noun can indicate where the person works: *el cocinero* (cook) works in *la cocina* (the kitchen). When the worker is female, the suffix becomes *-era*.

Formed Word	English Equivalent	Related to	English Equivalent
el banquero	banker	el banco¹	bank
el barbero	barber	la barba	beard
el basurero	garbage collector	la basura	refuse; rubbish; garbage; trash
el carnerero	shepherd	el carnero	sheep
el carnicero	butcher	la carne	meat
el cartero	mailman	la carta²	letter
el casero	landlord	la casa	house
el cervecero	brewer	la cerveza	beer
el cochero	driver	el coche	car
el cocinero	cook	la cocina	kitchen
el chispero	blacksmith	la chispa³	spark
el droguero	druggist	la droga	drug
el florero	florist; flower-seller	la flor	flower
el fontanero	plumber	la fontana	fountain
el granjero	farmer	la granja	farmer
el guerrero	warrior; fighter	la guerra	war
el jornalero	day laborer; journeyman	el jornal⁴	day work; day's work
el lechero	milkman	la leche	milk
el librero	bookseller	el libro	book

Formed Word	English Equivalent	Related to	English Equivalent
el maletero	suitcase maker or seller; porter	la maleta[5]	suitcase
el marinero	sailor	la marina	shore; sea-coast
el mensajero	messenger	el mensaje	message
el mesero	waiter	la mesa	table
el panadero	baker	el pan	bread
el peluquero	hairdresser	el pelo[6]	hair
el perrero	kennel-keeper; dog fancier	el perro	dog
el pistolero	gunman; gangster	la pistola	pistol
el platero	silversmith	la plata[7]	silver
el prisionero[8]	prisoner	la prisión	prison
el relojero	watchmaker; clockmaker	el reloj[9]	clock; watch; timepiece
el tejero	tile-maker	la teja	roof tile
el tendero	shopkeeper	la tienda	shop; store
el tesorero	treasurer	el tesoro	treasure
el tilichero	peddler	el tiliche	trinket
el torero	bullfighter	el toro	bull
el vaquero	cowherd; cowboy	la vaca	cow
el vidriero	glazier; glass-blower	el vidrio	glass
el zapatero	shoemaker; shoe salesman	el zapato	shoe

[1] banco de sangre = blood bank
[2] carta blanca = carte blanche
[3] estar chispa = to be tipsy
[4] a jornal = by the day
[5] hacer la maleta = to pack one's suitcase
[6] ser de pelo en pecho = to be a he-man
[7] como una plata = clean; bright; shining
[8] prisionero de guerra = prisoner of war
[9] reloj de bolsillo = pocket watch

-ero; -era

Meaning: *tree; plant; place where plants grow*
English equivalent: none
Found in: nouns

The ending -*ero,* or less commonly -*era,* is sometimes used to denote the name of a tree, a plant, or a place where it grows. The root noun usually is the name of the fruit, nut, vegetable, or product the tree or plant produces. Generally speaking, if this root noun ends in a vowel, drop that vowel and add -*ero* or -*era;* if the root noun ends in a consonant, add the suffix directly. Words ending with -*ero* are masculine, while those ending with -*era* are feminine.

Formed Word	English Equivalent	Related to	English Equivalent
el albaricoquero	apricot tree	el albaricoque	apricot
el alcachofero	artichoke plant	la alcachofa	artichoke
el algodonero	cotton plant	el algodón	cotton
la avellanera	hazel tree; filbert tree	la avellana	hazelnut; filbert
la castañera	*(prov.)* area rich in chestnut trees	el castaño[1]	chestnut tree
el clavero	clove tree	el clavo	clove
la datilera	date palm	el dátil	date
el fresero	strawberry plant	la fresa	strawberry
la higuera	fig tree	el higo[2]	fig
el limero	lime tree	la lima	lime
el limonero	lemon tree	el limón	lemon
el melocotonero	peach tree	el melocotón	peach
la noguera	grove of walnut trees	el nogal	walnut tree; walnut wood
el pimentero	pepper plant	el pimiento	pepper
el semillero	seedbed; seed-plot	la semilla	seed
el tomatero	tomato plant	el tomate[3]	tomato
el vivero	*(hort.)* nursery	el vivir	life

[1] castaño de Indias = horse-chestnut tree
[2] higo chumbo = prickly pear
[3] *(coll.)* aquí hay mucho tomate = there's plenty to be done here

-érrimo (-érrima)
Meaning: adjectival superlative
English equivalent: none
Found in: adjectives

The ending -érrimo is very uncommon and therefore often unrecognized. This is because -érrimo does exactly what the frequently used suffix -ísimo does, but in a specific
situation: note below that in all cases the adjectives in the Related to column have as
their final consonant the letter r. This is the prerequisite for using -érrimo; otherwise,
you will use -ísimo. As this is an adjectival ending, when these words describe feminine
nouns, the suffix becomes -érrima.

Formed Word	English Equivalent	Related to	English Equivalent
acérrimo	extremely bitter; sour	acre[1]	acrid; bitter; sour
aspérrimo	extremely rough; harsh	áspero	rough; harsh
beligérrimo	extremely belligerent; pugnacious	belígero	(poet.) warlike
celebérrimo	extremely famous	célebre[2]	celebrated; famous
celérrimo	extremely fast	célere	swift
integérrimo	most honest; upright	íntegro	integral; upright; honest
libérrimo	extremely free	libre[3]	free; detached
lugubérrimo	extremely mournful; sad	lúgubre	lugubrious; mournful
misérrimo	extremely miserable, miserly	mísero	miserable; miserly
paupérrimo	extremely poor	(Lat.) pauper	poor
salubérrimo	most salubrious	salubre	salubrious; healthy
ubérrimo	very fruitful; abundant	(Lat.) uber	rich; fruitful; fertile

---

[1]acre de condición = acrimonious by nature
[2]Juan es célebre = John is a (real) character
[3](com.) libre de derechos = duty free

-és (-esa)

Meaning: *native; native of; like; relating to*
English equivalent: *-ese*
Found in: nouns; adjectives

The suffix *-és* is one of a number of Spanish endings that denote origin. Like these other endings, *-és (-esa,* when denoting or describing a feminine noun) can function either as a noun or an adjective: *El japonés sirve el café francés a la barcelonesa* (The Japanese man serves the French coffee to the woman from Barcelona). Note that these terms are not capitalized, that when referring to a person, you need not mention man or woman (the gender of the ending makes that clear), and that the accent in the masculine form *(-és)* is not needed in the feminine form *(-esa).*

Formed Word	English Equivalent	Related to	English Equivalent
(el) aragonés	Aragonese (native)	Aragón	Aragon
(el) barcelonés	(native) of Barcelona	Barcelona	Barcelona
(el) berlinés	(native) of Berlin	Berlín	Berlin
(el) bernés	Bernese (native)	Berna	Bern
(el) burgués	(of or from) the middle class	el burgo	borough
(el) danés	Danish (native)	Dinamarca	Denmark
(el) escocés	Scottish (native)	Escocia	Scotland
(el) finlandés	Finnish (native)	Finlandia	Finland
(el) francés	French (native)	Francia	France
(el) groenlandés	(native) of Greenland	Groenlandia	Greenland
(el) hamburgués	(native) of Hamburg	Hamburgo	Hamburg
(el) holandés	(native) of Holland; Dutch	Holanda	Holland
(el) inglés	English (native)	Inglaterra	England
(el) irlandés	Irish (native)	Irlanda	Ireland
(el) japonés	Japanese (native)	Japón	Japan
(el) libanés	Lebanese (native)	Líbano	Lebanon
(el) lisbonés	(native) of Lisbon	Lisboa	Lisbon
(el) luxemburgués	(native) of Luxembourg	Luxemburgo	Luxembourg
(el) milanés	Milanese (native)	Milán	Milan
(el) montañés	(of or from) the mountain	la montaña	mountain
(el) neocelandés	(native) of New Zealand	Nueva Zelanda	New Zealand

Formed Word	English Equivalent	Related to	English Equivalent
(el) neoescocés	(native) of Nova Scotia	Nueva Escocia	Nova Scotia
(el) nepalés	(native) of Nepal	Nepal	Nepal
(el) pequinés	Pekingese (native)	Pequín	Peking
(el) polonés	Polish (native)	Polonia	Poland
(el) portugués	Portuguese (native)	Portugal	Portugal
(el) salamanqués	(native) of Salamanca	Salamanca	Salamanca
(el) siamés	Siamese (native)	Siam	Siam
(el) tailandés	(native) of Thailand	Tailandia	Thailand
(el) vienés	Viennese (native)	Viena	Vienna

-esco (-esca)

Meaning: *in the manner or style of; like; relating to; resembling*
English equivalent: *-esque*
Found in: adjectives

In the study of Spanish suffixes, one soon learns that there are several adjectival suffixes that mean *like, relating to,* etc. The suffix *-esco,* however, appears to be the strongest of these, for it often implies a capturing of the essence of the root noun. This is clearly seen in *sanchopancesco* and *jemsbondesco,* where the root nouns are the two famous literary characters *Sancho Panza* and *James Bond.* Because their personality traits are strong and focused, each can denote one characteristic, materialistic and glamorous, respectively. When such a word describes a feminine noun, the ending changes to *-esca.*

Formed Word	English Equivalent	Related to	English Equivalent
arabesco	arabesque; Arabian	Arabia	Arabia
brujesco	relating to witchcraft	la bruja	witch
bufonesco	buffoonish; farcical	el bufón	buffoon; clown; jester
burlesco	burlesque; comical	la burla[1]	hoax; mockery; scoff(ing)
caballeresco	chivalrous; gentlemanly	el caballero	knight; gentleman
camaleonesco	like a chameleon	el camaleón	chameleon
carnavalesco	carnival-like	el carnaval	carnival

Formed Word	English Equivalent	Related to	English Equivalent
cervantesco	in the style of Cervantes	Cervantes	(Miguel) Cervantes
chinesco	Chinese-like	chino	Chinese
dantesco	Dantesque; nightmarish	Dante	Dante (Alighieri)
gatesco	*(coll.)* feline; catlike	el gato[2]	cat
germanesco	relating to jargon	la germanía	jargon; cant; slang
gigantesco	like a giant; huge	el gigante	giant
gitanesco	gypsylike	el gitano	gypsy
goyesco	of Goya; Goyesque	Goya	(Francisco) Goya
guitarresco	*(coll.)* of or doing with guitars	la guitarra	guitar
hampesco	relating to the underworld	el hampa	underworld
jemsbondesco	like James Bond; glamorous	James Bond	James Bond
libresco	bookish	el libro[3]	book
marinesco	like a sailor	el marino	sailor; mariner
medievalesco	pertaining to medieval period	Edad Media	Middle Ages
monagesco	of or pertaining to Monaco	Mónaco	Monaco
monesco	apish; monkeyish	el mono[4]	monkey
novelesco	novelistic; like a novel	la novela	novel
oficinesco	clerical; bureaucratic	la oficina	office
pedantesco	absurdly pedantic	el pedante	pedant
picaresco	roguish; rascally	el pícaro[5]	rogue; schemer
pintoresco	picturesque; colorful	la pintura[6]	painting; picture; paint
quijotesco	quixotic	Don Quijote	Don Quixote

Formed Word	English Equivalent	Related to	English Equivalent
romanesco	Roman; Romanesque	Roma	Rome
rufianesco	of pimps or scoundrels	el rufián	pimp; rascal; pander
sanchopancesco	like Sancho Panza; materialistic	Sancho Panza	Sancho Panza
soldadesco	like a soldier	el soldado[7]	soldier
trovadoresco	like a troubadour	el trovador	troubadour
villanesco	boorish; crude; rustic	el villano	peasant; knave; scoundrel

---

[1]hacer burla de = to mock, make fun of
[2]gato montés = wildcat
[3]libro mayor = ledger
[4]mono sabio = trained monkey
[5]pícaro de cocina = scullion; kitchen-boy
[6]capa de pintura = coat of paint
[7]soldado raso = private soldier

-ésimo (-ésima); -imo (-ima)
Meaning: denotes ordinal number
English equivalent: -th
Found in: adjectives

To form ordinal numbers in English, generally we add -th to the cardinal number base (e.g., *seven; seventh; ten; tenth,* etc.). When you see a Spanish word with -*ésimo* or -*imo* at the end, or even inside the word (e.g., *decimosexto*), you can be quite certain that you have an ordinal number and that generally it relates to the Latin name of its base number. Because ordinal numbers are adjectives, when used to describe nouns of the feminine gender, the suffix becomes -*ésima* or -*ima*.

Formed Word	English Equivalent	Related to	English Equivalent
séptimo	seventh	*(Lat.)* septem	seven
décimo	tenth	*(Lat.)* decem	ten
undécimo	eleventh	*(Lat.)* undecim	eleven
duodécimo	twelfth	*(Lat.)* duodecim	twelve
decimocuarto	fourteenth	*(Lat.)* quattuordecim	fourteen
decimoquinto	fifteenth	*(Lat.)* quindecim	fifteen

Formed Word	English Equivalent	Related to	English Equivalent
decimosexto	sixteenth	(Lat.) sedecim	sixteen
decimoséptimo	seventeenth	(Lat.) septemdecim	seventeen
decimoctavo	eighteenth	(Lat.) decem et octo	eighteen
decimonoveno	nineteenth	(Lat.) decem et novem	nineteen
vigésimo	twentieth	(Lat.) viginti	twenty
trigésimo	thirtieth	(Lat.) triginta	thirty
cuadragésimo	fortieth	(Lat.) quadraginta	forty
quincuagésimo	fiftieth	(Lat.) quinquaginta	fifty
sexagésimo	sixtieth	(Lat.) sexaginta	sixty
septuagésimo	seventieth	(Lat.) septuaginta	seventy
octogésimo	eightieth	(Lat.) octoginta	eighty
nonagésimo	ninetieth	(Lat.) nonaginta	ninety
centésimo	one-hundredth	(Lat.) centum	one hundred
ducentésimo	two-hundredth	(Lat.) ducenti	two hundred
tricentésimo	three-hundredth	(Lat.) trecenti	three hundred
cuadringentésimo	four-hundredth	(Lat.) quadringenti	four hundred
quingentésimo	five-hundredth	(Lat.) quingenti	five hundred
sexcentésimo	six-hundredth	(Lat.) sescenti	six hundred
septingentésimo	seven-hundredth	(Lat.) septingenti	seven hundred
octingentésimo	eight-hundredth	(Lat.) octingenti	eight hundred
noningentésimo	nine-hundredth	(Lat.) nongenti	nine hundred
milésimo	one-thousandth	mil	one thousand

Formed Word	English Equivalent	Related to	English Equivalent
dosmilésimo	two-thousandth	dos mil	two thousand
tresmilésimo	three-thousandth	tres mil	three thousand
millonésimo	millionth	un millón	one million
billonésimo	billionth	un billón	one billion

-estre

Meaning: *like; relating to;* denotes period of time
English equivalent: *-estrian; -ester*
Found in: adjectives; nouns

The uncommon ending *-estre* usually is found in adjectives, indicating a relationship between the base term and the person or thing described. Note that while in English *pedestrian* can function either as an adjective or a noun, in Spanish, its counterpart *pedestre* is an adjective only (*el peatón* is the person walking across the street). As a noun ending, we see *-estre* as a time-marker of sorts: *el semestre* (semester) is generally half a school year. All nouns ending in *-estre* are masculine.

Formed Word	English Equivalent	Related to	English Equivalent
alpestre	alpine; Alpine	los Alpes	Alps; high mountains
campestre	country-like; rural; bucolic	el campo[1]	country; field
el cuatrimestre	period of four months	cuatro + mes	four + month
ecuestre	equestrian	*(Lat.)* equus	horse
pedestre	pedestrian	*(Lat.)* pes	foot
el semestre	semester	*(Lat.)* sex + mensis	six + month
silvestre	wild; uncivilized	la selva[2]	jungle; forest; tropical forest
terrestre	terrestrial	la tierra[3]	earth; land
el trimestre	trimester; academic quarter	*(Lat.)* tres + mensis	three + months

[1] campos Elíseos = Elysian fields
[2] Selva Negra = Black Forest
[3] tierra campa = treeless land

-eta

Meaning: diminutive
English equivalent: none
Found in: nouns

The suffix -eta is one of many Spanish word endings that act as diminutives. Its sister suffix, -ete, differs from -eta only in gender. All words ending with -eta are feminine.

Formed Word	English Equivalent	Related to	English Equivalent
la aleta	small wing	el ala (f.)[1]	wing
la avioneta	small airplane	el avión	airplane
la barreta	small bar	la barra	bar; beam
la buseta	small bus; van	el autobús	bus
la cajeta	small box	la caja[2]	box; case
la camioneta	van	el camión	truck
la camiseta	T-shirt; sport shirt	la camisa[3]	shirt
la capeta	short collarless cape or cloak	la capa	cape; cloak; mantle
la caseta	cabin	la casa	house
la cazoleta	small pan	el cazo	pan
la coleta	ponytail (hair)	la cola[4]	tail
la cuarteta	(poet.) quatrain	el cuarto[5]	fourth; fourth part
la cuchareta	small spoon	la cuchara	spoon
la faceta	facet; feature	la faz	face; (arch.) front
la faldeta	miniskirt	la falda	skirt
la hacheta	hatchet	el hacha	axe
la historieta	little story	la historia	story
la isleta	small isle; islet	la isla	isle; island
la lengüeta	small tongue	la lengua[6]	tongue
la libreta	bankbook; savings book; notebook	el libro	book
la manteleta	mantelet; small scarf or mantle	el mantel	tablecloth; altar cloth
la opereta	operetta	la ópera	opera
la orejeta	small ear	la oreja	ear
la paleta	small shovel; fire shovel; palette	la pala	shovel

Formed Word	English Equivalent	Related to	English Equivalent
la papeleta	scrap of paper	el papel	paper
la peineta	curved comb; back comb	el peine	comb
la pileta	small basin	la pila[7]	basin; water trough; font
la ropeta	short garment	la ropa	clothes; clothing
la serreta	small saw	la sierra	saw
la tarjeta[8]	card	la tarja	visiting card
la tijereta	small scissors	la tijera	scissors
la tineta	small tub	la tina	wooden vat; tub
la toalleta	small towel; hand towel	la toalla	towel
la veleta[9]	weathervane; pennant; streamer	la vela	sail; awning
la vinagreta	vinaigrette sauce	el vinagre[10]	vinegar
la voltereta	tumble; handspring; somersault	el volteo	whirling around

[1]dar alas = to protect, encourage
[2]caja del cuerpo = torso
[3]camisa de fuerza = straitjacket
[4]cola de caballo = ponytail
[5]cuarto creciente = first quarter of the moon
[6]de lengua en lengua = from mouth to mouth
[7]nombre de pila = Christian name; given name
[8]tarjeta postal = postcard
[9]veleta de manga = wind sleeve; wind sock
[10]*(coll.)* cara de vinagre = sourpuss

-ete
Meaning: diminutive
English equivalent: none
Found in: nouns

The suffix *-ete* is one of many Spanish word endings that indicate smallness of the root word. It has a sister suffix, *-eta,* which differs from *-ete* in gender only. All nouns ending with *-ete* are masculine.

Formed Word	English Equivalent	Related to	English Equivalent
el anillete	small ring	el anillo	ring
el arete	small earring	el aro	hoop
el atabalete	small kettle-drum	el atabal	kettle-drum
el asperete	sour taste	áspero	(fig.) sour; sharp
el banquete	banquet; feast	el banco	bench; pew
el barrilete	keg	el barril	barrel; cask
el blanquete	whitening skin cosmetic; whitewash	el blanco	white (color)
el bracete[1]	small arm	el brazo	arm
el caballete	small horse	el caballo	horse
el cañete	small tube	el caño	tube; pipe; gutter
el clarinete	clarinet	el clarín	clarion; organ-stop
el colorete	rouge	el color	color; complexion; blush
el gafete	clasp; hook and eye	la gafa	hook; cramp (for holding together)
el gorrete	small cap	la gorra	cap; baseball cap
el guantelete	gauntlet	el guante[2]	glove
el inglete	diagonal; angle of 45 degrees	la ingle	groin
el juguete[3]	toy	el juego	game
el librete	small book	el libro	book
el mollete	fleshy part (of the arm)	la molla	(coll.) fat (of a person)
el ojete	eyelet-hole	el ojo[4]	eye
el paquete[5]	packet; parcel	la paca	bundle; bale
el pelete[6]	poor man	el pelo[7]	hair; down

Formed Word	English Equivalent	Related to	English Equivalent
el saborete	slight taste or flavor	el sabor	taste; flavor
el sombrerete	small hat	el sombrero	hat
el soplete	blowpipe; blowtorch	el soplo[8]	blowing; blast; gust
el sorbete	sherbet	el sorbo	swallow; gulp
el templete[9]	small temple; niche	el templo	temple; church
el tenderete	(ramshackle) stall or stand	la tienda	shop
el tonelete	small cask; keg	el tonel	cask; barrel
el torete	bullock	el toro	bull
el zaguanete	small vestibule or entrance	el zaguán	entrance hallway

[1] ir del bracete = to go arm in arm
[2] recoger el guante = to take up the gauntlet
[3] por juguete = jestingly
[4] ¡ojo! = watch out!
[5] paquete turístico = package tour
[6] en pelete = naked
[7] montar a pelo *or* en pelo = to ride bareback
[8] ir con el soplo = to spill the beans
[9] el templete de música = bandstand

-ez

Meaning: *state of being;* forms abstract noun
English equivalent: *-ness; -ity*
Found in: nouns

Spanish nouns ending in *-ez* denote a state of being that relates to the root word, which almost always is an adjective. Generally speaking, if the root word ends in a vowel, that vowel is dropped and *-ez* is then added; if the root word ends in a consonant, the suffix *-ez* is added directly. The ending *-ez* has a sister suffix, *-eza,* which is similar in both meaning and formation. All nouns ending in *-ez* are feminine.

Formed Word	English Equivalent	Related to	English Equivalent
la adultez	adulthood	adulto	adult
la amarillez	yellowness	amarillo	yellow
la aridez	dryness; aridity; aridness	árido	arid; dry

Formed Word	English Equivalent	Related to	English Equivalent
la azulez	blueness	azul[1]	blue
la delgadez	leanness; slimness	delgado[2]	lean; slim
la escasez	scarcity	escaso[3]	scarce
la estupidez	stupidity	estúpido	stupid
la flaccidez/ flacidez	flaccidity; flabbiness	fláccido/flácido	flaccid; flabby
la frigidez	frigidity	frígido	frigid
la languidez	languor	lánguido	languid; languorous
la liquidez	liquidness; liquidity	líquido[4]	liquid; (com.) net amount; profit
la lividez	lividity; lividness	lívido	livid
la lobreguez	darkness; gloominess	lóbrego	dark; gloomy; murky; dingy
la lucidez	lucidity	lúcido	lucid
la madurez	maturity; ripeness	maduro	mature; ripe; middle-aged
la magrez	thinness; leanness	magro	lean; thin
la marchitez	withering; fading	marchito	faded; withered
la matidez	dullness (of light or sound)	mate	mat; dull; lusterless
la mentecatez	stupidity; dim-wittedness	mentecato	simple; foolish
la muchachez	childhood; puerility	el muchacho[5]	boy; lad; chap
la niñez	childhood	el niño[6]	child; little boy
la nitidez	clarity; brightness; sharpness	nítido	clear; bright; sharply defined

Formed Word	English Equivalent	Related to	English Equivalent
la pequeñez	littleness; smallness	pequeño	little; small
la pesadez	heaviness; sluggishness	pesado[7]	heavy; sluggish; sultry
la pulidez	neatness; cleanliness	pulido	neat; clean
la putridez	putridity; rottenness	pútrido	putrid
la rapidez	rapidity; swiftness	rápido	rapid; swift; fast
la robustez	hardiness; robustness	robusto	hardy; robust
la rojez	redness	rojo	red
la rosez	rosiness	roso[8]	red; rosy; threadbare
la salvajez	savageness; savagery	salvaje	savage; barbarous; wild
la sencillez	simplicity	sencillo	simple
la sensatez	sensibleness; good sense	sensato	sensible; level-headed
la timidez	timidity; shyness	tímido	timid; shy
la validez	validity	válido	valid
la vejez	oldness	viejo	old

[1] azul celeste = sky blue; azul turquí = indigo
[2] hilar demasiado delgado = to split hairs
[3] andar escaso de = to be short of
[4] líquido imponible = taxable net
[5] gran muchacho or buen muchacho = good chap; decent fellow; jolly good sort
[6] de niño = as a child
[7] broma pesada = nasty joke; practical joke
[8] a roso y velloso = without distinction

-eza

Meaning: *state of being;* forms abstract noun
English equivalent: *-ness ; -ity*
Found in: nouns

Spanish nouns ending in *-eza* denote a state of being that relates to the root word, which is almost always an adjective. Generally speaking, if the root term ends in a vowel, that vowel is dropped and the suffix is then added; if the root ends in a consonant, you add -eza directly. The ending -eza has a sister suffix, -ez, which is similar in both meaning and formation. All nouns ending in -eza are feminine.

Formed Word	English Equivalent	Related to	English Equivalent
la agudeza	acuteness; fineness; smartness	agudo[1]	acute; sharp; keen
la bajeza	baseness	bajo	base; low; short
la belleza	beauty; loveliness	bello[2]	beautiful; lovely
la certeza	certainty; certitude	cierto[3]	certain; sure; true
la dureza	hardness	duro	hard
la flaqueza	thinness	flaco	thin
la franqueza	candor; candidness	franco	candid; frank
la gentileza	gentility; gentleness; grace	gentil	gentle; genteel; graceful
la grandeza	greatness; grandeur	grande	great; grand; big
la graseza	fattiness	graso	fat; oily
la guapeza	(coll.) guts; daring	guapo	(coll.) having guts; showy
la largueza	length; liberality	largo[4]	long
la limpieza	cleanliness; cleanness	limpio	clean; clear
la lindeza	prettiness; neatness	lindo	pretty; neat; nice
la llaneza	simplicity; straight forwardness	llano	flat; plain; straight forward
la majeza	boldness; flamboyance	majo	free; nonchalant; sporty

Formed Word	English Equivalent	Related to	English Equivalent
la maleza	weeds; thicket; underbrush	malo	bad; evil
la naturaleza[5]	nature; temperament	natural	natural; usual
la nobleza	nobility; nobleness	noble	noble
la pobreza	poverty; want; lack	pobre	poor
la presteza	quickness; promptitude	presto[6]	quick; prompt; ready
la pureza	purity	puro[7]	pure
la rareza	rareness; rarity	raro[8]	rare
la riqueza	richness; wealth	rico	rich; wealthy
la rojeza	redness	rojo[9]	red
la rudeza	roughness; coarseness; crudeness	rudo	rough; coarse; crude
la sutileza	subtlety; subtility	sutil	subtle
la terneza	tenderness; softness	tierno	tender
la tibieza	lukewarmness; coolness	tibio	lukewarm
la torpeza	clumsiness	torpe	clumsy
la tristeza	sadness	triste	sad
la viveza	liveliness	vivo	alive; lively

[1]agudo de ingenio = quick-witted; *(geom.)* ángulo agudo = acute angle
[2]el bello sexo = the fair sex
[3]saber de cierto = to know for sure
[4]largo de lengua = over-free with the tongue
[5]naturaleza muerta = still life
[6]de presto = promptly; swiftly
[7]pura sangre = thoroughbred
[8]rara vez = seldom
[9]al rojo = red hot

-fobia

Meaning: *fear*
English equivalent: *-phobia*
Found in: nouns

The following words ending with *-fobia* should be very easy to recognize and use because they are almost perfect cognates of their English counterparts. The *ph* in English always appears as an *f* in Spanish: *el teléfono* (telephone); *el elefante* (elephant), and so on. All words ending with *-fobia* are feminine.

Formed Word	English Equivalent	Related to	English Equivalent
la acrofobia	acrophobia; fear of heights	*(Gr.)* akros	highest
la agorafobia	agoraphobia; fear of open places	*(Gr.)* agora	marketplace
la androfobia	androphobia; fear and hatred of men	*(Gr.)* aner	man
la anglofobia	Anglophobia; hatred of the English	*(Lat.)* Anglii	the English
la claustrofobia	claustrophobia; fear of small spaces	*(Lat.)* claustrum	confined place
la fotofobia	fear of light	*(Gr.)* phos	light
la hemofobia	fear of blood	*(Gr.)* haima	blood
la hidrofobia	hydrophobia; rabies; fear of water	*(Gr.)* hydor	water
la necrofobia	fear of death	*(Gr.)* nekros	dead body
la xenofobia	xenophobia; fear of strangers	*(Gr.)* xenos	stranger

-ible

Meaning: *able to; capable of*
English equivalent: *-ible; -able*
Found in: adjectives

The Spanish suffix *-ible* has as its English equivalents *-ible* and *-able,* and means what the latter implies, namely, *able to* or *capable of.* Spanish adjectives ending with *-ible* are derived from *-er* and *-ir* verbs (which generally are at the base of adjectives ending with *-able*). The one exception given below is *ostensible,* which comes from *ostentar,* an *-ar* verb. Generally, the suffix *-ible* simply is added to the root of the verb; however, at times, slight orthographic changes are made (e.g., *admisible,* from *admitir*). Nonetheless, the formed word remains a cognate of its English counterpart, leaving such words still easy to spot and translate.

Formed Word	English Equivalent	Related to	English Equivalent
abolible	abolishable	abolir	to abolish
aborrecible	detestable; hateful	aborrecer	to detest, abhor, hate
absorbible	absorbable	absorber	to absorb, drink in
acogible	receivable; acceptable	acoger	to welcome, receive
admisible	admissible; allowable	admitir	to admit, allow, receive
bebible	drinkable	beber[1]	to drink
comible	eatable	comer[2]	to eat
comprensible	comprehensible; understandable	comprender	to comprehend, understand
comprimible	compressible	comprimir	to compress
concebible	conceivable	concebir	to conceive
convenible	able to be agreed upon; reasonable	convenir[3]	to agree
convertible	convertible	convertir	to convert, turn
creíble	credible; believable	creer[4]	to believe
decible	expressible	decir[5]	to say, tell
deducible	deducible; inferable	deducir[6]	to deduce, infer
definible	definable	definir	to define
discutible	disputable; debatable	discutir	to discuss, debate
imponible	taxable; dutiable	imponer	to impose, deposit (money in a bank)
leíble	legible; readable	leer	to read
movible	movable; mobile	mover	to move

Formed Word	English Equivalent	Related to	English Equivalent
ostensible	ostensible; visible	ostentar	to show, display, bear
permisible	permissible	permitir	to permit, allow, enable
placible	agreeable; placid	placer	to please, content, gratify
producible	producible	producir	to produce
risible	laughable	reír(se)[7]	to laugh
rompible	breakable	romper	to break
sorbible	that can be sipped	sorber	to sip
suspendible	that can be suspended	suspender	to suspend
unible	that can be united, joined	unir	to unite, join, couple
vendible	salable; marketable	vender[8]	to sell

[1]beberse las lágrimas = to keep back one's tears
[2]quedarse sin comer = to go without one's lunch, food
[3]convenir en = to agree to, on, or about
[4]creer a ojos cerrados = to believe blindly, implicitly, firmly
[5]es decir = that is to say
[6]deducir de dicho or por lo dicho = to infer from what has been said
[7]reírse tontamente = to giggle, titter, snicker
[8]vender salud = to be bursting with health

-ica
Meaning: diminutive
English equivalent: none
Found in: nouns

The suffix -ica, like its sister suffix -ico, is among the more common Spanish diminutive endings. Usually this ending indicates physical smallness; however, it can also express endearment or familiarity, most notably at the end of a name, e.g., *Martica* (little Martha; "Marty"), from *Marta* (Marta). All diminutive nouns ending with -ica are feminine.

Formed Word	English Equivalent	Related to	English Equivalent
la abuelica	sweet little grandmother	la abuela	grandmother
la agujica	little needle	la aguja[1]	needle; knitting needle
la almendrica	small almond	la almendra	almond
la avecica	small bird	el ave[2]	bird
la aventurica	little adventure	la aventura	adventure; enterprise
la camisica	little shirt	la camisa	shirt
la cantarica	little pitcher	la cántara	large, narrow-mouthed pitcher
la ciruelica	small plum	la ciruela[3]	plum
la comidica	little meal	la comida	meal; food
la cuentica	little bill	la cuenta[4]	bill; tab; check; account
la estrellica	little star	la estrella	star
la fajica	small sash or band	la faja	sash; band
la fuentecica	small fountain	la fuente	fountain; spring; source
la hermanica	little sister	la hermana	sister
la lengüecica	small tongue	la lengua[5]	tongue
la liebrecica	young hare	la liebre	hare
la lucecica	little light	la luz	light
la lunica	little moon	la luna	moon
la manecica	small hand	la mano[6]	hand
la mañanica	daybreak; dawn; early morning	la mañana[7]	morning
la mariposica	little butterfly	la mariposa	butterfly
Martica	little Martha; "Marty"	Marta	Martha
la mesica	little table; end table	la mesa	table

Formed Word	English Equivalent	Related to	English Equivalent
la migajica	small, mere crumb or scrap	la migaja	crumb; scrap
la mujerica	little woman	la mujer	woman
la nochecica	twilight; nightfall	la noche[8]	night
la plumica	small feather	la pluma[9]	feather
la postalica	little postcard	la postal	postcard
la risica	giggle; titter; snicker	la risa[10]	laugh; laughter
la sombrica	little shade, shadow, or shelter	la sombra	shadow; shade; shelter
la sorpresica	little surprise	la sorpresa	surprise
la tacica	small cup	la taza	cup
la tintica	little bit of ink	la tinta[11]	ink; tint; dye
la ventanica	small window	la ventana[12]	window
la villica	small town	la villa	town; municipal council

[1]aguja de gancho = crochet hook
[2]ave de Paraíso = bird of Paradise
[3]ciruela pasa = prune
[4]cuenta de banco = bank account; checking account
[5]tener en la punta de la lengua = to have on the tip of one's tongue
[6]hecho a mano = handmade
[7]muy de mañana = very early in the morning
[8]de la noche a la mañana = overnight
[9]pluma viva = eiderdown
[10]no es cosa de risa = it's no laughing matter
[11]tinta simpática = invisible ink
[12]ventana de la nariz = nostril

-icia; -acia

Meaning: *state of being;* forms abstract noun
English equivalent: *-ice*
Found in: nouns

Nearly all of the following words that end *-icia* and *-acia* are related to adjectives. The addition of either suffix usually creates an abstract noun, something that cannot be touched or seen (one exception is *la farmacia*). Spanish words ending with *-icia* or *-acia* are feminine.

Formed Word	English Equivalent	Related to	English Equivalent
la audacia	audacity; boldness	audaz	audacious; bold
la avaricia	avarice; avariciousness	avaro	avaricious; miserly
la blandicia	softness; flattery	blando	soft; (too) easygoing; mild
la contumacia	obstinacy; obduracy; stubbornness	contumaz	contumacious; stubborn
la eficacia	efficacy; efficiency	eficaz	efficacious; effective; efficient
la estulticia	stupidity	estulto	stupid
la falacia	fallacy; deceit	(Lat.) fallere	to deceive
la farmacia	pharmacy; drug store	(Gr.) pharmakon	remedy; drug
la inmundicia	dirt; filth; filthiness; lewdness	inmundo	dirty; filthy; unclean; impure
la justicia[1]	justice	justo	just; fair; right
la malicia	slyness; artfulness; distrust	malo	bad; evil; naughty; mischievous
la mesticia	sadness	(Lat.) maestus	sad; sorrowful; dejected
la perspicacia	perspicacity; clearsightedness	perspicaz	perspicacious
la pertinacia	pertinacity; doggedness	pertinaz	pertinacious
la suspicacia	suspicion; mistrust	suspicaz	suspicious

[1]tomarse la justicia por su mano = to take justice into one's own hands

-icio; -acio

Meaning: *result of action or attribute;* forms abstract noun
English equivalent: *-ice; -ace*
Found in: nouns

The addition of *-icio* or *-acio* (*-icio* is found much more frequently) to the base term forms an abstract noun, often implying a result. Such words can be derived from a verb, an adjective, or a noun. All words ending with *-icio* and *-acio* are masculine.

Formed Word	English Equivalent	Related to	English Equivalent
el artificio	artifice; workmanship; craft	el artífice	artificer; artist; inventor
el beneficio[1]	benefit; favor; utility; profit	beneficiar	to benefit, be good to
el edificio	edifice; building	edificar	to construct, build, edify
el ejercicio[2]	practice; exercise	ejercer[3]	to exercise, practice, exert
el indicio	indication; mark; clue; sign	indicar	to indicate, point out, hint, suggest
el juicio	judgment; sense; opinion	juzgar[4]	to judge
el novicio	novice; beginner	nuevo[5]	new
el oficio[6]	work; occupation; job	oficiar	to officiate, minister
el palacio	palace	*(Lat.)* Palatium	Palatine Hill (Rome)
el perjuicio	detriment; damage; harm	perjudicar	to damage, hurt, injure, impair
el precipicio	precipice; chasm; abyss	precipitar	to precipitate, fling headlong

Formed Word	English Equivalent	Related to	English Equivalent
el prefacio	preface	(Lat.) praefari	to say beforehand
el prejuicio	prejudice; bias; prejudgment	prejuzgar	to prejudge
el sacrificio	sacrifice; slaughter	sacrificar	to sacrifice, slaughter (animals)
el servicio[7]	service; duty; dinner set	servir[8]	to serve, help
el solsticio	solstice	(Lat.) sol + stare	sun + to stand
el suplicio	torment; torture; execution	suplicar	to entreat, supplicate, beg
el vicio[9]	vice; defect; bad habit	viciar	to vitiate, adulterate, falsify
el vitalicio	life insurance policy	vital	vital; belonging to life; essential

[1] no tener oficio ni beneficio = to have neither profession nor means of support
[2] el ejercicio hace maestro = practice makes perfect
[3] ejercer influencia en or sobre = to exert influence on
[4] a juzgar por = to judge by; judging from
[5] nuevo flamante = brand-new; spanking new
[6] gajes del oficio = occupational hazards
[7] servicio de mesa = table service
[8] servir de = to serve as, act as, be good or useful for
[9] de vicio = from force of habit; for the sake of it

-ico
Meaning: diminutive
English equivalent: none
Found in: nouns

The suffix -ico, like its sister suffix -ica, is a common Spanish diminutive ending (-ico is more commonly found than -ica). Usually this ending simply denotes smallness of the root noun, e.g., el saltico (small hop), from el salto (jump; hop). At times, this ending implies diminished status (see el cieguecico and el pobrecico). Words ending with ico are masculine.

Formed Word	English Equivalent	Related to	English Equivalent
el angelico	little angel; baby	el ángel[1]	angel
el arbolico	miserable little tree	el árbol	tree
el asnico	little ass	el asno	ass
el cieguecico	poor little blind person	el ciego	blind person (male)
el corazoncico	dear little heart	el corazón	heart
el corpecico	small body	el cuerpo	body
el cuernecico	small horn	el cuerno[2]	horn; feeler; antenna
el gatico	little cat; kitty	el gato	cat
el ladroncico	petty thief; pickpocket	el ladrón	thief
el lebratico	young hare; leveret	la liebre[3]	hare
el leoncico	lion cub	el león	lion
el manojico	small bundle	el manojo	bundle (of twigs or grass)
el momentico	tiny bit of time	el momento[4]	moment; minute
el muchachico	little boy	el muchacho	boy
el pajarico	little bird	el pájaro	bird
el pedacico	small bit; small piece	el pedazo[5]	piece
el pobrecico	poor little fellow, thing, etc.	el pobre[6]	poor person; pauper; beggar
el saltico	little hop	el salto[7]	jump; hop; leap
el santico	regular little saint	el santo	saint
el sillico	stool	la silla	chair
el sombrerico	little hat	el sombrero	hat
el tontico	little dolt; twit	el tonto	fool; nincompoop

Formed Word	English Equivalent	Related to	English Equivalent
el torerico	miserable little bullfighter	el torero	bullfighter
el vasico	small glass	el vaso	drinking glass
el velico	small veil	el velo[8]	veil
el ventanico	small window	la ventana	window
el vientecico	little breeze	el viento	wind
el villancico	Christmas carol	el villano	old Spanish melody and dance
el zatico	small bit of bread	el zato	piece of bread

[1]ángel de la guarda = guardian angel
[2]cuerno de caza = hunting horn
[3]dar gato por liebre = to sell a pig in a poke
[4]por el momento = for the time being
[5]a pedazas *or* en pedazos = in bits; *(fig.)* me muero por tus pedazos = I'm crazy about you
[6]pobre de solemnidad = desperately poor person
[7]salto mortal = somersault
[8]correr el velo = to draw back the veil

-ico (-ica)

Meaning: *like; relating to*
English equivalent: *-ic*
Found in: adjectives

The adjectival suffix *-ico* translates into English as *-ic,* and most Spanish adjectives ending with *-ico* are cognates of their English counterparts. These formed words usually are related to nouns. Generally speaking, if the root noun ends with a vowel, that vowel is dropped and *-ico* is added; if the root noun ends in a consonant, *-ico* is added directly. When describing feminine nouns, adjectives ending with *-ico* take the ending *-ica.* Note that in these formed words the accent is on the antepenultimate syllable.

Formed Word	English Equivalent	Related to	English Equivalent
analítico	analytic	el análisis	analysis
angélico	angelic	el ángel[1]	angel
asmático	asthmatic	el asma	asthma
básico	basic	la base	base
bíblico	Biblical	la Biblia	Bible

Formed Word	English Equivalent	Related to	English Equivalent
caótico	chaotic; in disorder and confusion	el caos	chaos; *(fig.)* confusion; shambles
científico	scientific	la ciencia[2]	science
cúbico	cubic	el cubo	cube
dramático	dramatic	el drama	drama
enérgico	energetic; vigorous	la energía	energy; power
enfático	emphatic	el énfasis	emphasis
específico	specific	la especia	species; kind; class
estratégico	strategic	la estrategia	strategy
evangélico	evangelic; evangelical	el evangelio	gospel
fantástico	fantastic	la fantasía	fantasy
frenético	frenetic; frenzied; frantic; mad	el frenesí	frenzy; fury; madness
galáctico	galactic	la galaxia	galaxy
litúrgico	liturgic; liturgical	la liturgia	liturgy
mágico	magic	el mago[3]	Magus; magician; wizard
metálico	metallic	el metal[4]	metal
pacífico[5]	pacific; peaceful; peace-loving	la paz[6]	peace
panorámico	panoramic	el panorama	panorama
patriótico	patriotic	la patria[7]	fatherland
profético	prophetic	el profeta	prophet
sádico	sadistic	Marqués de Sade	Marquis de Sade
satánico	satanic	Satanás	Satan
semítico	Semitic	el/la semita	Semite
telefónico[8]	telephonic	el teléfono	telephone
telegráfico	telegraphic	el telégrafo[9]	telegraph
telepático	telepathic	la telepatía	telepathy
teórico	theoretic	la teoría	theory

Formed Word	English Equivalent	Related to	English Equivalent
terrorífico	horrific; bloodcurdling	el terror	terror; dread
teutónico	Teutonic	el teutón	Teuton
titánico	titanic	Titán	Titan
tóxico	toxic	la toxina	toxin
trágico	tragic	la tragedia	tragedy
único	one and only	el uno[10]	one (number)

[1]tener ángel = to have charm
[2]ciencia infusa = God-given knowledge
[3]los Reyes Magos = the Magi; the Wise Men of the East
[4]el vil metal = filthy lucre
[5]el Pacífico = the Pacific Ocean
[6]juez de paz = justice of the peace
[7]hacer patria = to boast about one's country
[8]la cabina telefónica = telephone booth
[9]hacer telégrafos = to talk by signs
[10]es todo uno = it's all the same

-idad

Meaning: *state of being; quality*
English equivalent: *-ity*
Found in: nouns

When you see *-idad* at the end of a Spanish word and change *-idad* to *-ity,* most likely you will have its English counterpart (or something very close to it) in front of you. The suffix *-idad* generally is attached to an existing adjective, as in all examples given below, to denote the quality or state of that adjective. This is a common suffix and appears in cognates of English words, making them easy to recognize and to translate. Words ending with *-idad* are feminine.

Formed Word	English Equivalent	Related to	English Equivalent
la absurdidad	absurdity	absurdo	absurd
la adversidad	adversity; calamity	adverso	adverse; calamitous
la atrocidad	atrocity; atrociousness	atroz	atrocious; heinous
la castidad	chastity	casto	chaste
la casualidad[1]	chance; coincidence	casual[2]	chance; coincidence

Formed Word	English Equivalent	Related to	English Equivalent
la claridad	clarity; brightness	claro	clear; bright
la conformidad[3]	conformity; agreement	conforme[4]	agreeing; in agreement
la debilidad	debility; weakness	débil	weak
la densidad	density; thickness	denso	dense; thick
la espiritualidad	spirituality	espiritual	spiritual
la eternidad	eternity	eterno	eternal
la fatalidad	fatality	fatal	fatal
la fecundidad	fecundity	fecundo	fecund; fertile; fruitful
la ferocidad	ferocity; ferociousness	feroz	ferocious; savage; fierce
la fragilidad	fragility	frágil	fragile
la fraternidad	fraternity; brotherhood	fraterno	fraternal; brotherly
la humanidad[5]	humanity	humano	human
la infinidad	infinity	infinito	infinite
la modicidad	moderateness; reasonableness	módico	moderate; reasonable
la morbosidad	morbidity; morbidness	morboso	morbid
la posibilidad	possibility	posible	possible
la potencialidad	potentiality	potencial	potential
la probidad	probity; honesty; integrity	probo	upright; honest
la productividad	productivity	productivo	productive
la profanidad	profanity; profaneness	profano	profane
la proximidad	proximity; vicinity	próximo	near; neighboring; next
la severidad	severity; strictness	severo	severe; strict

Formed Word	English Equivalent	Related to	English Equivalent
la superioridad	superiority	superior	superior; better; finer
la tenacidad	tenacity; tenaciousness	tenaz	tenacious
la utilidad[6]	utility; usefulness	útil	useful; serviceable; handy
la vanidad	vanity	vano	vain; idle
la velocidad	velocity	veloz	swift; fast
la veracidad	veracity; truthfulness	veraz	veracious; truthful
la virilidad	virility	viril	virile; manly
la visibilidad	visibility	visible	visible

[1]por casualidad = by chance
[2]por un casual = by any chance
[3]de or in conformidad con = in accordance with
[4]conforme con = complying with
[5]las humanidades = humanities
[6]ser de gran or mucha utilidad = to be extremely useful

-ido (-ida)

Meaning: *like; relating to*
English equivalent: *-id*
Found in: adjectives

The suffix *-ido* is a common one in Spanish: it is seen at the end of past participles of *-er* and *-ir* verbs, of adjectives, and of nouns. In the following list of formed words, all adjectives, you will find two distinct features. First, these words come directly to us from Latin. This, however, should not trouble you in working with and learning these words, for nearly all are cognates—Latin, Spanish, and English—of one another. Secondly, the antepenultimate syllable always is accented. When these formed words describe a feminine noun, *-ido* changes to *-ida*.

Formed Word	English Equivalent	Related to	English Equivalent
ácido[1]	acid	*(Lat.)* acidus	sharp
árido[2]	arid	*(Lat.)* aridus	dry
cándido	white; snowy; guileless; simple	*(Lat.)* candidus	shining

Formed Word	English Equivalent	Related to	English Equivalent
estólido	stolid	*(Lat.)* stolidus	dull; stolid; slow
estúpido	stupid; dense	*(Lat.)* stupidus	stupid
fétido	fetid	*(Lat.)* foetidus	fetid
flácido	flaccid	*(Lat.)* flaccidus	flaccid
frígido	frigid; extremely cold	*(Lat.)* frigidus	frigid
gélido	gelid; frigid; icy	*(Lat.)* gelidus	gelid
grávido	gravid; laden; heavy	*(Lat.)* gravidus	heavy
hórrido	horrid	*(Lat.)* horridus	rough
insípido	insipid	*(Lat.)* insipiens	foolish
lánguido	languid	*(Lat.)* languidus	faint
límpido	limpid; crystal clear	*(Lat.)* limpidus	limpid; clear
líquido	liquid	*(Lat.)* liquidus	liquid
lívido	livid	*(Lat.)* lividus	bluish; black; livid
lúcido	lucid	*(Lat.)* lucidus	lucid
pálido	pallid; pale; wan	*(Lat.)* pallidus	pallid
plácido	placid; calm	*(Lat.)* placidus	placid
rábido	rabid; raging	*(Lat.)* rabidus	rabid
rápido	rapid; fast	*(Lat.)* rapidus	violent; quick
sólido	solid	*(Lat.)* solidus	dense
sórdido	sordid	*(Lat.)* sordidus	dirty
tímido	timid; shy	*(Lat.)* timidus	timid
tórrido	torrid	*(Lat.)* torridus	torrid
translúcido	translucent	*(Lat.)* translucidus	translucent
túmido	tumid	*(Lat.)* tumidus	tumid; swollen
válido	valid	*(Lat.)* validus	valid

---

¹ácido cítrico = citric acid
²los áridos = dry goods

-ido; -ida

Meaning: *resulting action, object, person or sound*
English equivalent: none
Found in: nouns

Each of the following formed words, all derived from verbs, denotes the result of a particular verb's action, be it the action itself, an object, person, or sound. An unusual feature of the ending *-ido* is its frequent presence in words describing sounds that animals make, e.g., *el maullido* (meow). When the term refers to a person, e.g., *el nacido* (human being), the ending will change to *-ida* if that person is female. Words ending in *-ido* are masculine, while those ending in *-ida* are feminine.

Formed Word	English Equivalent	Related to	English Equivalent
el aparecido	ghost; specter	aparecer	to appear, show up
el apellido	surname; last or family name	apellidar	to call, name
el aullido	howl; howling	aullar	to howl
la bebida	drink; beverage	beber[1]	to drink
el cocido	stew	cocer	to cook, boil, bake
la comida[2]	food; meal	comer[3]	to eat
el contenido	contents	contener	to contain, comprise, hold
la corrida	run; sprint	correr	to run
el crujido	creak; crackle	crujir	to rustle, crackle, creak
el chillido	shriek; shrill sound	chillar	to scream, shriek, screech
el desagradecido	ungrateful person	desagradecer	to be ungrateful for
la despedida	leave-taking; farewell; send-off	despedir(se)	to take one's leave, say goodbye
el gruñido	pig grunt; dog growl; grumble	gruñir	to grunt, growl, grumble

Formed Word	English Equivalent	Related to	English Equivalent
la herida	injury; wound; insult	herir	to injure, hurt, wound, offend
el herido	injured or hurt person	herir	to injure, hurt, wound, offend
la huida	flight; escape	huir	to flee, run away
el ladrido	bark	ladrar[4]	to bark
el marido	husband	maridar	to marry
el maullido	mew; meow	maullar	to mew, meow
la mordida	bite	morder	to bite
el mordido	person bitten	morder	to bite
el mugido	moo; low; bellow	mugir	to moo, low, bellow
el nacido	human being	nacer	to be born
el oído[5]	ear	oír	to hear
el pedido	*(com.)* order; request	pedir	to ask (for), request
el prometido	fiancé; betrothed	prometer	to promise
el resoplido	puffing; snort	resoplar	to puff, snort
el roznido	braying; crunching noise	roznar	to crunch, crack with teeth
el rugido	roar	rugir	to roar
la sacudida	shake; jar; jolt	sacudir	to shake, jar, jolt
la salida	exit; egress; *(mil.)* sortie	salir[6]	to leave, go out
el sentido	sense	sentir	to sense, feel
el silbido[7]	whistle; hiss	silbar	to whistle, hiss

Formed Word	English Equivalent	Related to	English Equivalent
el sonido	sound; ring	sonar[8]	to sound, ring
el tañido	sound; tone	tañer	to play a musical instrument, ring a bell
el tronido	thunder; thunderclap	tronar	to thunder
el vestido	dress; garments; clothing	vestir(se)[9]	to dress (oneself)
el zumbido	buzz; buzzing	zumbar	to buzz

[1]beberse las lágrimas = to hold back one's tears
[2](fig.) cambiar la comida = to throw up
[3]comer a dos manos = to bolt down, eat like a wolf
[4]me ladra el estómago = I'm ravenous; my stomach is grumbling
[5]entrar por un oído y salir por el otro = to go in one ear and out the other
[6]salir con bien = to turn out well
[7]silbido de oídos = ringing in the ears
[8]sonarse = to blow one's nose
[9]vestirse bien = to dress properly

-iego (-iega)

Meaning: *like; relating to; fond of*
English equivalent: none
Found in: adjectives

The ending -iego is one of the less common adjectival suffixes meaning *like* or *relating to*. It also can mean *fond of,* as in *mujeriego* (keen on women). In rare instances, it can denote a specific action with regard to the root word (see *riberiego*); but generally, words ending with -iego refer broadly to features of the root term. When the root's final consonant is *ñ,* the *i* is dropped from the suffix: see *rebañego* and *cadañego.* Formed words describing feminine nouns will end with -iega.

Formed Word	English Equivalent	Related to	English Equivalent
aldeaniego	belonging to a village; rustic	la aldea	small village
alijariego	relating to wastelands	el alijar	uncultivated ground
andariego	wandering; roving	el andar[1]	gait; pace; walking
asperiego	sour	áspero	sour

Formed Word	English Equivalent	Related to	English Equivalent
cadañego	annual; yearly	cada + año	each + year
griego	Greek; Grecian	Grecia	Greece
moriego	Moorish	el moro	Moor; Mohammedan
mujeriego	keen on women; womanizing	la mujer[2]	woman
nocherniego	nocturnal	la noche[3]	night; evening
palaciego	relating to a palace or court	el palacio[4]	palace; mansion
palomariego	relating to domestic pigeons	la paloma	pigeon; dove
paniego	wheat producing; (coll.) keen on bread	el pan[5]	bread
piariego	owning a herd of pigs or mules	la piara	herd (of pigs, mules)
pinariego	relating to pines	el pino	pine; pine tree
rapiego	rapacious	rapar	to shave, shave close
rebañego	sheeplike; easily led	el rebaño	flock; herd; drove; crowd
riberiego	grazing on the banks of rivers	el ribero	bank (of a dam); river-wall; levee
serraniego	relating to highland, hills	la sierra	mountain range; range of hills
solariego	manorial; ancestral	el solar	manor house
veraniego	summery	el verano	summer

---

¹a largo andar = in the long run
²mujer de su casa = dutiful housewife
³Noche Buena = Christmas Eve; Noche Vieja = New Year's Eve
⁴las cosas de palacio van despacio = officialdom takes its time
⁵es pan comido = it's as easy as pie; it's a cinch

-iento (-ienta)

Meaning: *inclined to; tending to; full of; like; relating to*
English equivalent: *-y*
Found in: adjectives

If something is covered with grease, we say that it is *greasy,* the English suffix *-y* meaning *inclined to, tending to, full of,* or *like.* This is the function of the Spanish suffix *-iento:* it indicates that someone or something is filled with or strongly similar to the features of the base noun. One example, *amarillento,* drops the *i* from the ending to avoid an otherwise awkward pronunciation. As these are adjectives, the ending changes to *-ienta* when describing a feminine noun.

Formed Word	English Equivalent	Related to	English Equivalent
achaquiento	sickly; unhealthy	el achaque	(habitual) ailment; indisposition
alharaquiento	clamorous; strident	la alharaca	clamor; outcry
amarillento	yellowish	el amarillo	yellow (color)
avariento	avaricious; miserly	el avaro	miser; greedy person
calenturiento	feverish	la calentura	fever
catarriento	catarrhous	el catarro	catarrh; cold
cazcarriento	*(coll.)* splashed; bemired	la cazcarria	splashings of mud
ceniciento	ash-colored; ashen	la ceniza¹	ash
gargajiento	spitting frequently	el gargajo	phlegm; spit
granujiento	pimply	el granujo	pimple
grasiento	greasy; oily	la grasa²	grease; fat
guiñapiento	ragged; tattered	el guiñapo	rag; tatter
gusaniento	wormy; maggoty	el gusano	worm; maggot

Formed Word	English Equivalent	Related to	English Equivalent
hambriento	hungry; starving	el hambre[3]	hunger
harapiento	ragged; tattered	el harapo	rag; tatter
herrugiento	rusty	el herrín	rust
holliniento	sooty	el hollín	soot
mugriento	grimy; filthy; greasy	la mugre	grime; filth; greasy dirt
oriniento	rusty	el orín	rust
pizmiento	pitch-colored	la pez	pitch; tar
polvoriento	dusty	el polvo[4]	dust
sangriento	bloody; bloodstained	la sangre[5]	blood
soñoliento	sleepy; dreamy; drowsy	el sueño[6]	sleep; sleepiness; dream
sudoriento	perspiring	el sudor	sweat; perspiration; ooze
trapiento	raggedy; in rags	el trapo	rag
zancajiento	bandy-legged; bowlegged	la zanca	shank; long leg
zarriento	besmirched; bespattered	la zarria	dirt (on one's clothing)
zumiento	juicy	el zumo	juice

[1]Miércoles de ceniza = Ash Wednesday
[2]grasa de ballena = whale oil; blubber
[3]hambre canina = ravenous hunger
[4]estar hecho polvo = to be wiped out, extremely tired
[5]tener (mucha) sangre fría = to be cool as a cucumber, have plenty of sangfroid
[6]entre sueños = half-asleep

-ífero (-ífera)

Meaning: *bearing; producing; yielding*
English equivalent: *-iferous*
Found in: adjectives

The Spanish suffix *-ífero* and its English counterpart *-iferous* both indicate that something is bearing, producing, or yielding something specific. The suffix *-ífero* is derived from the Latin *ferre,* which means *to carry or bear.* Words ending in *-ífero* have at their base a noun: generally, if that noun ends in a vowel, that vowel is dropped and *-ífero* is added; if the root noun ends in a consonant, *-ífero* is added directly to the word. The ending changes to *-ífera* when these adjectives describe feminine nouns.

Formed Word	English Equivalent	Related to	English Equivalent
aerífero	air-conducting	*(Lat.)* aer	air
astrífero	*(poet.)* starry	el astro	heavenly body; *(fig.)* star
bacífero	berry-yielding	*(Lat.)* bacca	berry
conchífero	shell-bearing	la concha[1]	shell
coralífero	coral-bearing	el coral	coral
cristífero	wearing a crucifix	el cristo[2]	crucifix
ferrífero	iron-bearing	*(Lat.)* ferrum	iron
florífero	flower-bearing	la flor[3]	flower
frondífero	leaf-bearing	*(bot.)* el fronde	frond
fructífero	fructiferous; fruit-bearing	*(Lat.)* fructus	fruit
fumífero	*(poet.)* smoking; emitting smoke	*(Lat.)* fumus	smoke
lactífero	milk-producing	*(Lat.)* lac	milk
lanífero	wool-bearing	la lana[4]	wool
lucífero	shining	la luz[5]	light
melífero	honey-producing	la miel[6]	honey
metalífero	metalliferous	el metal	metal; brass
mortífero	lethal; death-dealing	la muerte	death
nectarífero	nectar-bearing	el néctar	nectar; exquisite drink
nubífero	*(poet.)* cloud-bearing	la nube[7]	cloud
palmífero	palm-bearing	*(bot.)* la palma	palm
pestífero	foul	la peste	plague; pestilence
petrolífero	oil-bearing	el petróleo	petroleum; oil
pilífero	*(bot.)* hairy	*(Lat.)* pilus	hair
plumífero	*(poet.)* feathered	la pluma	feather

Formed Word	English Equivalent	Related to	English Equivalent
pomífero	apple-bearing	*(Lat.)* pomum	fruit
salífero	*(chem.)* salt-bearing	la˙sal	salt
salutífero	healthful; salubrious	la salud[8]	health; welfare
sanguífero	blood-producing	*(Lat.)* sanguis	blood
soporífero	sleep-producing	el sopor	drowsiness; lethargy
sudorífero	sweat-producing	el sudor	sweat; perspiration; ooze

[1]meterse en su concha = to go into one's shell
[2]ni por un cristo = not on your life
[3]decir flores *or* echar flores = to pay compliments
[4]lana de vidrio = fiberglass
[5]a la luz del día = in the light of day; in broad daylight; openly
[6]miel de caña = molasses
[7]como caído de las nubes = out of the blue
[8]¡salud! = cheers!

-ificar

Meaning: *to make (like)*
English equivalent: *-ify*
Found in: verbs

The ending *-ificar* is unusual because infinitives rarely form a specific group. The suffix *-ificar* corresponds directly to the English *-ify*, which makes these words easy to recognize and use as they nearly always are cognates. Verbs ending with *-ificar* are regular, with the single orthographic change of *c* to *qu* before *e* when conjugated: *yo clasifico* (I classify); *yo clasifiqué* (I classified).

Formed Word	English Equivalent	Related to	English Equivalent
amplificar	to amplify	amplio	ample
beatificar	to beatify	beato	happy; blessed
calificar[1]	to qualify	la calidad[2]	quality
certificar	to certify	cierto	certain
clasificar	to classify	la clase[3]	class; kind
cosificar	to reduce to the level of an object	la cosa[4]	thing; matter

Formed Word	English Equivalent	Related to	English Equivalent
crucificar	to crucify	la cruz[5]	cross
cuantificar	to quantify	la cantidad	quantity
diversificar	to diversify	diverso	diverse
dosificar	to dose, proportion	la dosis	dose
electrificar	to electrify	eléctrico	electric
especificar	to specify	específico	specific
falsificar	to falsify	falso[6]	false
fortificar	to fortify	fuerte	strong; forceful
gasificar	to gasify	el gas	gas
glorificar	to glorify	la gloria[7]	glory; heaven; bliss
humidificar	to humidify	húmedo	humid
intensificar	to intensify	intenso	intense
justificar	to justify	justo	just; fair
mistificar	to mystify	místico	mystic
mortificar	to mortify	muerto[8]	dead
orificar	to fill with gold (dent.)	el oro	gold
osificar	to ossify	óseo	osseous
pacificar	to pacify	la paz[9]	peace
petrificar	to petrify	pétreo	stony
purificar	to purify	puro	pure
rectificar	to rectify	recto	right
santificar	to sanctify, make holy	santo	holy; blessed
simplificar	to simplify	simple[10]	simple
solidificar	to solidify	sólido	solid
tipificar	to typify	típico	typical
unificar	to unify	unido[11]	united
vivificar	to vivify	vivo	alive

[1]calificar de irresponsable = to call irresponsible, stamp as irresponsible
[2]las calidades = conditions; rules (in card games)
[3]de cualquier clase = of any kind or description
[4]eso es cosa mía = that's my business

[5] hacerse cruces (de) = to be shocked (at or by)
[6] puerta falsa = back or side door
[7] sabe a gloria = it tastes heavenly
[8] muerto de frío = frozen stiff
[9] dejar en paz = to leave alone
[10] a simple vista = at first sight
[11] Estados Unidos = United States

-iforme

Meaning: *shaped like; in the form of; like*
English equivalent: *-iform*
Found in: adjectives

The Spanish ending *-iforme* and its English counterpart, *-iform*, perform the same function, making these Spanish formed words easy to recognize and translate. The English suffix *-iform*, however, is more strictly tied to meaning *shaped like*, while the Spanish suffix *-iforme* can also mean *like*, e.g., *carniforme* (flesh-like). Generally speaking, if the base word ends in a vowel, drop that vowel and add *-iforme*. If the base word ends in a consonant, add *-iforme* directly.

Formed Word	English Equivalent	Related to	English Equivalent
aliforme	aliform; wing-shaped	el ala *(f.)*[1]	wing
anguiliforme	*(ichth.)* eel-like	la anguila	eel
arboriforme	shaped like a tree	el árbol[2]	tree
baciliforme	bacilliform	el bacilo	bacillus; bacterium
biforme	*(poet.)* biform; biformed	*(Lat.)* bis	twice
carniforme	fleshlike	la carne[3]	flesh; meat
cineriforme	ashlike	la ceniza[4]	ash
coniforme	coniform; conical; cone-shaped	el cono	cone
conquiforme	shell-shaped	la concha	shell; conch
corniforme	corniform; horn-shaped	el cuerno[5]	horn
criniforme	manelike	la crin	mane; horse hair
cruciforme	cruciform	la cruz	cross
cuadriforme	square-shaped	el cuadro[6]	square
cuneiforme	cuneiform; wedge-shaped	la cuña	wedge

Formed Word	English Equivalent	Related to	English Equivalent
deiforme	godlike; Godlike	*(Lat.)* deus	god; God
dentiforme	shaped like a tooth	el diente	tooth
estratiforme	stratiform	el estrato	stratum; layer
filiforme	threadlike	*(Lat.)* filum	thread
fungiforme	fungiform	el fungo	fungus
gaseiforme	in the form of gas; gaseous	el gas	gas
piriforme	pear-shaped	la pera	pear
pisciforme	fish-shaped	*(Lat.)* piscis	fish
semiforme	half-formed	*(Lat.)* semis	half
triforme	triform	*(Lat.)* tres	three
uniforme	uniform; standard	*(Lat.)* unus	one

[1] tomar alas = to take liberties
[2] los árboles = timber
[3] carne magra = lean meat
[4] convertir en cenizas = to reduce to ashes
[5] estar en los cuernos del toro = to be in jeopardy
[6] en cuadro = squared

-il

Meaning: *like; relating to; concerning; capable of*
English equivalent: *-ile; -able; -ible*
Found in: adjectives

Words taking the adjectival ending *-il* can have as a root either a noun or a verb, and in rare cases, an adjective, e.g., *femenil,* from *femenino.* When the formed adjective is derived from a noun, the meaning generally is *like* or *concerning.* When the formed word traces to a verb, its meaning will be *capable of,* as in *móvil* (capable of motion). As these adjectives end in a consonant, they will not change with regard to gender.

Formed Word	English Equivalent	Related to	English Equivalent
abogadil	lawyerish; like a lawyer	el abogado[1]	lawyer
aceitunil	olive-colored	la aceituna	olive
becerril	concerning cows	el/la becerro/a	young bull/ heifer
borreguil	concerning lambs	el borrego	young lamb

Formed Word	English Equivalent	Related to	English Equivalent
concejil	public; of the municipal council	el concejo[2]	municipal council; council board
conflátil	fusible	confluir	to join, meet, fuse
estudiantil	relating to students	el estudiante	student
fabril	manufacturing; industrial	la fábrica[3]	factory; works; plant
febril	feverish; febrile	la fiebre[4]	fever
femenil	feminine; womanly	femenino	feminine
grácil	graceful	la gracia[5]	grace
infantil	infantile; like a child	el infante	infant
juvenil	juvenile; relating to youth	joven	young
libreril	relating to books, book trade	el libro	book
manzanil	relating to apples	la manzana[6]	apple
monjil	nunlike; prudish	la monja	nun
móvil	capable of being moved	mover	to move
muchachil	youthful; like a child	el muchacho	young boy; lad
mujeril	womanly	la mujer	woman
portátil	portable	portar	to carry, bear
señoril	lordly; haughty; majestic	el señor[7]	sir; lord; master
servil	servile	servir[8]	to serve
tornátil	changeable; fickle	tornar	to return, turn, change back
varonil	manly	el varón	man; male

Formed Word	English Equivalent	Related to	English Equivalent
versátil	versatile; changeable	versar	to go round, turn
volátil	capable of flying	volar	to fly

[1] abogado de secano = charlatan; quack lawyer
[2] casa del concejo = town hall
[3] fábrica de tejidos = textile mill
[4] fiebre del heno = hay fever
[5] estar en gracia de Dios = to be in a state of grace
[6] manzana de Adán = Adam's apple
[7] Muy señor mío = Dear Sir (in letters)
[8] para servir a Vd. = at your service

-illa
Meaning: diminutive
English equivalent: -ette; usually none
Found in: nouns

The ending -illa, like its sister suffix -illo, is an extremely common diminutive. Words ending with -illa and -illo are so common that we've divided them into three groups. The first two (-illo and illa) deal with literal (physical) diminutives, and the third (-illo; -illa) contains words that are diminutive in status. Most of the terms in the first entry are merely names for the smaller version of the root noun, e.g., la cocinilla (kitchenette), from la cocina (kitchen). At times, however, the meaning changes significantly with the addition of -illa, e.g., la rodilla (knee), from la rueda (wheel; caster; roller); nonetheless, the relationship between these formed words and their respective roots generally is clear. Words ending with -illa are feminine.

Formed Word	English Equivalent	Related to	English Equivalent
la barbilla	point of the chin	la barba	chin
la bombilla	light bulb	la bomba	lamp globe
la cadenilla	small ornamental chain	la cadena[1]	(lit.; fig.) chain; chain-gang
la cajetilla	packet of cigarettes; cigarette box	la cajeta	small box
la camilla	stretcher; couch	la cama[2]	bed
la carretilla	small cart; wheelbarrow	la carreta	wagon
la cerilla	ear wax; cold cream	la cera	wax; wax candles

Formed Word	English Equivalent	Related to	English Equivalent
la cocinilla	kitchenette	la cocina	kitchen
la colilla	cigarette butt	la cola[3]	tail; tail-end; hind part
la cortinilla	small curtain	la cortina[4]	curtain; screen; covering
la escobilla	small broom; whisk broom	la escoba	broom
la estampilla	postage stamp	la estampa	printing stamp; engraving
la felpilla	chenille	la felpa[5]	plush
las fritillas	fritters	el frito	fried food
la frutilla	small fruit; rosary bead	la fruta	fruit
la gacetilla	personal news column	la gaceta[6]	gazette; political or literary newspaper
la gargantilla	necklace; bead (of a necklace)	la garganta[7]	throat; gullet
la gavetilla	small desk drawer	la gaveta	drawer (of writing desk)
la lanilla	nap (of cloth); fine flannel	la lana	wool; fleece
la manecilla	small hand; hand on a clock	la mano[8]	hand
la mantequilla	butter	la manteca	lard; grease; fat; pomade
la mariposilla	little butterfly	la mariposa	butterfly
la mesilla[9]	small table; sideboard	la mesa	table; desk
la papadilla	fleshy part under the chin	la papada	double chin; dewlap

Formed Word	English Equivalent	Related to	English Equivalent
la pastilla	tablet; pill; bar (of soap, chocolate)	la pasta	paste; batter; pastry
la plumilla	small feather	la pluma	feather
la rodilla	knee	la rueda	wheel; caster; roller
la sabanilla	small sheet; napkin; kerchief	la sábana	sheet (of a bed); altar cloth
la saetilla	small arrow; hand (of a watch)	la saeta	arrow; shaft
la semilla	seed	el semen	semen; sperm
la sortijilla	little ring	la sortija	ring
la tortilla[10]	tortilla; pancake; omelette	la torta	cake; pie
la zapatilla	slipper; little shoe	el zapato	shoe

[1]cadena perpetua = life imprisonment
[2]cama de matrimonio = double bed; cama camera or cama sencilla = single bed
[3]a la cola = at the end; right at the back; hacer cola = to line up
[4]correr la cortina = to draw the curtain
[5]toalla de felpa = thick towel; nap towel
[6]mentir más que la gaceta = to be an inveterate liar
[7]nudo en la garganta = lump in the throat
[8]tener mano izquierda = to have tact and *savoir faire,* know how to handle things adroitly
[9]mesilla de noche = bedside table
[10]tortilla francesa = plain omelette

-illo
Meaning: diminutive
English equivalent: *-ette;* usually none
Found in: nouns

In this grouping of words that end with *-illo*, this suffix indicates physical smallness. Most of the terms below are simply names for the smaller version of the root noun, e.g., *el platillo* (saucer; small dish), from *el plato* (plate; dish). At times, however, the meaning will change significantly with the addition of *-illo* or *-illa,* e.g., *el vespertillo* (bat), from *el véspero* (vesper; evening star); nonetheless, the relationship between the root and the formed words generally is clear. All nouns ending with *-illo* are masculine.

Formed Word	English Equivalent	Related to	English Equivalent
el banquillo	small bench	el banco	bench
el bocadillo[1]	sandwich; snack	el bocado	mouthful; morsel (of food)
el bolsillo[2]	pocket	la bolsa	purse; bag
el cachorrillo	small puppy	el cachorro	puppy
el caminillo	back road; path	el camino[3]	road; lane; way; route
el cerquillo	small circle or hoop	el cerco[4]	hoop; ring
el cervatillo	fawn	el ciervo	deer
el cigarillo	cigarette	el cigarro	cigar
el corralillo	small yard	el corral[5]	enclosure; yard; barnyard
el cuentecillo	little story	el cuento[6]	story; tale; short story
el cuernecillo	small horn	el cuerno	horn
el dedillo[7]	fingertip	el dedo[8]	finger
el dragoncillo	little dragon	el dragón	dragon; flying lizard
el espejillo	little mirror; hand-mirror	el espejo	mirror; lookingglass
el farolillo	lantern	el farol	streetlamp
el halconcillo	small or young falcon or hawk	el halcón	falcon; hawk
el hornillo	kitchen stove	el horno	oven; furnace
el humillo	thin smoke; vapor	el humo[9]	smoke; steam
el jaboncillo	soapstone; toilet soap	el jabón[10]	soap
el librillo	book of cigarette paper	el libro	book

Formed Word	English Equivalent	Related to	English Equivalent
el marranillo	little pig	el marrano	pig; swine (coll.) filthy creature
el nudillo	knuckle	el nudo[11]	joint; knot
el panecillo	roll	el pan	bread
el pasillo	aisle; hallway	el paseo	walk; avenue
el pastelillo[12]	small cake; meat pie	el pastel	cake; pastry
el pecadillo	small sin; peccadillo	el pecado	sin
el pececillo[13]	little fish	el pez	fish
el perrillo	small dog	el perro	dog
el platillo	saucer; small dish	el plato[14]	plate; dish
el plieguecillo	half-sheet of paper	el pliego	sheet of paper
el puntillo	small point; punctilio	el punto	point; period; dot
el torillo	little bull	el toro	bull
el tornillo[15]	screw	el torno	wheel; axletree
el trabajillo	small job; modest piece of work	el trabajo	work; job; labor
el versecillo	little verse	el verso	verse; line
el vespertillo	(zool.) bat	el véspero	vesper; evening star
el vientecillo	light wind; breeze	el viento	wind
el zarandillo	small sieve	la zaranda	sifter; sieve

[1]tomar un bocadillo = to have a snack
[2]de bolsillo = pocket-size
[3]camino trillado = beaten track
[4]en cerco = round about
[5]hacer corrales = to play truant
[6]cuento de nunca acabar = never-ending affair
[7]saberse al dedillo = to have at one's fingertips
[8]dedo cordial or dedo del corazón = middle finger; dedo índice = index finger
[9]cortina de humo = smokescreen

[10]dar jabón a = to softsoap, butter up
[11]nudo Gordiano = Gordian knot
[12]pastelillo de fruta = tart
[13]pececillos = small-fry
[14]comer en el mismo plato = to be bosom buddies
[15]*(coll.)* le falta un tornillo = he's a bit screwy; he's got a screw loose

-illo; -illa

Meaning: deprecative; *diminutive in status*
English equivalent: none
Found in: nouns

The overall function of *-illo* and *-illa* is to denote physical diminution of the root noun to which either ending is attached. This particular grouping of words ending in *-illo* or *-illa* denotes a lessened status of the base word, and thus the diminution is figurative, not literal or physical. Several of these words, especially those dealing with professions, are rather telling. Note that many of these terms have inserted the letter *c* between the root and the suffix. Those words ending in *-illo* are masculine, while those taking the suffix *-illa* are feminine. When the term refers to a person, the ending *-illo* becomes *-illa*: a male "quack" is *el mediquillo;* a female "quack" is *la mediquilla.*

Formed Word	English Equivalent	Related to	English Equivalent
el abogadillo	third-rate lawyer	el abogado	lawyer
el amorcillo	passing fancy; flirtation	el amor[1]	love; affection
el animalillo	wretched little animal or creature	el animal	animal; creature
el autorcillo	third-rate author	el autor	author
el baratillo	heap of junk for sale	el barato[2]	bargain; sale
el brocadillo	brocade of inferior quality	el brocado	brocade
el cieguillo	poor little blind person	el ciego[3]	blind person
la cosilla	miserable little thing	la cosa[4]	thing
el disgustillo	minor or petty upset	el disgusto[5]	displeasure; upset
el doctorcillo	third-rate doctor; "quack"	el doctor	doctor
la dudilla	sneaking doubt	la duda[6]	doubt
el escritorcillo	third-rate writer	el escritor	writer

Formed Word	English Equivalent	Related to	English Equivalent
el estanquillo	small, poor shop	el estanco	state-run shop
el estudiantillo	wretched student	el estudiante	student
el favorcillo	petty or minor favor or service	el favor	favor; good turn
la figurilla	*(coll.)* insignificant little person	la figura[7]	figure; person
el geniecillo	sharpish temper	el genio[8]	temperament; disposition; mood
la gentecilla	riffraff; rabble	la gente[9]	people
las hablillas	gossip; foolish talk; chitchat	el habla	speech; language; idiom
el hombrecillo	miserable little man	el hombre	man
el ladroncillo	petty thief	el ladrón	thief
el licenciadillo	wretched lawyer; fraud	el licenciado	lawyer
el maridillo	pitiful husband	el marido	husband
el mediquillo	third-rate doctor; "quack"	el médico	doctor; physician
la mentirilla[10]	white lie	la mentira	lie; falsehood
la mujercilla	wretched woman; slut	la mujer	woman
el pajarillo	miserable little bird; frail bird	el pájaro[11]	bird
el papelillo	scrap of paper; cigarette paper	el papel[12]	paper
la personilla	ridiculous little person	la persona[13]	person
el sabidillo	know-it-all	el sabio	sage, wise, learned person
el veranillo[14]	late or untimely summer	el verano	summer
el vinillo	weak wine	el vino[15]	wine

¹amor propio = self-esteem; pride; *amour propre*
²de barato = free; gratis
³ciego de ira = blind with rage
⁴cosa de oír *or* cosa de ver = thing worth hearing or seeing
⁵estar *or* sentirse a disgusto = not to feel at home; to feel uncomfortable
⁶sin duda alguna = beyond the shadow of a doubt
⁷figura de retórica = figure of speech
⁸mal genio = bad or ill temper; genio pronto *or* genio vivo = quick temper
⁹gente de bien = good, honest people; decent folk
¹⁰de mentirilla(s) = in fun; for fun
¹¹matar dos pájaros de un tiro = to kill two birds with one stone
¹²papel de seda = tissue paper; papel de estaño = tin-foil
¹³buena persona = decent person; mala persona = nasty individual
¹⁴veranillo de San Martín = Indian summer
¹⁵vino de Jerez = sherry; vino de Oporto = port wine

-ín

Meaning: diminutive
English equivalent: none
Found in: nouns; adjectives (rarely)

When added to a noun, the suffix -ín can reduce that noun either in physical size or in status (more commonly the reduction is physical). It can also denote a lesser result of the root noun, i.e., *el serrín* (sawdust) from *la sierra* (saw). Infrequently, -ín is an adjectival ending; in this capacity, -ín still acts as a diminutive, e.g., *colín*. All nouns ending with -ín are masculine.

Formed Word	English Equivalent	Related to	English Equivalent
el balín	small-bore bullet	la bala¹	bullet
el banderín	small flag	la bandera²	flag
el batín	dressing gown	la bata	bathrobe
el bolín	small ball	la bola	ball
el botín	half-boot; spat	la bota	boot
el botiquín	medicine chest; first-aid kit	la botica	apothecary's shop
el cafetín	small café; "dive"	el café	café
el cajetín	very small box	la cajeta	small box
el calabacín	gourd	la calabaza	pumpkin
el calcetín	sock	la calceta	stocking
el camarín	small room; boudoir	la cámara	room; chamber
el camisolín	dicky; shirt front	la camisola	laborer's shirt; blouse

Formed Word	English Equivalent	Related to	English Equivalent
colín (adj.)	short-tailed	la cola	tail
el collarín	small collar; priest's collar	el collar	collar
el copetín	cocktail	la copa³	drink (usually alcoholic)
el cornetín	small bugle	la corneta	bugle; cornet
el espadín	small dress sword; rapier	la espada	sword
el fajín	small band or sash	la faja	sash; girdle; band; swathing-band
el faldellín	short skirt; kilt	la falda	skirt
el herrín	rust	el hierro	iron
el labrantín	petty farmer	el labrador	laborer; farmer
el langostín	prawn	la langosta	lobster
el llavín	latchkey	la llave⁴	key
el magín	fancy; imagination	el mago	magician; wizard
el malandrín	rascal; scoundrel	el malandar	wild hog
el maletín	small suitcase; satchel	la maleta	suitcase
el patín	small courtyard	el patio⁵	court; courtyard
pequeñín (adj.)	wee	pequeño	small; little
el pilotín	pilot's mate; second pilot	el piloto⁶	pilot; mate; driver
el pizarrín	slate pencil	la pizarra	slate; blackboard
el polín	wooden roller	el polo	pole
el polvorín	very fine powder	el polvo	powder
el serrín	sawdust	la sierra⁷	saw
el sillín	bicycle seat	la silla⁸	chair

Formed Word	English Equivalent	Related to	English Equivalent
el verdín	pond scum; mold	el verde	green
el violín	violin; fiddle	la viola	viola; viol

---

[1] bala fría = spent or used bullet
[2] alzar *or* levantar bandera = to raise the flag
[3] tomar una copa = to have a drink
[4] echar la llave = to lock
[5] patio de recreo = playground
[6] piloto de altura = navigator
[7] sierra circular = buzz saw
[8] silla de tijera = folding chair; silla giratoria = swivel chair

-ina

Meaning: diminutive; *place where;* denotes feminine name
English equivalent: *-ine*
Found in: nouns

The noun ending *-ina* performs several functions. Its most common is to diminish the physical size of the base noun, e.g., *la neblina* (fine mist; haze), from *la niebla* (fog; mist; haze). The ending *-ina* also can take on the meaning of *place where,* indicating where the action of the root verb takes place, e.g., *la oficina* (office), from *oficiar* (to officiate, minister). Finally, *-ina* can denote the feminine counterpart of the masculine root noun, e.g., *la reina* (queen) from *el rey* (king). At times this ending is found in proper names, e.g., *Josefina* (Josephine) from *José* (Joseph). This suffix has a sister, *-ino,* which is similar in function, but less common. All nouns ending in *-ina* are feminine.

Formed Word	English Equivalent	Related to	English Equivalent
Agustina	Augustina	Agustín	Augustine
la bailarina	ballerina	el bailarín	male ballet dancer
la bronquina	*(fam.)* dispute; contention; quarrel	la bronca[1]	*(coll.)* wrangle; row; ticking off
la cabina[2]	cabin	caber	to fit, have room
Carolina	Caroline	Carlos	Charles
la cortina	curtain; screen; covering	la corte[3]	(royal) court; suite; retinue

Formed Word	English Equivalent	Related to	English Equivalent
Cristina	Christine	Cristo	Christ
la chocolatina	small chocolate bar	el chocolate	chocolate
la escarlatina	(med.) scarlet fever	la escarlata	scarlet (color)
la filmina	filmstrip	el filme	film
la gallina	(fig.) chicken; hen	el gallo[4]	rooster
Guillermina	Wilhelmina	Guillermo	William
la heroína	heroine	el héroe	hero
Josefina	Josephine	José	Joseph
la llantina	fit of weeping	el llanto	crying; weeping; flood of tears
la madrina	godmother	la madre[5]	mother
la marina	shore; seacoast	el mar	sea
la neblina	fine mist; haze	la niebla	fog; mist; haze
la oficina	office	oficiar[6]	to officiate, minister
la palomina	pigeon dung	la paloma[7]	pigeon; dove
la piscina	small swimming pool; fish pond	(Lat.) piscis	fish
la reina[8]	queen	el rey[9]	king
Serafina	Serafina	el serafín	seraph; angel (beautiful person)
la sonatina	sonatina	la sonata	sonata
la sordina[10]	mute; damper (of a piano)	sordo (adj.)	deaf; mute; noiseless
Tomasina	Thomasina	Tomás	Thomas
la turbina	turbine	turbar	to upset; trouble; disturb

Formed Word	English Equivalent	Related to	English Equivalent
la vitrina	glass case; showcase	*(Lat.)* vitrum	glass
la zarina	tsarina	el zar	czar; tsar

[1] echarle a alguien una bronca = to tick someone off
[2] cabina telefónica = phone booth
[3] las Cortes = legislative assembly of Spain
[4] tener mucho gallo = to be very cocky
[5] madre de leche = wet nurse
[6] oficiar de = to act as
[7] paloma casera = domestic pigeon
[8] reina mora = hopscotch
[9] ni rey ni roque = nobody
[10] a la sordina = secretly; on the quiet

-ino

Meaning: diminutive; *place where*
English equivalent: none
Found in: nouns

The noun ending -*ino* usually denotes smallness of the root noun, e.g., *el ansarino* (gosling), from *el ánsar (goose; gander)*. This ending, however, also can indicate the place where the action of the root verb takes place, e.g., *el molino* (mill), from *moler* (to grind). This suffix has a sister suffix, -*ina,* which is more commonly used, but essentially identical in function. Nouns ending with -*ino* are masculine.

Formed Word	English Equivalent	Related to	English Equivalent
el abanino	pleated collar; ruffle; frill	el abano	fan
el ansarino	gosling	el ánsar	goose; gander
el camino[1]	road	caminar	to walk
el casino[2]	men's club	la cása[3]	house; home; business house
el cebollino[4]	onion seedling; chive	la cebolla	onion; onion bulb
el colino	cabbage seed	el col[5]	cabbage
el michino	kitten; pussy	el micho	puss
el molino[6]	mill	moler	to grind
el padrino	godfather	el padre[7]	father

Formed Word	English Equivalent	Related to	English Equivalent
el palomino	young pigeon	la paloma[8]	pigeon; dove
el pollino	young chap or fellow	el pollo	(fig.) chap; fellow
el porrino	tender leek plant	el porro	leek
el vellocino[9]	fleece	el vello	down; nap; soft hair; gossamer

[1]camino trillado = beaten track
[2]casino de juego = casino
[3]casa de préstamos = pawnshop
[4]escardar cebollinos = to do nothing useful
[5]entre col y col = every now and again
[6]molino de viento = windmill
[7]padre de familia = head of a family
[8]paloma mensajera = carrier pigeon
[9]vellocino de oro = the Golden Fleece

-ino (-ina)

Meaning: *like; relating to; native; native of*
English equivalent: *-ine*
Found in: adjectives; nouns

The adjectival suffix *-ino*, which means *like* and *relating to*, also is one of several endings that denote origin. Like other endings signifying origin (e.g., *-és* or *-ano*), *-ino* in this context functions as a noun as well as an adjective: *El andino sirve el café argentino a la neoyorquina* (The Andean man serves the coffee from Argentina to the woman from New York). Note that these words are not capitalized, as they are in English, and that words ending in *-ino* take the feminine form *-ina* when denoting or describing a feminine noun.

Formed Word	English Equivalent	Related to	English Equivalent
alpino	Alpine; alpine	los Alpes	the Alps
ambarino	relating to amber	el ámbar	amber
(el) andino	(native) of the Andes	los Andes	the Andes
(el) argelino	(native) of Algeria	Argelia	Algeria
(el) argentino	(native) of Argentina	Argentina	Argentina
azulino	bluish	el azul[1]	blue (color)
blanquecino	whitish	el blanco[2]	white (color); blank space

Formed Word	English Equivalent	Related to	English Equivalent
caballino	relating to horses; equine	el caballo	horse
(el) campesino	peasant; of the country	el campo	country; countryside
canino	canine; relating to dogs	(Lat.) canis	dog
cedrino	(made) of cedar; cedar	el cedro[3]	cedar
cochino	(coll.) filthy; rotten; vile	el cocho	(prov.) pig; filthy person
corderino	relating to lambs	el cordero	lamb
cristalino	crystalline	el cristal	crystal
dañino	harmful; destructive; noxious	el daño[4]	damage; harm
elefantino	elephantine; (of) ivory	el elefante	elephant
esmeraldino	emeraldlike	la esmeralda	emerald
ferino[5]	wild; savage; ferocious	(Lat.) fera	a wild animal
(el) florentino	(native) of Florence; Florentine	Florencia	Florence
(el) granadino	(native) of Granada	Granada	Granada
mortecino	dying	la muerte[6]	death
(el) neoyorquino	(native) of New York	Nueva York	New York
purpurino	purplish	la púrpura	purple (color)
repentino	sudden; unexpected	el repente[7]	start; sudden movement
(el) salmantino	(native) of Salamanca	Salamanca	Salamanca
(el) santiaguino	(native) of Santiago	Santiago	Santiago
septembrino	of September	septiembre	September
serpentino	serpentine; snakelike	la serpiente[8]	serpent; snake

Formed Word	English Equivalent	Related to	English Equivalent
(el) tangerino	(native) of Tangiers	Tánger	Tangiers
(el) tunecino	(native) of Tunis or Tunisia	Túnez	Tunis; Tunisia
zucarino	sugary	el azúcar[9]	sugar

[1]azul marino = navy blue
[2]blanco de la uña = half-moon of the fingernail
[3]cedro del Líbano = cedar of Lebanon
[4](com.) daños y perjuicios = damages
[5]tos ferina = whooping cough
[6]estar a la muerte = to be at death's door
[7]de repente = suddenly
[8]serpiente de cascabel = rattlesnake
[9]azúcar en polvo = powdered sugar

-isco (-isca)

Meaning: *like; relating to; result of action*
English equivalent: none
Found in: adjectives; nouns

The ending -*isco* is used infrequently and is found in both adjectives and nouns. As an adjectival ending, the resulting word will indicate that the person or thing described holds characteristics of the base term, usually a noun (-*isco* will change to -*isca* when the adjective describes a feminine noun). As a noun ending, the base word is a verb, and the formed word will indicate the result of that action. Note that some of the nouns below are related to verbs ending with -*iscar.* All nouns ending with -*isco* are masculine; those ending with -*isca* are feminine.

Formed Word	English Equivalent	Related to	English Equivalent
alemanisco	made in Germany	Alemania	Germany
arenisco	sandy; gritty; like sand	la arena[1]	sand; grit
arisco	churlish; surly; evasive	ariscarse	to become sullen, standoffish
levantisco[2]	turbulent; restless; Levantine	el levante	east coast of Spain; east wind; Levant
el mordisco	bite; pinch	morder[3]	to bite, nip
morisco	Moorish	el moro	Moor

Formed Word	English Equivalent	Related to	English Equivalent
el ventisco/la ventisca	snowstorm; snowdrift	ventiscar	to snow hard

[1]arena movediza = quicksand
[2]soplan vientos levantiscos = difficult times are coming
[3]morderse la lengua = to mince one's words

-ísimo (-ísima)

Meaning: adjectival superlative
English equivalent: none
Found in: adjectives

The most common superlative ending for Spanish adjectives is *-ísimo* (*-ísima* when describing feminine nouns). It can be added to most adjectives (except those whose final consonant is *r:* see *-érrimo*), and its formation is simple: if the root adjective ends with a vowel (or vowels), drop the vowel(s) and add *-ísimo;* if the root adjective ends with a consonant, add *-ísimo* directly. The exception is with base adjectives ending with *-ble,* where an *i* is added between the *b* and the *l: amable - amabilísimo.* The standard orthographic changes of *c* to *qu (rico - riquísimo), z* to *c (feliz - felicísimo),* and *g* to *gu (largo - larguísimo)* should be noted, because this suffix begins with the letter *i.*

Formed Word	English Equivalent	Related to	English Equivalent
amabilísimo	extremely kind	amable	kind
beatísimo	most holy	beato	blessed; pious; devout
bellísimo	extremely fair, beautiful	bello[1]	fair; beautiful
bonísimo/ buenísimo	extremely good	bueno[2]	good
clarísimo	extremely clear	claro	clear
delgadísimo	extremely thin	delgado	thin; lean
delicadísimo	extremely delicate	delicado	delicate; dainty
excelentísimo	most excellent	excelente	excellent
feísimo	extremely ugly; hideous	feo	ugly
felicísimo	extremely happy	feliz[3]	happy; merry; glad

Formed Word	English Equivalent	Related to	English Equivalent
ferventísimo	extremely fervent	ferviente	fervent
grandísimo	extremely large; huge	grande	big; large
guapísimo	extremely handsome	guapo	handsome
hermosísimo	extremely beautiful	hermoso	beautiful
horribilísimo	extremely horrible	horrible	horrible
ilustrísimo	most illustrious	ilustre	illustrious
importantísimo	extremely important	importante	important
jovencísimo	extremely young	joven	young
larguísimo	extremely long	largo[4]	long
limpísimo	extremely clean	limpio	clean
malísimo	extremely bad	malo	bad; evil
mismísimo	very same; selfsame	mismo[5]	same
muchísimo	enormous amount; very much	mucho	much; a lot
nobilísimo	most noble	noble	noble
notabilísimo	most notable	notable	notable
palidísimo	extremely pale; white as a sheet	pálido	pale
pequeñísimo	extremely small, tiny	pequeño	small; tiny
poquísimo	miserable little (amount)	poco[6]	small (amount)
riquísimo	extremely rich, wealthy	rico	rich
santísimo[7]	most holy	santo[8]	holy; blessed
sucísimo	extremely dirty, filthy	sucio	dirty; filthy
valentísimo	most valiant	valiente	valiant
venerabilísimo	most venerable	venerable	venerable

[1] bellas artes = fine arts
[2] a buena de Dios = at random; on chance
[3] Feliz Navidad = Merry Christmas
[4] de dos pies de largo = two feet long
[5] ahora mismo = right now
[6] poco antes = shortly before
[7] el Santísimo = the holy sacrament
[8] santo titular = patron saint

-ismo

Meaning: *system; doctrine; loyalty to; act; characteristic*
English equivalent: *-ism*
Found in: nouns

Though it has a number of specific meanings, the suffix *-ismo* can be reduced to one general function, that of expanding upon the particular. For example, from *el vándalo* (vandal), we get *el vandalismo* (vandalism), which encompasses all vandals and their actions. Note the expansive effect this suffix has on the base term in the following examples. Words ending with *-ismo* are masculine.

Formed Word	English Equivalent	Related to	English Equivalent
el alcoholismo	alcoholism	el alcohol[1]	alcohol
el analfabetismo	illiteracy	el alfabeto	alphabet
el argentinismo	Argentinism	Argentina	Argentina
el caciquismo	control by political "machine"	el cacique	political leader
el conservadurismo	conservatism	el conservador	*(polit.)* conservative
el despotismo	despotism	el déspota	despot
el dogmatismo	dogmatism	el dogma	dogma
el egoísmo	egoism; selfishness	el ego	ego; self
el esnobismo	snobbery	el esnob	snob
el españolismo	love of *or* devotion to Spain	España	Spain
el evangelismo	evangelism	el Evangelio[2]	gospel
el feísmo	cult of the ugly or hideous	feo[3]	ugly; nasty
el gitanismo	gypsyism; gypsy life	el gitano	gypsy
el hipnotismo	hypnotism	la hipnosis	hypnosis
el idealismo	idealism	el ideal	ideal
el idiotismo	ignorance	el idiota	idiot
el liberalismo	liberalism	el liberal	liberal
el machismo	glorification of masculinity	el macho	male
el magnetismo	magnetism	el magneto	magnet
el materialismo	materialism	el material	material
el mejicanismo	Mexicanism	Méjico	Mexico
el nacionalismo	nationalism	el nacional	nationalist

Formed Word	English Equivalent	Related to	English Equivalent
el narcisismo	narcissism	Narciso	Narcissus
el narcotismo	drug addiction	el narcótico	narcotic
el obrerismo	labor movement	el obrero	laborer
el paganismo	paganism	el pagano	pagan
el patriotismo	patriotism	la patria[4]	native land; fatherland
el radicalismo	radicalism	el radical	radical
el salvajismo	savagery	el salvaje	savage
el tabaquismo	addiction to cigarettes	el tabaco	tobacco; cigarettes
el terrorismo	terrorism	el terror	terror
el vandalismo	vandalism	el vándalo	vandal
el ventajismo	(political) one-upmanship	la ventaja	advantage; good point
el verbalismo	verbalism	el verbo[5]	word; *(gram.)* verb

[1] alcohol de grano = grain alcohol; alcohol de fricciones = rubbing alcohol
[2] es el Evangelio = it's (the) gospel truth
[3] eso está feo = it looks bad; it's not done
[4] hacer patria = to boast about one's country
[5] echar verbos = to curse, swear

-ista

Meaning: *one who*; denotes profession
English equivalent: *-ist*
Found in: nouns

Generally speaking, endings that indicate *one who* have both masculine and feminine forms (e.g., *-ero/-era; -dor/-dora,* etc.). The suffix *-ista,* however, is both masculine and feminine (*el dentista; la dentista*), and thus the gender of the person referred to is determined from context. Words ending in *-ista,* though usually derived from nouns, can be derived from verbs and adjectives as well.

Formed Word	English Equivalent	Related to	English Equivalent
el acuarelista	watercolor artist	la acuarela	watercolor
el andinista	mountain climber	los Andes	the Andes
el artista	artist	el arte[1]	art

Formed Word	English Equivalent	Related to	English Equivalent
el ascensionista	balloonist; climber	ascender	to ascend, climb
el bautista[2]	one who baptizes; Baptist	bautizar	to baptize
el budista	Buddhist	Buda	Buddha
el capitalista	capitalist	el capital	capital
el carterista	pickpocket	la cartera	pocketbook; wallet
el ciclista	cyclist	el ciclo	cycle
el cientista	scientist	la ciencia[3]	science
el clarinetista	clarinet player	el clarinete	clarinet
el dentista	dentist	el diente[4]	tooth
el deportista	sportsman	el deporte	sport; pastime
el espiritualista	spiritualist	el espíritu	spirit
el fatalista	fatalist	fatal	fatal
el flautista	flautist	la flauta	flute
el florista	florist	la flor	flower
el formalista	formalist	formal	formal
el humanista	humanist	el humano	human
el inversionista	investor	la inversión	(com.) investment
el licorista	liquor dealer or seller	el licor	liquor
el literalista	literalist; adherent to the letter	literal	literal
el maquinista	machinist	la máquina[5]	machine
el marxista	Marxist	Marx	Karl Marx
el optimista	optimist	óptimo	best; first-class
el pacifista	pacifist	la paz[6]	peace
el paisajista	landscape painter	el paisaje	landscape; scenery
el perfeccionista	perfectionist	la perfección	perfection
el periodista	journalist	el periódico	newspaper

Formed Word	English Equivalent	Related to	English Equivalent
el pesimista	pessimist	pésimo	atrocious; abominable
el pianista	pianist	el piano[7]	piano
el realista	realist	real	real
el terrorista	terrorist	el terror	terror
el violinista	violinist	el violín	violin
el vocabulista	lexicographer; student of words	el vocablo	word; term

[1] arte manual = craft
[2] San Juan Bautista *or* El Bautista = St. John the Baptist
[3] ciencia infusa = God-given knowledge
[4] apretar los dientes = to grit one's teeth
[5] máquina de escribir = typewriter
[6] bandera de paz = flag of truce
[7] piano de cola = grand piano; piano vertical = upright piano

-ita

Meaning: diminutive
English equivalent: none
Found in: nouns

The suffix -ita indicates smallness of the root noun to which it is attached. At times, the addition of -ita changes not only the size, but *also* the meaning of the term itself, e.g., *la animita* (firefly), from *el ánimo* (soul; spirit). This ending has a sister suffix, -ito, which performs the same function. Words ending in -ita are feminine.

Formed Word	English Equivalent	Related to	English Equivalent
la animita	firefly	el ánimo[1]	soul; spirit
la cajita	small box	la caja[2]	box
la cancioncita	(delightful) little song, tune, ditty	la canción	song; tune
la caperucita[3]	little hood or cap	la caperuza	pointed hood or cap
la chiquita	little girl	la chica	girl; lass
la cunita	little cradle	la cuna[4]	cradle; crib
la espadita	small sword	la espada	sword
la estrellita	small star	la estrella	star

Formed Word	English Equivalent	Related to	English Equivalent
la florecita	little flower	la flor[5]	flower
la hormiguita	tiny little ant	la hormiga	ant
la lentejita	small lentil	la lenteja	lentil
la manecita	small hand	la mano	hand
la mariquita	ladybird; (coll.) sissy	la marica	(orn.) magpie
la mosquita[6]	small fly	la mosca	fly
la nochecita	twilight; nightfull	la noche	night
la notita	short note	la nota	note; bill; statement
la ollita	small pot	la olla	pot
la pajita	drinking straw	la paja[7]	straw (crop)
la palabrita	brief or gentle word	la palabra[8]	word
la patita	small foot	la pata[9]	foot; paw
la pesita	small weight	el peso	weight
la pollita	chick; young chicken; (coll.) girl	el pollo	chicken; (fig.) young fellow
la ramita	sprig; twig	la rama	branch
la señorita	Miss; young lady	la señora	Mrs.; lady; gentlewoman
la sorpresita	little surprise	la sorpresa	surprise
la sortijita	little ring; ringlet	la sortija[10]	ring; curl (of hair)
la trencita	braid; plait	la trenza	braided hair; tresses
la vaquita	small cow	la vaca	cow
la velita	small candle; votive candle	la vela	candle
la viejecita	little old woman	la vieja	old woman
la viudita	merry little widow	la viuda	widow

[1]estado de ánimo = state or frame of mind
[2]caja de música = music box
[3]Caperucita Roja = Little Red Riding Hood

4de humilde cuna = of humble birth
5en flor = in blossom
6*(coll., fig.)* mosquita muerta = one who looks as if butter wouldn't melt in his mouth
7echar pajas = to draw lots with straws
8¡palabra! = I promise!; I give you my word!
9patas de gallos = crow's feet; wrinkles
10sortija de sello = signet ring

-itis

Meaning: *disease; inflammation*
English equivalent: *-itis*
Found in: nouns

Words ending with *-itis,* in English as in Spanish, often are medical terms that indicate inflammation of the base term. Although frequently such words are not related directly to other Spanish terms, they are easy to recognize because they are cognates of their English counterparts. Spanish words ending with *-itis* are feminine.

Formed Word	English Equivalent	Related to	English Equivalent
la amigdalitis	tonsillitis	la amígdala	tonsil
la apendicitis	appendicitis	el apéndice	appendix
la artritis	arthritis	*(Gr.)* arthron	joint
la bronquitis	bronchitis	*(Gr.)* bronchos	windpipe
la celulitis	cellulitis	la célula	cell; cellule
la colitis	colitis	el colon	*(anat.)* colon
la conjuntivitis	conjunctivitis	*(Lat.)* conjunctivus	serving to connect
la dermatitis	dermatitis	*(Gr.)* derma	skin
la diverticulitis	diverticulitis	*(Lat.)* diverticulum	a bypath
la esplenitis	splenitis	el esplín	spleen
la estomatitis	stomatitis	*(Gr.)* stoma	mouth
la flebitis	phlebitis	*(Gr.)* phleps	vein
la frenitis	phrenitis; delirium	*(Gr.)* phren	the mind
la gastritis	gastritis	*(Gr.)* gaster	belly
la gingivitis	gingivitis	*(Lat.)* gingiva	the gum
la glositis	glossitis	*(Gr.)* glossa	tongue
la hepatitis	hepatitis	*(Gr.)* hepar	liver
la laringitis	laryngitis	la laringe	larynx

Formed Word	English Equivalent	Related to	English Equivalent
la meningitis	meningitis	*(Gr.)* meninx	membrane
la nefritis	nephritis	*(Gr.)* nephros	kidney
la neumonitis	pneumonitis	*(Gr.)* pneumon	lung
la neuritis	neuritis	*(Gr.)* neuron	nerve
la oftalmitis	ophthalmitis	*(Gr.)* ophthalmos	eye
la otitis	otitis	*(Gr.)* ous	ear
la ovaritis	ovaritis	*(Lat.)* ovarium	egg
la pancreatitis	pancreatitis	el páncreas	pancreas
la pericarditis	pericarditis	*(Gr.)* peri + kardia	around + heart
la peritonitis	peritonitis	*(Gr.)* peri + teinein	around + to stretch
la queratitis	keratitis	*(Gr.)* keras	horn
la rinitis	rhinitis	*(Gr.)* rhis	nose
la sinusitis	sinusitis	el seno	*(med.)* sinus
la tendinitis	tendinitis	el tendón	tendon
la timpanitis	tympanitis	*(Gr.)* tympanon	drum
la vaginitis	vaginitis	la vagina	vagina

-ito

Meaning: diminutive
English equivalent: none
Found in: nouns

The suffix *-ito* indicates physical smallness of the root noun to which it is attached. This ending can also express endearment or familiarity, as in *Miguelito* (Mike; "Mikey"), from *Miguel* (Michael). One colloquial exception is the term *adiosito* (from *adiós*), said in the same spirit as the English *ta-ta*. The ending *-ito* is a common one, and has a sister suffix, *-ita,* which performs the same function. Words ending in *-ito* are masculine.

Formed Word	English Equivalent	Related to	English Equivalent
el abuelito	little grandfather; "gramps"	el abuelo	grandfather
adiosito *(interj.)*	ta-ta	adiós	good-bye
el besito	(delightful) little kiss	el beso	kiss
el bracito	little arm	el brazo	arm

Formed Word	English Equivalent	Related to	English Equivalent
el braserito	small pan to hold coals	el brasero	brazier; fire-pan
el burrito	(attractive or nice) little donkey	el burro	donkey; ass; burro
el caballito	small horse; pony	el caballo	horse
el cajoncito	small drawer; desk drawer	el cajón	drawer
el cerdito	piglet; (dear) little pig; piggy	el cerdo	*(lit., fig.)* pig; hog
el cochecito	pram; baby carriage	el coche	coach; carriage; car
el conejito	small rabbit	el conejo	rabbit
el corazoncito	dear little heart	el corazón	heart
el cordelito	fine, thin cord	el cordel	cord; thin rope; line
el corralito	playpen	el corral	enclosure; yard; barnyard
Danielito	little Daniel; "Danny"	Daniel	Daniel
despacito *(adv.)*[1]	*(coll.)* very slowly; nice and gently	despacio *(adv.)*	slowly; carefully; with attention
el dientecito	little tooth	el diente	tooth
el gatito	kitten	el gato	cat
el granito	small grain	el grano	grain
el halconcito	small or young falcon or hawk	el halcón	falcon; hawk
el huerfanito	little orphan	el huérfano	orphan
el jueguecito	little game	el juego	game
Miguelito	little Michael; Mike; "Mikey"	Miguel[2]	Michael
el momentito	tiny bit of time	el momento[3]	moment; minute
el palito	little stick	el palo[4]	stick; pole
el patito	duckling	el pato	duck

Formed Word	English Equivalent	Related to	English Equivalent
el pedacito	small bit; small piece	el pedazo[5]	piece; bit; lump
el perrito	puppy	el perro	dog
el pobrecito	poor little poor person or thing	el pobre[6]	poor person; pauper; beggar
el poquito[7]	very small amount	el poco	little amount
el puentecito	small bridge; footbridge	el puente[8]	bridge
el ratito	very short time; little while	el rato[9]	short time; while
el regalito	small gift or present	el regalo	gift; present
el saltito	little hop	el salto[10]	jump; spring; leap
el santito	regular little saint; image of a saint	el santo	saint
el sueñecito	nap	el sueño[11]	sleep; sleepiness; dream
el traguito	short swig	el trago[12]	swallow; gulp; swig; drink
el trapito	small rag	el trapo	rag
el trenecito	little train; toy train	el tren[13]	train
el viejecito	little old man	el viejo[14]	old man

[1] despacito y buena letra = take it nice and easy
[2] Miguel Angel = Michelangelo
[3] por momentos = constantly; continually; all the time
[4] estar del mismo palo = to be in the same boat
[5] hacerse pedazos = to fall to bits or be smashed to pieces
[6] más pobre que una rata = poor as a churchmouse
[7] un poquito = a little bit
[8] puente colgante = suspension bridge
[9] buen rato = quite a while; quite some time
[10] salto mortal = somersault
[11] entre sueños = half-asleep
[12] echar un trago = to have a drink
[13] tren de vida = pace of life; rate of spending
[14] viejo verde = dirty old man

-ito; -ita

Meaning: *like; relating to; quality; mineral product; native; native of; one who*
English equivalent: *-ite*
Found in: adjectives; nouns

Spanish words ending in *-ito* or *-ita* nearly always have as their English counterparts cognates ending with *-ite* or *-yte* (those ending in *-yte* are derived from Greek). This pair of suffixes is found in adjectives as well as in nouns, and can indicate several different meanings. Most words ending with *-ito* follow the usual pattern whereby the final o becomes *a* when denoting or describing a feminine noun; however, three examples given below, *semita* (Semite), *israelita* (Israelite), and vietnamita (Vietnamese), always end with *-ita,* whether masculine or feminine *(el semita; la semita).* These terms are not capitalized as they are in English and they function as both adjectives and nouns. Otherwise, all nouns ending with *-ito* are masculine, while those ending with *-ita* are feminine. Note that this is a common ending for minerals.

Formed Word	English Equivalent	Related to	English Equivalent
el acólito	acolyte; assistant	*(Gr.)* akolouthos	follower; attendant
el apetito[1]	appetite	*(Lat.)* appetere	to strive after, long for
contrito	contrite	*(Lat.)* conterere	to rub away, grind
el crédito[2]	credit	*(Lat.)* credere	to trust
decrépito	decrepit; fallen into decay	decrepitar	to decrepitate, crackle
el depósito	deposit	depositar	to deposit
la dinamita	dynamite	*(Gr.)* dynamis	power
emérito	emeritus	*(Lat.)* emerere	to obtain by service
erudito	erudite; learned; scholarly	*(Lat.)* erudire	to free from rudeness
la estalactita	stalactite	*(Gr.)* stalaktos	oozing out in drops
la estalagmita	stalagmite	*(Gr.)* stalagmos	a dropping; dripping
exquisito	exquisite	*(Lat.)* exquirere	to search out
favorito	favorite	el favor	favor
finito	finite	el fin[3]	end

Formed Word	English Equivalent	Related to	English Equivalent
el grafito	graphite	*(Gr.)* graphein	to write
el granito	granite	el grano	grain
gratuito	gratuitous	grato	pleasing; pleasant
el hábito[4]	habit	habitar	to inhabit
ilícito	illicit; unlawful	*(Lat.)* il + licet	not + to permit
infinito[5]	infinite	in + el fin	not + end
ingénito	innate; inborn	*(Lat.)* ingignere	to implant by birth
(el) islamita	Islamic; Islamite	islam	Islam
(el) israelita	Israelite	Israel	Israel
lícito	licit; lawful	*(Lat.)* licet	it is permitted
el mérito	merit	merecer	to deserve, merit
el meteorito	meteorite	el meteoro	meteor
el neófito	neophyte	*(Gr.)* neos + phytos	new + grown
el nitrito	nitrite	*(Lat.)* nitrum	natron; natural soda
la pirita	pyrite	la pira	pyre
el pretérito	past; preterite	preterir	to pass over, leave out
recóndito	recondite; hidden; concealed	*(Lat.)* recondere	to put away, store
(el) semita	Semite	Shem	Shem (son of Noah)
solícito	solicitous; eager to please	solicitar	to solicit, request, apply for
el sulfito	sulphite	*(Lat.)* sulfur	sulfur; sulphur

Formed Word	English Equivalent	Related to	English Equivalent
el tránsito[6]	transit; traffic; passage	*(Lat.)* transitus	transit; a passing over or across
(el) vietnamita	Vietnamese	Vietnam	Vietnam

[1]abrir el apetito = to whet the appetite
[2]créditos activos = assets
[3]al fin y al cabo = after all; when all is said and done
[4]tener por hábito = to be in the habit (of)
[5]hasta lo infinito = ad infinitum
[6]de tránsito = passing through; in transit

-itud

Meaning: *state of being; condition*
English equivalent: *-tude*
Found in: nouns

A Spanish word that ends in -*itud* is a noun that denotes the state or condition of the base word. Usually the base is an adjective: *la ineptitud* (ineptitude) indicates the state of being *inepto* (inept). Infrequently, these formed words are derived from nouns: *la actitud* (attitude) comes from *el acto* (action; deed); however, -*itud* still indicates the state or condition of that root. All words ending with -*itud* are feminine.

Formed Word	English Equivalent	Related to	English Equivalent
la actitud	attitude; posture; pose	el acto[1]	act; deed
la amplitud	amplitude; roominess	amplio	ample; spacious; roomy
la aptitud	aptitude; fitness; ability	apto	able; competent; apt; fit
la beatitud	beatitude	beato	blessed
la decrepitud	decrepitude	decrépito	decrepit; fallen into decay
la esclavitud	slavery; bondage	el esclavo	slave
la exactitud	exactness; accuracy	exacto	exact; accurate

Formed Word	English Equivalent	Related to	English Equivalent
la excelsitud	loftiness	excelso	lofty; sublime
la habitud	relationship; convention; custom	el hábito[2]	habit
la ilicitud	illicitness	ilícito	illicit
la ineptitud	ineptitude; incompetency	inepto	inept; incompetent
la inexactitud	inexactness; inaccuracy	inexacto	inexact; inaccurate
la inverosimilitud	unlikelihood; incredibleness	inverosímil	unlikely; incredible
la juventud	youth; state of being young	joven	young
la lasitud	lassitude; weariness; languor	laso	weary; weak; languid
la latitud	latitude; breadth; width	lato	broad; wide; large
la laxitud	laxness; laxity	laxo	lax; slack
la lentitud	slowness	lento	slow
la longitud	longitude; length	luengo (obs.)	long; far
la magnitud	magnitude	magno[3]	great
la plenitud	plenitude; fullness	pleno[4]	full
la prontitud	promptitude; promptness	pronto[5]	prompt; soon
la pulcritud	pulchritude; neatness	pulcro	neat; tidy; fastidious
la rectitud	rectitude	recto	right; upright; precise
la similitud	similitude; similarity	símil	similar
la solicitud	solicitude; diligence; care	solícito	solicitous; diligent; careful
la verosimilitud	verisimilitude	verosímil	likely; probable; verisimilar

Formed Word	English Equivalent	Related to	English Equivalent
la vicisitud	vicissitude	el vicio[6]	vice

---

[1]en el acto = at once; instantly
[2]tomar el hábito = to profess, take vows
[3]Alejandro Magno = Alexander the Great
[4]en pleno día = in broad daylight
[5]tan pronto como = as soon as
[6]de vicio = from force of habit; for the sake of it

-ivo (-iva)

Meaning: *causing; making*
English equivalent: *-ive*
Found in: adjectives

Spanish adjectives ending in *-ivo* nearly always have an English counterpart ending in *-ive*. The examples given below, all derived from verbs, indicate that someone or something behaves in a manner related to the particular base verb. As with adjectives ending in *-o,* when describing a noun of feminine gender, *-ivo* becomes *-iva.*

Formed Word	English Equivalent	Related to	English Equivalent
abusivo	abusive	abusar[1]	to abuse
administrativo	administrative	administrar	to administer, manage
admirativo	admiring; wondering	admirar	to admire, marvel, or wonder at
calculativo	calculative	calcular	to calculate
declarativo	declarative	declarar[2]	to declare, state; *(law)* to find
defensivo[3]	defensive	defender	to defend, shield
descriptivo	descriptive	describir	to describe
digestivo	digestive	digerir	to digest, take in
educativo	educational	educar	to educate
efectivo[4]	effective	efectuar	to effect

Formed Word	English Equivalent	Related to	English Equivalent
ejecutivo	executive	ejecutar	to execute, carry out, perform
evocativo	evocative	evocar	to evoke
evolutivo	evolutionary; evolving	evolucionar	to evolve
exagerativo	exaggerating	exagerar	to exaggerate
exclamativo	exclamatory	exclamar	to exclaim, cry out
exclusivo	exclusive	excluir	to exclude
expansivo	expansive	expansionar	to expand
expeditivo	expeditious; prompt	expedir	to facilitate, expedite
germinativo	germinative	germinar	to germinate, bud
gubernativo	administrative; governmental	gobernar	to govern, rule
ilusivo	illusive	ilusionar	to delude, have illusions
ilustrativo	illustrative	ilustrar	to illustrate
imaginativo	imaginative	imaginar	to imagine
imperativo	imperative	imperar	to rule, reign, command
inclusivo	inclusive	incluir	to include
indicativo	indicative	indicar	to indicate
meditativo	meditative	meditar	to meditate (on)
nutritivo	nutritive	nutrir	to nourish, feed
ofensivo	offensive	ofender	to offend, slight
regenerativo	regenerative	regenerar	to regenerate

Formed Word	English Equivalent	Related to	English Equivalent
regitivo	ruling; governing	regir	to rule, govern
regresivo	regressive	regresar	to return
representativo	representative	representar[5]	to represent
repulsivo	repulsive	repulsar	to rebuff, reject

[1]abusar de = to make bad use of, take advantage of, impose upon
[2]declarar culpable = to find guilty
[3]estar *or* ponerse a la defensiva = to be or go on the defensive
[4]hacer efectivo = to put into effect
[5]tiene cincuenta años, pero representa menos = he is fifty years old, but he looks younger

-ívoro (-ívora)

Meaning: *tending to eat*
English equivalent: *-ivorous*
Found in: adjectives

Those few adjectives ending with *-ívoro* (*-ívora* when describing feminine nouns) are cognates of their English counterparts. In both languages these words indicate that some person or animal tends to eat a particular foodstuff.

Formed Word	English Equivalent	Related to	English Equivalent
carnívoro	carnivorous	la carne[1]	meat; flesh
herbívoro	herbivorous	la hierba[2]	grass; herb
omnívoro	omnivorous	*(Lat.)* omnis	all; every kind
piscívoro	piscivorous	*(Lat.)* piscis	fish

[1]ser de carne y hueso = to be flesh and blood
[2]mala hierba = weed

-izar

Meaning: *to make (like)*
English equivalent: *-ize*
Found in: verbs

When you see a verb ending with *-izar,* note that it means *to make* or *to make like* the root noun or adjective. As you will see below, many of the roots to which *-izar* is attached are cognates of English words; you therefore should find these verbs relatively easy to learn and use. Verbs ending with *-izar* are regular, and when conjugated make the standard orthographic change from *z* to *c* before the vowel *e*: *yo organizo* (I organize); *yo organicé* (I organized).

Formed Word	English Equivalent	Related to	English Equivalent
alfabetizar	to alphabetize	el alfabeto	alphabet
amenizar	to make pleasant, cheer	ameno[1]	pleasant; agreeable
arborizar	to make treelike	el árbol[2]	tree
autorizar	to authorize	el autor	author
centralizar	to centralize	central	central
climatizar	to air-condition	el clima (artificial)	air conditioning
familiarizar	to familiarize	familiar	familiar
fertilizar	to fertilize	fértil	fertile
finalizar	to finalize	final[3]	final
humanizar	to humanize, soften	el humano	human (being)
legalizar	to legalize	legal	legal
liberalizar	to liberalize	liberal	liberal
magnetizar	to magnetize	el magneto	magnet
memorizar	to memorize	la memoria[4]	memory
nasalizar	to nasalize	nasal	nasal
naturalizar	to naturalize	natural[5]	natural
neutralizar	to neutralize	neutral	neutral
organizar	to organize	el órgano	organ; part
paralizar	to paralyze	la parálisis	paralysis
polemizar	to engage in argument	la polémica	polemics; dispute
polvorizar	to pulverize	el polvo[6]	powder; dust
psicoanalizar	to psychoanalyze	el psicoanálisis	psychoanalysis
realizar	to realize, accomplish	real	real
ruborizar	to make blush	el rubor	blush; flush
satirizar	to satirize	la sátira	satire
suavizar	to make smooth	suave	smooth
teorizar	to theorize	la teoría	theory

Formed Word	English Equivalent	Related to	English Equivalent
tranquilizar	to tranquilize	tranquilo[7]	tranquil
utilizar	to utilize, make use of	útil	useful
valorizar	to make more valuable	el valor[8]	value; worth
vaporizar	to vaporize	el vapor	vapor
vocalizar	*(mus.)* to vocalize, articulate	vocal	vocal; oral

[1] una película amena = an entertaining film
[2] *(Bib.)* árbol de la ciencia del bien y del mal = tree of the knowledge of good and evil
[3] Juicio Final = Last Judgment
[4] ser flaco de memoria = to have a poor or short memory
[5] es natural = it stands to reason; it's understandable
[6] hacer polvo = to wreck, smash up
[7] ¡tranquilo! = calm down!; take it easy!
[8] valor adquisitivo = purchasing value or power

-izo (-iza)

Meaning: *like; relating to; made of*
English equivalent: none
Found in: adjectives

The adjectival ending *-izo* is one of many Spanish suffixes meaning *like* or *relating to*. However, *-izo* also can mean *made of:* from *el cobre* (copper), we get *cobrizo* (made of copper). Adjectives ending in *-izo* can be derived either from nouns or from other adjectives. When used to describe feminine nouns, words ending with *-izo* take the ending *-iza*.

Formed Word	English Equivalent	Related to	English Equivalent
agostizo	born in August	agosto	August
banderizo	factious	el bando	faction; party
bermejizo	tending to vermilion	bermejo	vermilion
cabrerizo	goatish; like a goat	el cabrón	goat
calverizo	having many barren spots (ground)	calvo	barren; treeless; bald
castizo	of noble descent; pure-blooded	casto	pure; chaste
cenizo	ash-colored	le ceniza[1]	ash

Formed Word	English Equivalent	Related to	English Equivalent
cobrizo	made of copper	el cobre[2]	copper; brass kitchen utensils
enfermizo	sickly; unhealthy	enfermo	sick
estadizo	stagnant; stationary	el estado	state; condition
ferrizo	made of iron; ferrous	el fierro	iron
fronterizo	relating to a frontier or border	la frontera	frontier
hechizo	artificial; homemade	hecho[3]	made; done; ready-made
macizo	solid; massive	la masa[4]	mass
otoñizo	autumnal	el otoño	autumn
pajizo	made of straw	la paja	straw
plomizo	leaden; made of lead	el plomo	lead
primerizo	first	primero[5]	first; former; prime
roblizo	oaken; hard; strong	el roble	oak; oak tree
rojizo	reddish	rojo[6]	red
sequizo	dryish	seco	dry
vaquerizo	relating to cattle	la vaca	cow

[1]tomar uno la ccniza = to receive ashes on Ash Wednesday
[2]los cobres = brass (instruments of an orchestra)
[3]dicho y hecho = said and done
[4]en masa = en masse
[5]primera cura = first aid
[6]al rojo = red-hot

-lento (-lenta)

Meaning: *like; relating to; full of*
English equivalent: *-lent*
Found in: adjectives

Spanish adjectives ending with -*lento* have at their base a noun, and indicate that the person or thing described has characteristics of that noun. When describing a feminine noun, these adjectives take the ending -*lenta*.

Formed Word	English Equivalent	Related to	English Equivalent
corpulento	corpulent; fat; fleshy	el cuerpo[1]	body
flatulento	flatulent; windy	el flato	flatus; wind
fraudulento	fraudulent	el fraude	fraud
friolento	chilly; sensitive to cold	el frío[2]	cold; coldness; coolness
pulverulento	powdery; dusty	el polvo[3]	powder; dust
sanguinolento	bloody; dripping blood	(Lat.) sanguis	blood
suculento	succulent	el suco	sap; juice
vinolento	fond of drinking wine	el vino[4]	wine
violento	violent	la violencia	violence
virolento	having smallpox; pockmarked	la viruela[5]	smallpox; pockmark
virulento	virulent	el virus	virus

[1]cuerpo sin alma = dull, lifeless person
[2]tener frío = to be cold
[3]morder el polvo = to bite the dust
[4]vino de coco = coconut milk
[5]viruelas locas = chicken pox

-manía
Meaning: *insane excitement; madness*
English equivalent: -*mania*
Found in: nouns

Spanish words ending with -*manía* are nearly perfect cognates of their English counterparts. These terms refer to madness or excitement with regard to the root term. All words ending with -*manía* are feminine.

Formed Word	English Equivalent	Related to	English Equivalent
la anglomanía	Anglomania; enthusiasm for England	(Lat.) Anglii	the English

Formed Word	English Equivalent	Related to	English Equivalent
la cleptomanía	kleptomania	(Gr.) kleptes	thief
la erotomanía	erotomania	Eros	Eros
la lipemanía	(med.) melancholia	(Gr.) lipos	fat
la megalomanía	megalomania	(Gr.) megas	great; mighty
la monomanía	monomania	(Gr.) monos	one; single; alone
la ninfomanía	nymphomania	la ninfa	nymph; young lady
la piromanía	pyromania	la pira	pyre
la toxicomanía	drug addiction	el tóxico	poison

-mano; -mana

Meaning: *one who is mad; having insane tendencies*
English equivalent: *-maniac*
Found in: nouns; adjectives

As nouns, Spanish words taking the suffix *-mano* refer to persons with overwhelming desires who often gratify them. These same terms also can function as adjectives and are used in describing such persons. When the referent is masculine, the ending is *-mano;* when feminine, the ending is *-mana*.

Formed Word	English Equivalent	Related to	English Equivalent
(el) anglómano	Anglomaniac; in love with England	(Lat.) Anglii	the English
(el) cleptómano	kleptomaniac	(Gr.) kleptes	thief
(el) erotómano	erotomaniac	Eros	Eros
(el) megalómano	megalomaniac	(Gr.) megas	great; mighty
(el) monómano	monomaniac	(Gr.) monos	one; single; alone
(la) ninfómana	nymphomaniac	la ninfa	nymph; young lady
(el) pirómano	pyromaniac	la pira	pyre
(el) toxicómano	drug addict(ed)	el tóxico	poison

-mente
Meaning: forms adverbs
English equivalent: *-ly*
Found in: adverbs

Just as nearly all English adverbs end in *-ly,* nearly all adverbs in Spanish take *-mente* as the ending. Adverbs, which modify verbs, adjectives, and other adverbs, are derived from adjectives. Note that when the root adjective ends with the letter *o,* that *o* changes to *a* before *-mente* is added. All other adjectives simply add *-mente* to become an adverb.

Formed Word	English Equivalent	Related to	English Equivalent
actualmente	presently; nowadays	actual	present; present-day
afortunadamente	fortunately; luckily	afortunado	fortunate; lucky
aparentemente	apparently; seemingly	aparente	apparent; seeming
ciegamente	blindly	ciego[1]	blind
claramente	clearly	claro[2]	clear
culpablemente	guiltily	culpable	guilty; culpable; blameworthy
desgraciadamente	unfortunately; unhappily	desgraciado	unfortunate; luckless
enfáticamente	emphatically	enfático	emphatic
estupendamente	extremely well; perfectly	estupendo	fine; great; super
evidentemente	evidently	evidente	evident
exactamente	exactly	exacto	exact
fácilmente	easily	fácil	easy
felizmente	happily	feliz	happy
finalmente	finally	final	final
frecuentemente	frequently	frecuente	frequent
inculpablemente	blamelessly	inculpable	blameless; inculpable
justamente	precisely; just so	justo	just; fair; right
lentamente	slowly	lento	slow

Formed Word	English Equivalent	Related to	English Equivalent
malamente	in an evil manner	malo[3]	bad; evil
mentalmente	mentally	mental	mental
naturalmente	naturally	natural	natural
necesariamente	necessarily	necesario	necessary
neutralmente	neutrally	neutral	neutral
normalmente	normally	normal[4]	normal
notablemente	notably	notable	notable
nuevamente	again; anew	nuevo[5]	new
obviamente	obviously	obvio	obvious
perfectamente	perfectly	perfecto	perfect
precisamente[6]	precisely; exactly	preciso	precise; accurate; just right
probablemente	probably	probable	probable
rápidamente	rapidly; fast	rápido	rapid; fast
relativamente	relatively; comparatively	relativo	relative; comparative
seguramente	surely; very likely	seguro[7]	sure; secure; certain
tristemente	sadly	triste	sad
usualmente	usually	usual	usual
valientemente	valiantly; bravely	valiente[8]	valiant; brave

[1] obediencia ciega = blind obedience
[2] colores claros = light colors
[3] mala fama = ill fame; bad reputation
[4] línea normal = perpendicular line
[5] de nuevo = again; anew
[6] precisamente en ese momento = at that very moment
[7] seguro social = social security
[8] ¡valiente amigo! = a fine friend!

-miento
Meaning: *act; state of being; result of action*
English equivalent: *-ment*
Found in: nouns

The suffix *-miento* marks the achievement of an action. A word ending with *-miento* has at its root a verb. Infinitives ending in *-ar* retain the *a* (*tratar* becomes *tratamiento*); *-er* and *-ir* verbs take an *i* before this suffix (*envolver* becomes *envolvimiento; sentir* gives us *sentimiento*). All words ending with *-miento* are masculine.

Formed Word	English Equivalent	Related to	English Equivalent
el agrandamiento	enlargement	agrandar	to enlarge
el amillaramiento	tax assessment	amillarar	to assess the tax on
el aplazamiento	postpone- ment	aplazar	to postpone
el aquietamiento	appeasement	aquietar	to appease
el atrincheramiento	entrenchment	atrincherar	to entrench
el aturdimiento	bewilder- ment; daze; confusion	aturdir	to bewilder; daze; stun
el avasallamiento	enslavement	avasallar	to enslave
el confinamiento	confinement	confinar	to confine
el embellecimiento	embellishment	embellecer	to embellish
el empobrecimiento	impoverish- ment	empobrecer	to impoverish
el encadenamiento	enchainment	encadenar	to enchain
el encantamiento	enchantment	encantar[1]	to enchant
el encarcelamiento	imprisonment	encarcelar	to imprison
el enriquecimiento	enrichment	enriquecer	to enrich
el entretenimiento	amusement; entertainment	entretener	to amuse, entertain
el envilecimiento	abasement	envilecer	to abase
el envolvimiento	envelopment	envolver	to envelop
el esclarecimiento	enlightenment	esclarecer	to light up
el establecimiento	establishment	establecer	to establish
el incitamiento	incitement	incitar	to incite
el limpiamiento	cleaning	limpiar	to clean, cleanse
el mejoramiento	improvement	mejorar[2]	to improve
el movimiento	movement	mover	to move
el nombramiento	appointment	nombrar	to appoint, name

Formed Word	English Equivalent	Related to	English Equivalent
el ofrecimiento	offer	ofrecer	to offer
el pagamiento	payment	pagar[3]	to pay
el pensamiento[4]	thought	pensar[5]	to think
el reclutamiento	recruitment	reclutar	to recruit
el seguimiento	pursuit; chase; continuation	seguir[6]	to follow, come after, continue
el sentimiento	sentiment; feeling; emotion; grief	sentir[7]	to sense, feel; regret
el señalamiento	appointed day; marking with signs	señalar	to mark out (with signs)
el tratamiento	treatment	tratar[8]	to treat

[1]encantado (de conocerle) = delighted (to meet you)
[2]mejorando lo presente = present company excepted
[3]pagar al contado = to pay cash (down)
[4]tener el pensamiento de = to intend to
[5]pensar en = to think about
[6]suma y sigue = carry on
[7]lo siento = I'm sorry
[8]tratar de hacer algo = to try to do something

-o

Meaning: *resulting object; resulting action*
English equivalent: none
Found in: nouns

Many of the following formed words are extremely common—so common, in fact, that it is easy to overlook the properties they share. First, notice that they all come from -*ar* verbs: -*er* and -*ir* verbs generally do not produce nouns that indicate result of action in this fashion. Next, while it is obvious that they all end in -*o*, you will see upon closer inspection that such words always are the same as the verb's first-person, singular *(yo)* form in the present indicative, e.g., *yo trabajo* (I work); *el trabajo* (the work). Thus, when the root is a stem-changing verb, the change will take place in the noun as well as in the verb: *yo almuerzo; el almuerzo*. All words ending in -*o* derived from -*ar* verbs are masculine.

Formed Word	English Equivalent	Related to	English Equivalent
el abrazo	embrace; hug	abrazar	to embrace, hug

Formed Word	English Equivalent	Related to	English Equivalent
el abrigo	overcoat; shelter	abrigar	to shelter, protect, cover
el almuerzo	lunch; luncheon	almorzar	to eat lunch
el atajo	shortcut	atajar	to cut short, interrupt
el atraco	holdup; robbery	atracar	to hold up, rob
el atraso	backward-ness; delay; slowness	atrasar	to slow (down), retard
el aumento[1]	increase; salary raise	aumentar	to increase, augment, magnify
el auxilio[2]	aid; assistance; help	auxiliar	to aid, help, assist
el ayuno	fast; abstinence	ayunar	to fast
el beso	kiss	besar	to kiss
el brillo	brilliancy; luster; shine	brillar[3]	to shine, sparkle, glisten
el castigo	punishment; chastisement	castigar[4]	to punish, castigate, chastise
el comienzo	beginning	comenzar	to begin, commence
el cuento[5]	tale; story	contar	to tell (a story)
el desarrollo	development; growth; expansion	desarrollar	to develop, expand
el desayuno	breakfast	desayunar	to eat breakfast
el descanso	rest; pause; break	descansar	to rest, pause
el ejército[6]	army	ejercitar	to exercise, practice, train, drill

Formed Word	English Equivalent	Related to	English Equivalent
el estudio	study; learning	estudiar	to study
el fracaso	failure; collapse; "flop"	fracasar	to fail, be unsuccessful
el gasto[7]	expenditure; expense	gastar	to spend (time, money, etc.)
el gobierno	government	gobernar	to govern, rule
el gozo	joy; pleasure; enjoyment	gozar	to enjoy
el grito	shout; scream	gritar	to shout, scream
el gusto[8]	taste; pleasure; liking	gustar	to be pleasing (to), like
el hado	fate; destiny	hadar	to divine, foretell, fate
el juego[9]	game; play; playing; gambling	jugar	to play (a game)
el logro	gain; profit; achievement	lograr	to get, achieve
el objeto	object	objetar	to object
el odio	hatred	odiar	to hate
el pago[10]	payment	pagar	to pay, pay for, repay
el paso[11]	step; gait; walk	pasar	to pass, go across
el regreso	return	regresar	to return
el reino	kingdom; realm	reinar	to reign, prevail
el saludo	greeting; wave; salute	saludar[12]	to greet, welcome, salute
el silencio[13]	silence; *(mus.)* rest	silenciar	to silence

Formed Word	English Equivalent	Related to	English Equivalent
el sueño	dream; sleep; sleepiness	soñar[14]	to dream, dream about
el trabajo[15]	work; labor; job	trabajar	to work, labor
el vómito[16]	vomit; vomiting	vomitar	to vomit
el voto[17]	vote; ballot; vow; wish	votar	to vote, vow
el vuelo	flight; flying	volar	to fly

[1]ir en aumento = to increase, grow
[2]auxilio social = social work
[3]brillar por su ausencia = to be conspicuous by one's absence
[4]castigar la vista = to strain one's sight
[5]cuento de viejas = old wives' tale
[6]ejércitos de tierra, mar y aire = armed forces
[7]pagar los gastos = to foot the bill
[8]de buen gusto = in good taste
[9]juego limpio = fair play; juego sucio = foul play
[10](com.) suspender el pago = to stop payment
[11]paso a paso = step by step
[12]saludar militarmente = to salute
[13]pasar en silencio = to pass over, omit
[14]soñar con or soñar en = to dream of
[15]cuesta (mucho) trabajo = it's (very) hard
[16]provocar a vómito = to nauseate
[17]voto de calidad or decisivo = casting vote

-o

Meaning: *tree; plant*
English equivalent: none
Found in: nouns

Several Spanish names for trees and bushes take the suffix -o. An interesting feature of these words is that the name of the relevant fruit or nut often ends with an -a, and this suffix replaces that final letter. In other words, the plant is the masculine form of the fruit it bears: *la cereza* (cherry); *el cerezo* (cherry tree). The only exceptions below are *el cafeto,* from el café and *el cedro* from *la cedria.* All words taking this ending are masculine.

Formed Word	English Equivalent	Related to	English Equivalent
el aceituno	olive tree	la aceituna[1]	olive
el almendro	almond tree	la almendra	almond
el banano	banana tree	la banana	banana

Formed Word	English Equivalent	Related to	English Equivalent
el bergamoto	bergamot tree	la bergamota	bergamot
el cafeto	coffee tree	el café	coffee
el calabazo	pumpkin plant	la calabaza[2]	pumpkin; *(fig.)* bumpkin; clod
el canelo	cinnamon tree	la canela	cinnamon
el castaño	chestnut tree	la castaña[3]	chestnut
el cedro	cedar tree	la cedria	resin from the cedar
el cermeño	pear tree	la cermeña	pear
el cerezo	cherry tree	la cereza	cherry
el ciruelo	plum tree	la ciruela[4]	plum
el frambueso	raspberry bush	la frambuesa	raspberry
el granado	pomegranate tree	la granada	pomegranate
el majuelo	white hawthorn	la majuela	fruit of the white hawthorn
el manzano	apple tree	la manzana[5]	apple
el naranjo	orange tree	la naranja	orange
el olivo	olive tree	la oliva	olive; *(fig.)* olive branch
el sangüeso	raspberry bush	la sangüesa	raspberry
el toronjo	grapefruit tree	la toronja	grapefruit

[1]aceituna rellena = stuffed olive
[2]llevar calabazas = to be jilted
[3]castaña de Pará *or* del Brasil = Brazil nut
[4]ciruela pasa = prune
[5]manzana silvestre = crab apple

-o (-a)
Meaning: *one who;* denotes profession
English equivalent: *-er; -ist*
Found in: nouns

There are thousands of Spanish words ending in *-o*. What distinguishes these words, however, is that they all are derived from a science or calling of sorts and denote the person who practices it. All the examples in the *Related to* column end with *-ía* or *-ia* (with the exception of *la medicina*): from there, simply drop the *-ía* or *ia* and add *-o* (an exception is *el anatómico*, from *la anatomía,* which adds *-ic* before the suffix *-o*). Note that all the formed words have an accent on the antepenultimate syllable. Finally, if the person performing the action is a woman, the ending is *-a: el filósofo; la filósofa.*

Formed Word	English Equivalent	Related to	English Equivalent
el anatómico	anatomist	la anatomía	anatomy
el arqueólogo	archaeologist	la arqueología	archaeology
el astrólogo	astrologist	la astrología	astrology
el astrónomo	astronomer	la astronomía	astronomy
el bígamo	bigamist	la bigamia	bigamy
el biólogo	biologist	la biología	biology
el calígrafo	calligrapher	la caligrafía	calligraphy
el cartógrafo	cartographer; mapmaker	la cartografía	cartography
el coreógrafo	choreographer	la coreografía	choreography
el craneólogo	craniologist	la craneología	craniology
el criptógrafo	cryptographer	la criptografía	cryptography
el cronólogo	chronologist	la cronología	chronology
el ecólogo	ecologist	la ecología	ecology
el filósofo	philosopher	la filosofía	philosophy
el fotógrafo	photographer	la fotografía	photography
el gastrónomo	gastronome; gourmet	la gastronomía	gastronomy
el geógrafo	geographer	la geografía	geography
el geólogo	geologist	la geología	geology
el ginecólogo	gynecologist	la ginecología	gynecology
el médico	doctor; physician	la medicina[1]	medicine
el microbiólogo	microbiologist	la microbiología	microbiology
el misántropo	misanthropist; misanthrope	la misantropía	misanthropy
el mitólogo	mythologist	la mitología	mythology
el monógamo	monogamist	la monogamia	monogamy
el neurólogo	neurologist	la neurología	neurology
el oftalmólogo	ophthalmologist	la oftalmología	ophthalmology

Formed Word	English Equivalent	Related to	English Equivalent
el paleontólogo	paleontologist	la paleontología	paleontology
el patólogo	pathologist	la patología	pathology
el polígamo	polygamist	la poligamia	polygamy
el pornógrafo	pornographer	la pornografía	pornography
el psicólogo	psychologist	la psicología	psychology
el radiólogo	radiologist	la radiología	radiology
el sociólogo	sociologist	la sociología	sociology
el teólogo	theologian	la teología	theology
el tipógrafo	typographer; typesetter	la tipografía	typography; typesetting
el topógrafo	topographer; surveyor	la topografía	topography
el toxicólogo	toxicologist	la toxicología	toxicology

¹medicina casera = home remedies

-ón

Meaning: denotes suddenness or intensity of an action
English equivalent: none
Found in: nouns

One of the meanings the suffix -ón takes is that of denoting a sudden movement or action. Such words all are masculine and are derived from verbs, most of which themselves denote intense or violent actions. When these formed words are made plural, words taking this suffix no longer require an accent mark: *el jalón; los jalones.*

Formed Word	English Equivalent	Related to	English Equivalent
el acelerón¹	acceleration; burst of speed	acelerar	to accelerate, hasten, hurry forward
el achuchón	*(coll.)* squeeze	achuchar	*(coll.)* to squeeze
el aguijón	sting; pinch; goad	aguijar	to goad, incite

Formed Word	English Equivalent	Related to	English Equivalent
el apagón	blackout	apagar[2]	to extinguish, put out, quench
el apretón	sharp pressure; pain; twinge	apretar	to press, tighten, squeeze
el atracón	stuffing; gluttony	atracarse	to stuff oneself with food
el baldón	insult; blot; disgrace	baldonar	to insult, stain, disgrace
el barzón	stroll; saunter	barzonear	to saunter, loiter about
el bebezón	drunken spree	beber[3]	to drink
el chapuzón	(coll.) duck; ducking	chapuzar(se)	to duck
el empujón[4]	hard push; shove	empujar	to push
el encontrón	collision; clash; crash	encontrar(se)	to collide, crash
el estirón	jerk; tug; sharp pull	estirar	to stretch, pull taut
el hinchazón	swelling; vanity; inflation	hinchar[5]	to blow up, inflate, swell
el hurgón	thrust; stab	hurgar	to poke
el jalón	jerk; pull; tug	jalar	to pull, haul, tug
el lametón	hard lick; strong lick	lamer	to lick
el nevazón	snowfall	nevar	to snow
el peleón	fight; fracas; scuffle	pelear	to fight
el pregón	proclamation	pregonar	to cry or proclaim publicly
el punzón	punch	punzar	to punch, puncture, prick

Formed Word	English Equivalent	Related to	English Equivalent
el rascazón	prickling; tickling; itching	rascar	to scratch, itch
el relumbrón	flash; glare; tinsel	relumbrar	to shine brightly
el remesón	plucking out of hair	remesar	to pull out (hair)
el repelón[6]	tug or yank on hair	repelar	to pull hair out
el restregón	hard rubbing; scrubbing	restregar	to rub (hard); to scrub
el retortijón	twisting; contortion	retortijar	to twist, curl
el reventón	burst; blowout	reventar	to explode
el tachón	erasure; crossing out	tachar	to cross out, strike through
el trompicón	stumbling; stumble	trompicar	to trip, trip up
el turbión	squall; heavy rain shower	turbar	to disturb, trouble, stir up
el vomitón	violent vomiting	vomitar	to vomit; *(fig.)* to cough up

[1]dar *or* pegar acelerones = to rev hard, speed
[2]apagar la sed = to quench one's thirst
[3]beber como una cuba = to drink like a fish
[4]a empujones = pushing; shoving; by fits and starts
[5]hincharle a alguien cl ojo = to give someone a black eye
[6]a repelones = by fits and starts

-ón (-ona)

Meaning: *(person) tending to; (person) given to*
English equivalent: none
Found in: adjectives and nouns

In this group, *-ón* can always serve as an adjectival ending, but in many of these words, this suffix also can denote a noun. Thus, one could say, though redundantly, *El preguntón es preguntón* (The nosy man is nosy). Most of these terms are derived from verbs, but can also derive from nouns or other adjectives. All words ending with -*ón* are masculine; when referring to or denoting a feminine noun, these words take the suffix -*ona*. When made plural, the accent on the masculine form no longer is necessary: *el pidón; los pidones.*

Formed Word	English Equivalent	Related to	English Equivalent
abusón	*(coll.)* given to taking advantage of	abusar	to misuse, take advantage
(el) adulón	fawning; groveling (person)	adular	to flatter, dote upon
(el) barbullón	babbling (person)	barbullar	to babble
(el) besucón	heavy kissing; necking (person)	besucar	to kiss, neck with
(el) bocón	wide-mouthed (person)	la boca	mouth
(el) burlón	given to mocking (joker)	burlar	to mock, laugh at
(el) cabezón	fatheaded; egomaniacal (person)	la cabeza[1]	head
calentón	unpleasantly warm or hot	caliente[2]	warm; hot
(el) cincuentón	fifty years old or fiftyish (person)	cincuenta	fifty
(el) comilón	heavy eating (big eater)	comer	to eat
(el) criticón	critical; faultfinding (person)	criticar	to criticize
(el) cuarentón	forty years old or fortyish (person)	cuarenta	forty
gordón	*(coll.)* pretty fat or hefty	gordo[3]	fat
gritón	*(coll.)* vociferous; bawling	gritar	to shout, cry out, scream
guapetón	tall, dark, and handsome	guapo	handsome
holgachón	*(coll.)* fond of ease and little work	holgar[4]	to rest, be idle, have free time

Formed Word	English Equivalent	Related to	English Equivalent
juguetón	playful; frolicsome	jugar	to play (a game)
(el) llorón	weepy (crybaby)	llorar	to cry, weep
(el) mandón	domineering; bossy (person)	mandar	to order, command
(el) mirón	gazing; gawking (onlooker)	mirar[5]	to look at, watch
(el) narizón	big-nosed (person)	la nariz	nose
(el) orejón	big-eared (person)	la oreja	ear
peleón	given to fighting	pelear	to fight
(el) pidón	greedy (person)	pedir[6]	to request, ask for
politicón	keen on politics; overly polite	político[7]	polite; diplomatic
(el) preguntón	nosy, questioning (person)	preguntar	to ask (a question)
regalón	(coll.) luxury loving; spoiled	regalar	to give a present
replicón	(coll.) given to answering back	replicar	to answer back, argue back
reservón	very reserved, secretive	reservar	to reserve, keep secret
respondón	(coll.) cheeky; saucy	responder	to answer, reply
temblón	shaky; tremulous	temblar	to shake, tremble
(el) tomón	"sticky-fingered" (thief)	tomar[8]	to take
(el) tragón	greedy; gluttonous (person)	tragar[9]	to swallow, gulp down
vomitón	given to vomiting	vomitar	to vomit

[1] no levantar cabeza = to have one's nose to the grindstone
[2] hacer algo en caliente = to do something in the heat of the moment
[3] premio gordo = first prize
[4] huelga decir que = needless to say
[5] mirar de hito en hito = to look up and down

⁶pedir limosna = to ask (for) alms, beg
⁷padre político = father-in-law
⁸tomar el sol = to sunbathe
⁹tragar quina = to lump it, grin and bear it

-ón; -ona
Meaning: augmentative; pejorative
English equivalent: none
Found in: nouns

The suffix -*ón,* or -*ona* when the referent is a feminine noun, is a common augmentative ending in Spanish. In addition to the increase in physical size, this suffix also can hold pejorative connotations, e.g., *la novela* (novel) leads to *el novelón* (long, tedious third-rate novel). Gender change with this suffix can yield markedly different meanings, as illustrated by the examples *el moscón* and *la moscona,* both derived from *la mosca.*

Formed Word	English Equivalent	Related to	English Equivalent
el avispón	hornet	la avispa	wasp
el barbón	full-bearded man	la barba	beard
el barcón	big boat	el barco	boat
el bolsón	large purse; tote bag	la bolsa[1]	purse; bag; money-bag
el cajón	drawer; crate	la caja[2]	box; case
el calenturón	violent fever	la calentura	fever; temperature
el camón	large bed; portable throne	la cama	bed
el caserón	big run-down house	la casa	house
el cochostrón	*(coll.)* filthy or revolting person	el cocho	*(prov.)* pig; filthy person
el comedión	long, tedious comedy or play	la comedia	comedy; play
el cortezón	thick bark or rind or crust	la corteza	bark; peel; rind; crust
el cortinón	large curtain	la cortina	curtain
el culebrón	large snake	la culebra[3]	snake
el gigantón	enormous giant	el gigante	giant
el goterón	large raindrop	la gota	drop; raindrop

Formed Word	English Equivalent	Related to	English Equivalent
el guión	leader (of a dance)	el guía	guide; leader
el hombretón	hefty fellow	el hombre	man
el hombrón	big, lusty man; he-man	el hombre[4]	man
el manchón	big dirty spot or stain	la mancha	spot; stain
el memorión	phenomenal memory	la memoria[5]	memory
el moscón	big fly	la mosca[6]	fly
la mujerona	stout, lusty woman; hefty creature	la mujer	woman
el narigón	big nose	la nariz	nose
el novelón	long, tedious third-rate novel	la novela	novel
el pavón	peacock	el pavo[7]	turkey
el rodeón	long detour; complete turn	el rodeo[8]	detour; roundabout way
el sillón	big overstuffed easy chair	la silla	chair
la solterona	spinster	la soltera	unmarried woman
el tazón	basin	la taza	cup
el vocejón	harsh voice	la voz	voice
el zapatón	big shoe; "gunboat"	el zapato[9]	shoe

[1] bolsa de agua caliente = hot-water bottle
[2] caja de música = music box
[3] saber más que las culebras = to be very crafty
[4] hombre de pelo en pecho = real he-man
[5] encomendar a la memoria = to commit to memory
[6] mosca de burro or mosca de caballo = horsefly
[7] la edad del pavo = the teens
[8] andarse con rodeos = to beat around the bush
[9] como tres en un zapato = like sardines in a tin

-or (-ora)

Meaning: *one who;* denotes profession or machine
English equivalent: *-or*
Found in: nouns

Among the several Spanish suffixes that indicate a person who does something is the ending *-or*. This ending also can denote a machine, as in *el interruptor* (electrical switch). Such terms are derived from verbs, and nearly always have as their English counterparts close cognates, which makes these terms easy to learn and use. When the referent is female, the ending is *-ora*.

Formed Word	English Equivalent	Related to	English Equivalent
el actor	actor; performer; player	actuar	to act, perform
el ascensor	elevator	ascender	to ascend, go up, rise
el auditor[1]	judge; auditor; adviser	*(Lat.)* audire	to hear
el autor	author; writer; composer	*(Lat.)* augere	to increase, produce
el compositor	composer	componer[2]	to compose
el comprensor	one who understands	comprender	to understand, comprehend
el compresor[3]	compressor	comprimir	to compress, condense, constrain
el conductor	leader; driver; conductor	conducir	to conduct, guide, drive (a vehicle)
el confesor	confessor	confesar[4]	to confess
el consultor	consultant; consultor; adviser	consultar[5]	to consult
el depresor	oppressor; *(anat., surg.)* depressor	deprimir	to depress; *(fig.)* to humiliate
el destructor	destroyer	destruir	to destroy
el detector	detector	detectar	to detect, spot
el director	director; manager; chief	dirigir	to direct, manage, govern, control

Formed Word	English Equivalent	Related to	English Equivalent
el editor	publisher	editar	to publish
el ejecutor	executor	ejecutar	to execute
el escritor	writer	escribir[6]	to write
el escultor	sculptor; carver	esculpir	to sculpt, carve
el eyector	ejector	eyectar	to eject
el expositor	expounder; exhibitor	exponer	to expound, exhibit, cxposc
el impresor	printer	imprimir	to print, imprint, impress
el inspector	inspector	inspeccionar	to inspect
el instructor	instructor	instruir	to instruct, teach, train
el interruptor[7]	interrupter; *(elec.)* switch	interrumpir	to interrupt, discontinue
el interventor	comptroller; supervisor; auditor	intervenir	to audit, inspect, tap (a telephone line)
el inventor	inventor; fabricator	inventar	to invent, fabricate
el lector	reader; teaching assistant	leer[8]	to read
el mentor	mentor	*(Lat.)* monere	to admonish
el opositor	opponent; competitor	oponer	to oppose
el pastor	shepherd; (Prostestant) clergyman	pastorear	to pasture, graze
el pintor	painter	pintar[9]	to paint, depict
el profesor	professor; teacher	profesar	to profess, practice

Formed Word	English Equivalent	Related to	English Equivalent
el rector	rector; principal	rectorar	to attain the office of rector
el redactor	editor; copy editor	redactar	to edit, word, draw up
el seductor	seducer; charmer	seducir[10]	to seduce, allure, tempt, entice
el subdirector	assistant manager	sub + dirigir	under + to direct, manage, govern, control

[1]auditor de guerra (de marina) = military (naval) adviser
[2]componer el semblante = to compose one's countenance
[3]compresor de aire = air compressor
[4]confesarse = to make a confession
[5]consultar con la almohada = to sleep on it
[6]escribir a máquina = to type (out)
[7]interruptor de dos (tres) direcciones = two- (three-)way switch
[8]leer cátedra = to occupy a university chair
[9]ella se pinta mucho = she wears a lot of makeup
[10]no me seduce la idea = the idea doesn't appeal to me

-orio
Meaning: *place where; means by which*
English equivalent: *-ory*
Found in: nouns

The Spanish noun ending *-orio* has two distinct meanings: (1) *place where,* and (2) *means by which.* In the former, we find mostly rooms and buildings whose names generally are derived from the verb expressing the action performed in them: *el lavatorio* (lavatory; washroom) comes from *lavar* (to wash). The second meaning, *means by which,* indicates the thing necessary for carrying out the action denoted in the root verb: *el aspersorio* (water sprinkler) is needed in order to sprinkle *(aspergear).* All nouns ending in *-orio* are masculine.

Formed Word	English Equivalent	Related to	English Equivalent
el adoratorio	Indian temple	adorar[1]	to adore, worship

Formed Word	English Equivalent	Related to	English Equivalent
el aspersorio	water sprinkler	aspergear	to sprinkle, spray
el auditorio	auditorium	*(Lat.)* audire	to hear
el conservatorio	conservatory	conservar[2]	to conserve
el convictorio	students' quarters	el convictor	boarder; pensioner
el declinatorio	declinator (instrument)	declinar	to decline
el dedicatorio	dedication; inscription	dedicar[3]	to dedicate
el defensorio	plea; defense	defender	to defend, shield
el depilatorio	depilatory	depilar	to depilate
el destilatorio	distillery	destilar	to distill
el directorio	directory; directorate	dirigir	to direct, manage, govern
el divisorio	geological divide	dividir[4]	to divide
el dormitorio	bedroom; dormitory	dormir[5]	to sleep
el enjuagatorio	mouthwash	enjuagar	to rinse
el escritorio	writing desk; office; study	escribir[6]	to write
el laboratorio	laboratory	laborar	to labor, work
el lavatorio	lavatory; washstand	lavar	to wash
el nalgatorio	*(coll.)* posterior; seat; buttocks	la nalga	buttock; rump
el observatorio	observatory	observar	to observe
el ofertorio	offertory	ofrecer[7]	to offer
el parlatorio	parlor	parlar	to chatter, babble
el purgatorio	purgatory	purgar	to purge, cleanse
el reformatorio	reformatory	reformar	to reform, amend

Formed Word	English Equivalent	Related to	English Equivalent
el sanatorio	sanatorium	sanar	to heal, cure
el territorio	territory	la tierra[8]	land; earth

[1]adorar a Dios = to worship God
[2]está (muy) bien conservado = he looks (very) young for his age
[3]dedicarse a = to dedicate oneself to
[4]no me puedo dividir = I can't be in two places at the same time
[5]dormir la mona = to sleep it off
[6]¿Cómo se escribe? = How do you spell it?
[7]ofrecerse (a) = to volunteer (to)
[8]ver tierras = to see the world

-orio (-oria)

Meaning: *like; relating to*
English equivalent: *-ory*
Found in: adjectives

As an adjectival ending, *-orio* has two salient features. First, note below that all the examples are derived from verbs (except *textorio,* which comes from the noun *el texto*) and that nearly all of them are *-ar* verbs. Second, when the derivation is an *-ar* verb, the *-ar* is replaced by *-at* before adding *-orio* (*inflamar* gives us *inflamatorio*); there is no standard formation rule for those adjectives derived from *-er* and *-ir* verbs. Words ending with *-orio* take *-oria* when describing feminine nouns.

Formed Word	English Equivalent	Related to	English Equivalent
aclamatorio	with acclaim	aclamar	to acclaim, applaud
aclaratorio	explanatory	aclarar	to make clear, explain
acusatorio	accusatory	acusar	to accuse, charge, prosecute
adivinatorio	divinatory	adivinar	to guess, divine, solve
aprobatorio	approbatory; approving	aprobar	to approve
circulatorio	circulatory	circular	to circulate
cobratorio	pertaining to collecting	cobrar[1]	to collect

Formed Word	English Equivalent	Related to	English Equivalent
conciliatorio[2]	conciliatory	conciliar	to conciliate, reconcile
decisorio	(law) decisive	decidir	to decide
declamatorio	declamatory	declamar	to declaim, recite
dedicatorio	dedicatory	dedicar	to dedicate
depilatorio	depilatory	depilar	to depilate, remove hair
discriminatorio	discriminatory	discriminar	to discriminate
giratorio[3]	rotatory; revolving	girar	to rotate, revolve
gratulatorio	congratulatory	gratular	to congratulate
inflamatorio	inflammatory	inflamar	to inflame, set afire
laudatorio	laudatory	laudar	(law) to give judgment on
masticatorio	chewing	masticar	to chew, masticate
meritorio	meritorious	merecer[4]	to deserve, merit
mortuorio	of the dead	morir[5]	to die
obligatorio	obligatory	obligar	to oblige
operatorio	operative	operar	to operate
oscilatorio	oscillatory	oscilar	to oscillate, fluctuate
prohibitorio	prohibitory	prohibir[6]	to prohibit
promisorio	promissory	prometer	to promise
purificatorio	purificatory	purificar	to purify
recomendatorio	recommendatory	recomendar	to recommend
satisfactorio	satisfactory	satisfacer	to satisfy
sublimatorio	sublimatory	sublimar	to sublimate

Formed Word	English Equivalent	Related to	English Equivalent
sudatorio	sudorific; pertaining to sweat	sudar	to sweat, perspire
textorio	textorial	el texto	text; textbook
undulatorio	undulatory	undular	to undulate, rise in waves
vibratorio	vibratory	vibrar	to vibrate, shake

---

[1]cobrar un cheque = to cash a check
[2]palabras conciliatorias = conciliatory words
[3]puerta giratoria = revolving door
[4]merece la pena = it's worth it, worth the trouble
[5]morir de viejo = to die of old age
[6]se prohibe el paso = no thoroughfare

-osis

Meaning: *condition; process; disease*
English equivalent: *-osis*
Found in: nouns

Words ending with *-osis,* in English as well as in Spanish, often are medical terms that denote a diseased condition. Below are listed several such terms, many of which are commonly used. As you will see, not all refer to a sickness, e.g., *la ósmosis* (osmosis). Though these words are not related directly to other Spanish terms, they are easy to recognize as cognates of their English counterparts. All words ending with *-osis* are feminine.

Formed Word	English Equivalent	Related to	English Equivalent
la acidosis	acidosis	*(Lat.)* acidus	sour
la alcalosis	alkalosis	el álcali	*(chem.)* alkali
la amaurosis	amaurosis	*(Gr.)* amauros	dim
la arteriosclerosis	arteriosclerosis	*(Lat.)* arteria + *(Gr.)* skleros	artery + hard
la cirrosis	cirrhosis	*(Gr.)* kirrhos	orange-colored
la endometriosis	endometri-osis	*(Gr.)* endon + metra	within + uterus
la esclerosis	sclerosis	*(Gr.)* skleros	hard

Formed Word	English Equivalent	Related to	English Equivalent
la estenosis	stenosis	(Gr.) stenos	narrow
la fibrosis	fibrosis	(Lat.) fibra	fiber
la halitosis	halitosis	(Lat.) halitus	breath
la hipnosis	hypnosis	(Gr.) hypnos	sleep
la melanosis	melanosis	(Gr.) melas	black
la metamorfosis	metamorphosis	(Gr.) meta + morphe	beyond + form
la miosis	miosis	(Gr.) meiosis	diminution
la nefrosis	nephrosis	(Gr.) nephros	kidney
la neurosis	neurosis	(Gr.) neuron	nerve
la ósmosis	osmosis	(Gr.) osmos	impulse
la psicosis	psychosis	(Gr.) psyche	the mind
la queratosis	keratosis	(Gr.) keras	horn
la silicosis	silicosis	(Lat.) silex	flint
la simbiosis	symbiosis	(Gr.) syn + bios	with + life
la triquinosis	trichinosis	(Gr.) trichinos	hairlike
la trombosis	thrombosis	(Gr.) thrombos	clot
la tuberculosis	tuberculosis	(Lat.) tuberculum	small swelling

-oso (-osa)
Meaning: *full of; having*
English equivalent: *-ous; -ful; -y*
Found in: adjectives

A Spanish word ending in *-oso* signifies that the person or object described possesses characteristics of the root noun. Nouns ending in a vowel generally drop that vowel and take on the *-oso* ending, while *-oso* is added directly to words ending with a consonant. In some cases, the root noun will undergo a slight spelling change (e.g., *temeroso* from *el temor*); but the root still is recognizable. Remember that as *-oso* is an adjectival ending, it will become *-osa* when the formed word describes a feminine noun.

Formed Word	English Equivalent	Related to	English Equivalent
carnoso	fleshy	la carne	flesh; meat
codicioso	covetous; greedy	la codicia	greed
cuidadoso	careful	el cuidado[1]	care

Formed Word	English Equivalent	Related to	English Equivalent
doloroso	painful; distressing	el dolor[2]	pain; sorrow; regret
dudoso	doubtful	la duda	doubt
escandaloso	scandalous	el escándalo	scandal
espantoso	frightful	el espanto	fright
fabuloso	fabulous	la fábula	fable
gozoso	joyful	el gozo	joy; enjoyment
huesoso	bony	el hueso	bone
humoso	smoky	el humo	smoke
jubiloso	jubilant; joyful	el júbilo	jubilation; joy
lastimoso	pitiful	la lástima[3]	pity
lujoso	luxurious	el lujo[4]	luxury
lloroso	tearful	el lloro	crying; weeping
mantecoso	buttery; greasy; fatty	la manteca	lard; grease; fat; pomade
maravilloso	wonderful; marvelous	la maravilla	wonder; marvel
mentiroso	lying	la mentira[5]	lie
milagroso	miraculous; marvelous	el milagro[6]	miracle
misterioso	mysterious	el misterio	mystery
mocoso	(coll.) snot-nosed; dirty-nosed	el moco	mucus
nervioso	nervous	el nervio	nerve
odioso	hateful	el odio	hatred; hate
pegajoso	sticky	la pega	sticking; cementing
peligroso	dangerous	el peligro[7]	danger; peril
perezoso	lazy; slothful	la pereza	sloth

Formed Word	English Equivalent	Related to	English Equivalent
poderoso[8]	powerful; mighty	el poder	power; might
polvoroso	dusty	el polvo	dust
pomposo	pompous	la pompa[9]	pomp
pulgoso	flea-ridden	la pulga	flea
rencoroso	spiteful	el rencor	spite
respetuoso	respectful	el respeto	respect
sabroso	tasty; delicious	el sabor[10]	taste; flavor; relish
temeroso	fearful	el temor	fear
venenoso	poisonous	el veneno	poison
ventoso	windy	el viento[11]	wind

[1] a cuidado de = in care of
[2] ¡Qué dolor! = How sad!
[3] ¡Qué lástima! = What a pity! What a shame!
[4] de lujo = deluxe
[5] coger a alguien en una mentira = to catch someone in a lie
[6] vida y milagros = life and times
[7] correr peligro = to be in danger
[8] poderoso caballero es don dinero = money is power
[9] pompas fúnebres = funeral ceremony
[10] a sabor = to one's liking
[11] vientos alisios = trade winds

-ote; -ota

Meaning: augmentative; pejorative; *like; relating to*
English equivalent: none
Found in: nouns; adjectives

The suffix *-ote* or *-ota* serves as an augmentative that sometimes carries negative connotations: *el pajarote* is a big clumsy bird (from *el pájaro*). This ending is more commonly a noun ending, but performs essentially the same function as an adjectival ending, namely, enlarging upon the root: from *feo* (ugly), we get *feote* (big and ugly). Nouns ending with *-ote* are masculine, while those ending with *-ota* are feminine. An adjective ending with *-ote* takes the ending *-ota* when describing a feminine noun.

Formed Word	English Equivalent	Related to	English Equivalent
el amigote	*(coll.)* pal; buddy; crony	el amigo[1]	friend

Formed Word	English Equivalent	Related to	English Equivalent
el angelote	large figure of an angel	el ángel[2]	angel
el animalote	big animal; (coll.) ignorant person	el animal	animal; creature
la bancarrota	bankruptcy; failure	el banco	bank
barbarote	utterly rude; coarse	bárbaro	barbaric; savage
el barcote	big boat	el barco	boat
blancote	excessively white or pale	blanco[3]	white
el bobote	great idiot or simpleton	el bobo	fool; dimwit
el borricote	(coll.) utter ass; plodder	el borrico	ass
el bravote	(sl.) bully	bravo	brave; valiant; manly
el caballerote	clumsy, loutish knight	el caballero[4]	knight; gentleman
el camarote	(naut.) stateroom	la cámara	chamber; room
el cerote	shoemaker's wax	la cera	wax
el chicote	husky youngster	el chico	boy; youngster; lad
feote	big and ugly	feo	ugly
el frailote	big, coarse friar	el fraile	friar; monk
francote	plainspoken	franco[5]	frank; open; candid
el gatote	big cat	el gato[6]	cat
grandote	very big; hulking great	grande	big; large
guapote	(coll.) really good-looking	guapo	handsome
el librote	huge book	el libro	book

Formed Word	English Equivalent	Related to	English Equivalent
el lugarote	ugly, sprawling village	el lugar[7]	place; village; spot
la machota	mannish woman	el macho	male
el machote	real he-man; tough guy	el macho	male
la muchachota	tomboy	la muchacha	girl; lass
el muchachote	hefty lad	el muchacho	boy; lad
la narizota	ugly, huge nose	la nariz[8]	nose
el pajarote	clumsy, big bird	el pájaro	bird
el papelote	wretched piece of paper; rubbish	el papel[9]	paper
el perrote	big dog	el perro	dog
el pipote	keg	la pipa	cask
el villanote	great villain	el villano	villain

[1] amigo del alma *or* amigo del corazón = bosom buddy
[2] ángel malo = evil genius
[3] Blanca Nieves = Snow White
[4] ser todo un caballero = to be every inch a gentleman
[5] franco de servicio = off-duty
[6] a gatas = on all fours
[7] en primer lugar = in the first place
[8] meter la nariz en = to stick one's nose in
[9] papel de lija = sandpaper

-sión

Meaning: *state of being; result of action; act*
English equivalent: *-sion*
Found in: nouns

Words ending with *-sión* are derived from verbs. Generally speaking, the *-ar, -er* or *-ir,* along with the final consonant of the infinitive are dropped, and then *-sión* is added. Very rarely does a Spanish word ending with *-sión* have as its English equivalent *-tion.* Only two examples are given below in which this is the case: *la contorsión* (contortion) and *la distorsión* (distortion); otherwise, the English ending virtually always is *-sion.* All words ending in *-sión* are feminine, and drop the accent mark when made plural: *la decisión; las decisiones.*

Formed Word	English Equivalent	Related to	English Equivalent
la accesión	accession	acceder[1]	to accede, agree, consent

Formed Word	English Equivalent	Related to	English Equivalent
la aspersión	aspersion; sprinkling; spraying	aspergear	to sprinkle
la comisión[2]	commission; trust	cometer	to commit, entrust
la concesión	concession	conceder	to concede
la confusión	confusion	confundir	to confuse
la contorsión	contortion	contornar	to contour, wind around a place
la decisión	decision	decidir	to decide
la depresión	depression	deprimir	to depress
la difusión	diffusion; diffuseness; vagueness	difundir[3]	to diffuse, spread
la distorsión	distortion; twisting; spraining	distorsionar	to distort, twist
la expansión	expansion	expansionar	to expand
la extensión	extension	extender[4]	to extend, enlarge, spread (out)
la fusión	fusion	fusionar	to fuse, amalgamate
la incisión	incision	incidir	to incise, cut into
la invasión	invasion	invadir	to invade
la inversión	inversion; investment	invertir	to invert, reverse, invest
la oclusión	occlusion	ocluir	to occlude, close
la percusión	percussion	percutir	to percuss, strike
la posesión	possession	poseer	to possess, own
la precisión	precision; preciseness	precisar	to specify

Formed Word	English Equivalent	Related to	English Equivalent
la progresión	progression	progresar	to progress
la propulsión[5]	propulsion	propulsar	to propel, drive
la repulsión	repulsion	repulsar	to check, rebuff, reject
la subversión	subversion	subvertir	to subvert
la suspensión	suspension	suspender	to suspend
la televisión	television	televisar	to televise
la transfusión[6]	transfusion	transfundir	to transfuse, transmit, spread
la transgresión	transgression	transgredir	to transgress, sin
la transmisión	transmission	transmitir	to transmit, broadcast
la visión[7]	vision	*(Lat.)* videre	to see

[1]acceder a la petición = to accede or grant the request
[2]*(com.)* comisión mercantil = commission; percentage
[3]está muy difundido = it's very widespread
[4]extender un cheque = to write out a check
[5]avión de propulsión a chorro = jet-propelled aircraft
[6]transfusión de sangre = blood transfusion
[7]ver visiones = to see things

-tad; -stad

Meaning: *state of being;* forms abstract noun
English equivalent: *-ty*
Found in: nouns

The endings *-tad* and *-stad* are relatively uncommon in Spanish. Words taking these endings generally refer to an abstraction or intangible quality, e.g., *la lealtad* (loyalty), from the adjective *leal* (loyal). All words ending in *-tad* or *-stad* are feminine.

Formed Word	English Equivalent	Related to	English Equivalent
la amistad[1]	friendship; amity	el amigo	friend
la dificultad[2]	difficulty	difícil	difficult
la enemistad	hatred; enmity	el enemigo[3]	enemy

Formed Word	English Equivalent	Related to	English Equivalent
la facultad	school; faculty; power	(Lat.) facultas	feasibility; power; means
la lealtad	loyalty	leal[4]	loyal; faithful
la libertad[5]	liberty; freedom	libre[6]	free; detached
la majestad	majesty	majo	boasting; blustering; swaggering
la voluntad[7]	will; willpower; willingness	(Lat.) voluntas	will; wish; inclination

[1]trabar amistad = to strike up a friendship
[2]tener muchas dificultades = to have a great deal of trouble
[3]ser enemigo de = to be against
[4]según su leal saber y entender = to the best of his knowledge
[5]libertad de palabra = freedom of speech
[6]al aire libre = in the open (air)
[7]a voluntad = at will

-teca
Meaning: *place where things are collected and stored*
English equivalent: none
Found in: nouns

Those few Spanish words ending with *-teca* indicate a kind of library or place where a specific object is stored. Such words always are feminine.

Formed Word	English Equivalent	Related to	English Equivalent
la biblioteca[1]	library	(Gr.) biblion	book
la discoteca	discotheque; record library	el disco	record
la filmoteca	film library	el filme	film
la hemeroteca	newspaper, magazine, and periodical library	(Gr.) hemero	day
la pinacoteca	picture gallery; place where paintings are stored	la pintura	painting

[1]biblioteca de consulta = reference library; biblioteca circulante = lending library

-triz

Meaning: denotes profession or role of female
English equivalent: *-ess*
Found in: nouns

Spanish words ending with *-triz* denote an occupation or role held by a woman. In English, we usually use *-ess* to make such a distinction, although current common usage does not always distinguish between the two (*poetess* has now generally fallen out of usage). In Spanish, however, the distinction continues and *-triz* is one suffix to demonstrate it, usually by adding this ending to the stem of the root verb. As would be expected, all such terms are feminine.

Formed Word	English Equivalent	Related to	English Equivalent
la actriz[1]	actress	actuar[2]	to act
la adoratriz	cloistered nun	adorar[3]	to adore, worship
la cantatriz	female singer	cantar[4]	to sing
la emperatriz	empress	el emperador	emperor
la fregatriz	kitchen maid	fregar	to scrub, scour, swab, mop (floor)
la institutriz	governess	instituir	to instruct, teach, train, educate
la mediatriz	female mediator	mediar	to mediate
la meretriz	prostitute	*(Lat.)* merere	to earn
la protectriz	protectress	proteger	to protect, favor, patronize
la saltatriz	female ballet dancer	saltar[5]	to jump, leap, spring

[1]primera actriz = leading lady
[2]actuar de = to act as
[3]adorar a Dios = to worship God
[4]quien canta mal, bien le suena = we are all blind to our own defects
[5]saltarse una línea = to skip a line

-uco; -uca
Meaning: diminutive; endearing; deprecative
English equivalent: none
Found in: nouns

Included among the many diminutive and/or deprecative suffixes in Spanish are *-uco* and *-uca*. As with many diminutive endings, the smallness can be physical, e.g., *el ventanuco* (small window), from *la ventana* (window); at times it can also be deprecative, with diminution in quality as well, e.g., *el cuartuco* (miserable little room), from *el cuarto* (room). The diminutive aspect also can express a charming quality, as in the references to animals below, e.g., *el gatuco* (cute little kitty), from *el gato* (cat). Words ending with *-uco* are masculine, while those taking *-uca* are feminine.

Formed Word	English Equivalent	Related to	English Equivalent
el abejaruco	*(orn.)* bee eater	la abeja[1]	bee
el almendruco	green almond	la almendra	almond
el animaluco	cute little animal	el animal	animal
el becerruco	cute little bull	el becerro	young bull
el caballuco	cute little horse	el caballo	horse
el carruco	small cart	el carro[2]	cart; carriage; car
la casuca	miserable house; hovel	la casa[3]	house
el cuartuco	miserable little room	el cuarto[4]	room
el frailuco	despicable friar	el fraile	friar; monk
el gatuco	cute little cat; kitty	el gato	cat
la gitanuca	little gypsy woman	la gitana	gypsy woman
el hermanuco	*(contempt.)* lay brother	el hermano[5]	brother
el ladronuco	petty thief; pickpocket	el ladrón	thief
el maizuco	little ear of corn	el maíz	maize; corn; Indian corn
el muchachuco	cute little boy	el muchacho	boy; lad
la mujeruca	slovenly woman	la mujer[6]	woman
el niduco	little nest	el nido	nest

Formed Word	English Equivalent	Related to	English Equivalent
la obruca	little piece of work; small task	la obra	work; piece of work; task; chore
el pajarruco	cute little bird	el pájaro	bird
el pastuco	little plot of grass	el pasto[7]	pasture; pasture-ground
la patatuca	little potato	la patata[8]	potato
la peluca	wig	el pelo	hair
el perruco	cute little dog; doggie	el perro	dog
el postruco	little dessert	el postre[9]	dessert; sweet
la puertuca	little door	la puerta	door
la sobruca	little bit left over	la sobra[10]	surplus; excess
la tienduca	little store or shop	la tienda	store; shop
la tierruca	small piece of land; garden bed	la tierra	land; earth
el tontuco	cute, silly little person	el tonto	silly person
el ventanuco	small window	la ventana[11]	window
el vientuco	little breeze	el viento	wind

[1] abeja madre *or* abeja reina = queen bee
[2] ¡alto el carro! = hold your horses!
[3] casa flotante = houseboat
[4] cuarto de costura = sewing room
[5] hermano político = brother-in-law
[6] tomar mujer = to take a wife
[7] a pasto = galore
[8] patatas fritas = potato chips
[9] llegar a los postres = to arrive (too) late
[10] las sobras = leftovers (food)
[11] echar por la ventana = to throw away, squander

-ucho; -ucha
Meaning: pejorative; diminutive (nouns); augmentative (adjectives); *like*
English equivalent: none
Found in: nouns; adjectives

The ending -*ucho* or -*ucha* could be termed the "too much of a good thing" suffix. As you will see below, when -*ucho* or -*ucha* is added to the base word, the resulting word often suggests excess or something that has gotten out of hand: from *el café,* we get *el cafetucho,* which is a dump, a terrible place to go for coffee. Or consider *blando* (soft) and the resulting *blanducho* (flabby). When the root word is a noun, the formed word also will be a noun; similarly, when the base word is an adjective, it will remain an adjective when this suffix is added. At times this suffix is merely a diminutive, as in *el aguilucho* (eaglet), from *el águila* (eagle). Adjectives ending with -*ucho* will take -*ucha* when describing nouns of the feminine gender. Words ending in -*ucho* are masculine, while those ending in -*ucha* are feminine.

Formed Word	English Equivalent	Related to	English Equivalent
el aguaducho	stream; stall for selling water	el agua *(f.)*[1]	water
el animalucho	wretched, ugly little creature	el animal[2]	animal
el avechucho	wretched, ugly bird	el ave *(f.)*[3]	bird
blanducho	overly soft; flabby	blando	soft
el cafetucho	wretched little café; dump	el café	café
el calducho	thin, tasteless soup or stock	el caldo	broth; clear soup
calentucho	revoltingly warm or hot	caliente[4]	warm; hot
la camucha	wretched little bed	la cama	bed
el capirucho	dunce cap	el capirote[5]	academic hood
el carrucho	wretched little cart	el carro	cart; car; carriage
la casucha	run-down house	la casa[6]	house
clarucho	watery; thin	claro	clear
el cuartucho	miserable little room	el cuarto	room
delgaducho	overly thin; scrawny	delgado	thin; slim
endeblucho	very weak or flimsy	endeble	feeble; flimsy
enfermucho	a bit off color; groggy	enfermo	sick; ill
feúcho	*(coll.)* rather ugly; plain	feo	ugly
flacucho	scrawny; overly thin	flaco[7]	thin; lean; weak

Formed Word	English Equivalent	Related to	English Equivalent
flojucho	rather loose, on the floppy side	flojo	loose; slack
larguirucho	*(coll.)* lanky; gangling	largo	long
malucho	*(coll.)* sickly; groggy	malo[8]	ill; sick; bad
el medicucho	third-rate doctor; quack	el médico[9]	doctor
el papelucho	wretched piece of paper; rubbish	el papel[10]	paper
el periodicucho	tabloid; "rag"	el periódico	newspaper; periodical
el santucho	*(coll.)* hypocrite	el santo	saint
el serrucho	handsaw	la sierra	saw
templaducho	tepid	templado	temperate; moderate; warm
la tenducha	wretched little shop; "dump"	la tienda	shop; store

[1]agua bendita = holy water
[2]¡qué animal! = what a brute *or* beast!
[3]ave de rapiña = bird of prey
[4]caliente de cascos = hot-headed
[5]tonto de capirote = dunce
[6]casa de moneda = mint
[7]punto flaco = weak point
[8]ser malo = to be bad or naughty; estar malo = to be sick, feel lousy
[9]médico partero = obstetrician
[10]papel pintado = wallpaper

-udo (-uda)

Meaning: augmentative; having (a great deal of the root noun)
English equivalent: none
Found in: adjectives

The augmentative suffix -*udo* indicates that the person or thing being described possesses a lot of the root term: *un hombre peludo* is a man with a lot of hair. As you will see below, this suffix often is attached to names of body parts. Remember that when describing a noun of feminine gender, the suffix will change to -*uda,* as in M*aría es narizuda* (Mary has a big nose).

Formed Word	English Equivalent	Related to	English Equivalent
barbudo	full-bearded	la barba[1]	beard
barrigudo	(coll.)big-bellied; pot-bellied	la barriga	belly; bulge (in a wall)
bigotudo[2]	heavily mustached	el bigote	mustache
bocudo	having a big mouth	la boca[3]	mouth
cabezudo	having a big head	la cabeza	head
caderudo	having large hips	la cadera	hip
cejudo	having bushy eyebrows	la ceja	eyebrow
ceñudo	frowning	el ceño	frown
cornudo	horned	el cuerno	horn
dentudo	having big teeth	el diente[4]	tooth
espaldudo	having broad shoulders	las espaldas[5]	shoulders; back
felpudo[6]	plushy; downy	la felpa	plush
huesudo	bony; big-boned	el hueso[7]	bone
jetudo	snouted; big-lipped	la jeta	hog's snout; big lips
juanetudo	having bunions	el juanete	bunion
lanudo	woolly; fleecy	la lana[8]	wool
mantudo	having drooping wings (bird)	el manto	mantle; cloak; robe
molletudo	chubby-cheeked	la molla	(coll.) fat (of a person)
nalgudo	having big buttocks	la nalga	buttock
narizudo	having a big nose	la nariz	nose
orejudo	flap-eared; long-eared	la oreja	ear
pantorrilludo	having large or thick calves	la pantorrilla	calf (of the leg)
panzudo	having a big belly	la panza	belly
papudo	having a double chin	el papo	double chin
patudo	having big feet or paws	la pata[9]	foot; paw

Formed Word	English Equivalent	Related to	English Equivalent
peludo	hairy; hirsute	el pelo	hair
picudo	beaked	el pico	beak; bill
rodilludo	having big knees	la rodilla	knee
talludo	grown-up; overgrown	el tallo	stem; stalk
tetuda	having large breasts; busty	la teta	breast; teat
tozudo	obstinate; stubborn; pigheaded	la toza	block of wood; stump
zancudo	having long legs	el zanco	stilt
zapatudo	wearing big shoes	el zapato	shoe

[1] por barba = per cápita; apiece
[2] ser bigotudo = (fig.) to be tough, have guts
[3] andar de boca en boca = to be the talk of the town
[4] echar los dientes = to teethe, cut (one's) teeth
[5] a espaldas de alguien = behind someone's back
[6] el felpudo = doormat
[7] estar en los huesos = to be extremely thin, skin and bones
[8] ser un Juan Lanas = to be a nobody
[9] pata de palo = wooden or peg leg

-uelo; -uela
Meaning: diminutive
English equivalent: none
Found in: nouns

The endings -uelo and -uela indicate smallness of the root noun. At times this smallness can be figurative, as in el embusteruelo (little fibber), which is derived from el embustero (fibber); however, most of the time it means small in the literal sense, e.g., la hojuela (small leaf) from la hoja (leaf). Note below the slight difference in meaning between el hoyuelo and la hoyuela. This pair of suffixes has sister suffixes, -zuelo and -zuela, which are similar in function. Nouns ending in -uelo are masculine, while those ending with -uela are feminine.

Formed Word	English Equivalent	Related to	English Equivalent
la abejuela	little bee	la abeja[1]	bee
la callejuela	alley	la calle[2]	street
la cejuela	small eyebrow	la ceja	eyebrow
la corderuela	little ewe-lamb	el cordero	lamb
el chicuelo	small boy	el chico	boy

Formed Word	English Equivalent	Related to	English Equivalent
la chicuela	small girl	la chica	girl
el embusteruelo	little fibber	el embustero	fibber
el espejuelo	looking glass	el espejo[3]	mirror
la habichuela	kidney bean	la haba	bean
la hachuela	hatchet	el hacha *(f.)*	axe
el hijuelo	*(bot.)* shoot	el hijo	son; child; offspring
la hojuela	small leaf	la hoja[4]	leaf; petal; sheet; blade
la hoyuela	hollow (in the neck)	la hoya	hole
el hoyuelo	little hole; dimple	el hoyo	hole
la lentejuela[5]	spangle; sequin	la lenteja	lentil
la meajuela	small crumb	la meaja	crumb
la migajuela	small crumb or scrap	la migaja	crumb; scrap
el ojuelo	small eye	el ojo[6]	eye
la pajuela	sulfur match; short straw	la paja	straw
el pañuelo	handkerchief	el paño[7]	cloth
el patrañuelo	little story; white lie	la patraña	cock-and-bull story; yarn; lie
el polluelo	chick	el pollo	chicken
la portañuela	fly (of trousers)	la portañola	porthole
la sortijuela	little ring; ringlet	la sortija[8]	ring; curl (of hair)
el vallejuelo	tiny valley; dell	el valle[9]	valley; vale; glen
la viñuela	small vineyard	la viña	vineyard
la viruela[10]	smallpox; pockmark	el virus	virus

[1] abeja madre *or* abeja reina = queen bee; abeja neutra *or* abeja obrera = worker bee
[2] calle arriba *or* abajo = up or down the street
[3] espejo de cuerpo entero = full-length mirror
[4] hoja de afeitar = razor blade
[5] vestir de lentejuelas = to be very pompous, showy

⁶no pegar ojo = not to sleep a wink
⁷ser del mismo paño = to be of the same ilk
⁸sortija de sello = signet ring
⁹valle de lágrimas = vale of tears
¹⁰viruelas locas = chicken pox

-undo (-unda)
Meaning: *like; relating to*
English equivalent: *-und*
Found in: adjectives

The suffix *-undo* is an adjectival ending implying that someone or something has characteristics of the root term. Many words ending in *-undo* come directly from Latin, and at times the formed word and the base term are mere translations of one another. When a Spanish root does exist, a consonant often is inserted between that root and the ending *-undo,* the most common being the letter *b*, e.g., *nauseabundo* (nauseating), from *la nausea* (nausea). When used to describe feminine nouns, words ending with *-undo* take *-unda.*

[AU]
English

English Formed Word	Equivalent	Related to	Equivalent
cogitabundo	pensive; musing	cogitar	to reflect, meditate
errabundo	wandering; aimless	errar¹	to miss, get wrong, mistake
facundo	eloquent; loquacious	(*Lat.*) facundus	eloquent
fecundo	fecund; fertile	(*Lat.*) fecundare	to fertilize
furibundo	furious; raging	la furia	fury; rage
gemebundo	groaning; moaning	gemir	to groan, moan, wail, whine
infacundo	ineloquent	(*Lat.*) infacundus	not eloquent
infecundo	infertile; sterile	(*Lat.*) in + fecundare	not + to fertilize
inmundo	dirty; filthy; unclean; impure	(*Lat.*) in + mundus	not + neat; clean; nice
iracundo	ireful; wrathful	la ira	ire; wrath
jocundo	jocund	(*Lat.*) jocus	joke
meditabundo	meditative	meditar	to meditate

Formed Word	English Equivalent	Related to	English Equivalent
moribundo	moribund; dying	morir	to die
nauseabundo	loathsome; nauseating	la nausea	nausea; seasickness
oriundo	native of; coming from	*(Lat.)* oriundus	descended; sprung; born
profundo	profound	*(Lat.)* profundus	deep; boundless; vast
pudibundo	modest; bashful; shy	el pudor	modesty; bashfulness
rotundo	rotund; round	*(Lat.)* rotundus	rounded; circular
rubicundo	rubicund; red; rosy	el rubí	ruby
segundo[2]	second	*(Lat.)* secundus	second; next; following
tremebundo	dreadful; fearful	*(Lat.)* tremebundus	trembling
vagabundo	vagabond	vagar	to wander, roam
verecundo	bashful; shy	*(Lat.)* verecundus	bashful; shy; modest

[1]errar el camino = to take the wrong road, miss one's way
[2]de segunda mano = secondhand

-uno (-una)

Meaning: *like; relating to; pertaining to*
English equivalent: none
Found in: adjectives

The adjectival suffix *-uno* is interesting not so much for what it does (there are several endings meaning *like* and *relating to*) but instead for its specialized use in reference to animals. While this suffix is not restricted solely to the animal kingdom, it is generally the suffix of choice where animals are concerned. When used to describe a feminine noun, words ending with *-uno* take *-una*.

Formed Word	English Equivalent	Related to	English Equivalent
abejuno	pertaining to bees	la abeja[1]	bee
bajuno	base; low; vile	el bajo[2]	deep place
boquiconejuno	harelipped	la boca; el conejo	mouth; rabbit
boyuno	bovine	el buey	ox
caballuno	pertaining to horses; equine	el caballo[3]	horse
cabrituno	pertaining to a kid	el cabrito	kid; young goat
cabruno	goatish; goatlike	el cabrón	buck; he-goat
carneruno	pertaining to sheep; ovine	el carnero	sheep (ram)
cervuno	pertaining to deer	el ciervo	deer; stag; hart
conejuno	pertaining to rabbits	el conejo[4]	rabbit
corderuno	pertaining to lambs	el cordero[5]	lamb
gatuno	pertaining to cats; feline	el gato	cat
hombruno	mannish	el hombre[6]	man
lebruno	harelike	la liebre	hare
lobuno	wolfish	el lobo	wolf
machuno	mannish; manly	el macho	male
montuno	pertaining to the mountain; wild	el monte	mountain
moruno	Moorish	el moro	Moor; Mohammedan
osuno	pertaining to bears; osine	el oso[7]	bear
ovejuno	pertaining to sheep; ovine	la oveja	sheep (ram)
perruno	pertaining to dogs; canine	el perro[8]	dog
porcuno	pertaining to pigs; porcine	el puerco[9]	pig; hog
raposuno	of the fox	el reposo	dog-fox

Formed Word	English Equivalent	Related to	English Equivalent
vacuno	pertaining to cows; bovine	la vaca	cow
zorruno	foxlike	el zorro	fox

¹abeja de miel = honey bee
²bajo relieve = bas-relief
³a caballo regalado no le mires el diente = don't look a gift horse in the mouth
⁴es una coneja = she breeds like a rabbit; she's always having children
⁵cordero pascual = paschal lamb
⁶hombre de mundo = man of the world
⁷oso blanco = polar bear
⁸perro braco = setter; perro cobrador = retriever
⁹puerco espín = porcupine

-uo (-ua)

Meaning: *like; relating to*
English equivalent: *-uous*
Found in: adjectives

Spanish adjectives ending in *-uo* nearly always correspond to English cognates ending in *-uous*. Although such words are derived from Latin, there are very few Spanish words that employ the same root. Because this is an adjectival ending, words ending in *-uo* take *-ua* to modify feminine nouns. Note that one term below, *el residuo,* is a noun.

Formed Word	English Equivalent	Related to	English Equivalent
ambiguo	ambiguous	*(Lat.)* ambigere	to wander about, waver
arduo	arduous	*(Lat.)* arduus	steep; high
asiduo	assiduous	*(Lat.)* assidere	to sit near
congruo	congruous	*(Lat.)* congruere	to come together, agree
conspicuo	conspicuous	*(Lat.)* conspicere	to get sight of, perceive
contiguo¹	contiguous; next; adjacent	*(Lat.)* contiguus	contiguous; near; touching
continuo	continuous	*(Lat.)* continere	to hold together

Formed Word	English Equivalent	Related to	English Equivalent
discontinuo	discontinuous	(Lat.) dis + continuus	not + continuous
estrenuo	strenuous	(Lat.) strenuus	strenuous
fatuo	fatuous; conceited; foolish	(Lat.) fatuus	fatuous; foolish; inane
incongruo	incongruous	(Lat.) in + congruus	not + congruous; incompatible
individuo	individual	(Lat.) in + dividuus	not + divisible
ingenuo	ingenuous	(Lat.) ingenuus	inborn; freeborn; noble; frank
inocuo	innocuous; harmless	(Lat.) in + nocere	not + to hurt
longincuo	distant; remote	(Lat.) longe	long; far off; distant; remote
melifluo	mellifluous	(Lat.) mel + fluere	honey + to flow
menstruo	menstruous	(Lat.) mensis	month
oblicuo	oblique	(Lat.) obliquus	slanting; inclined
occiduo	occidental	(Lat.) occidere	to fall, set
perpetuo	perpetual; everlasting	(Lat.) perpetuus	continuous; throughout
perspicuo	perspicuous	(Lat.) perspicere	to look through
precipuo	principal; chief	(Lat.) praecipuus	special; chief; principal
promiscuo	promiscuous	(Lat.) promiscuus	mixed
el residuo	residue; remainder	(Lat.) residuus	remaining

Formed Word	English Equivalent	Related to	English Equivalent
somnílocuo	talking in sleep	*(i.)* somnus + loquor	sleep + to speak
superfluo	superfluous	*(Lat.)* super + fluere	over + to flow
ubicuo	ubiquitous; omnipresent	*(Lat.)* ubique	everywhere
vacuo	vacuous	*(Lat.)* vacuus	empty

[1]contiguo al garaje = next to the garage

-ura

Meaning: *state of being;* forms abstract noun
English equivalent: *-ness*
Found in: nouns

The following words that end in *-ura* all are derived from adjectives. The addition of this suffix forms an abstract noun, an intangible that refers to the state or qualities of the root adjective. All words ending with *-ura* are feminine.

Formed Word	English Equivalent	Related to	English Equivalent
la albura	perfect whiteness; white of egg	albo	*(poet.)* snow white
la altura[1]	height; altitude	alto[2]	high; tall
la amargura	bitterness	amargo	bitter
la anchura	width	ancho	wide
la bajura	shortness; lowness	bajo[3]	short; low
la blancura[4]	whiteness	blanco	white
la blandura	softness	blando	soft
la bravura	courage; fierceness; manliness	bravo	brave; valiant; manly
la dulzura	sweetness	dulce	sweet
la espesura	thickness; denseness	espeso	thick; dense
la estrechura	narrowness; closeness; tight spot	estrecho[5]	tight; narrow; close
la finura	fineness; delicacy	fino	fine; delicate

Formed Word	English Equivalent	Related to	English Equivalent
la flacura	thinness	flaco	thin
la gordura	fatness	gordo[6]	fat; corpulent; stout; thick; big
la grosura	grossness; crudeness	grosero	gross; crude; coarse
la hermosura	beauty; handsomeness	hermoso	beautiful; handsome
la holgura	roominess	huelgo	room; space
la hondura	depth	hondo	deep
la largura	length	largo	long
la listura	smartness; quickness	listo[7]	smart; quick
la lisura	smoothness; evenness; glibness	liso[8]	smooth; plain
la locura	madness; insanity	loco[9]	mad; crazy; insane
la llanura	evenness; flatness	llano	even; flat
la negrura	blackness	negro	black
la rojura	redness	rojo	red
la secura	dryness	seco	dry
la soltura	looseness	suelto	loose
la ternura	tenderness	tierno	tender
la tersura	smoothness	terso	smooth
la tiesura	stiffness	tieso[10]	stiff; rigid; firm
la verdura[11]	greenness	verde	green

---

[1]pesca de altura = deep-sea fishing
[2]hablar en voz alta = to speak aloud, out loud
[3]hablar en voz baja = to speak quietly, in a low voice
[4]blancura del ojo = white of the eye
[5]de manga estrecha = strict; narrow-minded
[6]agua gorda = hard water
[7]ser listo = to be smart, sharp, astute; estar listo = to be ready, prepared
[8]liso y llano = plain and simple
[9]estar loco de remate = to be stark raving mad
[10]tenerse tieso = to stick to one's guns
[11]las verduras = greens; vegetables

-ura; -uro; -urar

Meaning: *result of action; state of being; process; (to) act*
English equivalent: *-ure*
Found in: nouns; adjectives; verbs *(-urar)*

English words ending in *-ure*—which may be nouns, adjectives, or verbs—nearly always are cognates of their Spanish counterparts. Spanish words ending with *-ura, -uro* or *-urar,* nearly all of which come directly from Latin, are therefore easy to recognize, use, and learn. Thus, a few tips: (1) The nouns almost always are feminine, and end with *-ura* (the only masculine term below is *el futuro*). (2) Adjectives, as would be expected, end with *-uro,* and take the ending *-ura* when describing feminine nouns. (3) English verbs ending with *-ure* almost always will take the verb ending *-urar* in Spanish, e.g., *fracturar* (to fracture). Verbs ending with *-urar* are regular.

Formed Word	English Equivalent	Related to	English Equivalent
la abertura	opening (physical)	*(Lat.)* aperire	to open
la apertura	opening (figurative)	*(Lat.)* aperire	to open
la aventura	adventure	*(Lat.)* advenire	to reach, arrive
la captura	capture	*(Lat.)* capere	to capture
capturar	to capture	*(Lat.)* capere	to capture
caricatura	caricature	*(Lat.)* carricare	to charge, overload, exaggerate
la censura	censure	*(Lat.)* censere	to give an opinion
censurar	to censure, censor	*(Lat.)* censere	to give an opinion
la criatura	creature	criar[1]	to create, breed, foster
la cultura	culture	*(Lat.)* colere	to till, cultivate
la cura[2]	cure	*(Lat.)* curare	to care for
curar[3]	to cure, heal	*(Lat.)* curare	to care for
la escultura	sculpture	esculpir	to sculpt, carve
la estatura	stature	*(Lat.)* stare	to stand
la estructura	structure	*(Lat.)* struere	to arrange, construct
la fractura[4]	fracture; breaking	*(Lat.)* frangere	to break

Formed Word	English Equivalent	Related to	English Equivalent
fracturar	to fracture	*(Lat.)* frangere	to break
el futuro	future	*(Lat.)* futura	future
impuro	impure	*(Lat.)* in + purus	not + pure
inseguro	insecure	*(Lat.)* in + securus	not + free from care
la lectura	lecture	*(Lat.)* legere	to pick
la literatura	literature	*(Lat.)* litera	letter (of the alphabet)
madurar	to mature, ripen, mellow	*(Lat.)* maturare	to mature, ripen
maduro	mature; ripe	*(Lat.)* maturus	ripe; seasonable
la manicura	manicure	*(Lat.)* manus + cura	hand + care
oscuro	dark; obscure	*(Lat.)* obscurus	covered
la pastura	pasture	*(Lat.)* pascere	to pasture, feed
perjurar	to perjure	*(Lat.)* per + jurare	through + to swear
la pintura	painting; picture; paint	*(Lat.)* pingere	to paint
la postura	posture	*(Lat.)* ponere	to place, put, posit
puro[5]	pure	*(Lat.)* purus	pure
seguro[6]	secure; sure; safe	*(Lat.)* securus	without care
la signatura	signature	*(Lat.)* signare	to mark
la temperatura	temperature	*(Lat.)* temperare	to temper, blend, regulate

[1]Dios los cría y ellos se juntan = birds of a feather flock together
[2]no tiene cura = it (he/she) is hopeless
[3]curar al humo = to smoke (meat, etc.)
[4]fractura complicada = compound fracture
[5]a puro trabajar = by sheer hard work
[6]de seguro = for sure; very probably

-usco (-usca); -uzco (-uzca)

Meaning: *like; relating to*
English equivalent: *-ish*
Found in: adjectives

Words ending in *-usco* and *-uzco* occur infrequently. Note that they often have names of colors as base terms. As they are adjectives, when used to describe feminine nouns, the endings become *-usca* and *-uzca,* respectively.

Formed Word	English Equivalent	Related to	English Equivalent
blancuzco	whitish	blanco[1]	white
corusco	shining	coruscar	to shine, coruscate
negruzco	blackish	negro[2]	black
pardusco	drab; dark brown	pardo	dull grayish-brown
verdusco	greenish	verde[3]	green

[1]blanco del ojo = white of the eye
[2]negro de humo = lamp-black; soot
[3]chiste verde = dirty joke

-uto; -uta

Meaning: *relating to; result of action*
English equivalent: *-ute*
Found in: adjectives; nouns

A Spanish word ending in *-uto* or *-uta* nearly always has an English counterpart that ends with *-ute.* Such suffixes can be found at the end of adjectives or nouns (*-uto* is a more common noun ending than *-uta*). Spanish adjectives ending in *-uto* are almost always derived from Latin, while most nouns ending in *-uto* or *-uta* have a Spanish base (at times a verb ending with *-utar*). One term below, *(el) minuto,* can perform as either a noun or an adjective; the derivation is the same for both formed words. Nouns ending with *-uto* are masculine, while those ending with *-uta* are feminine. Adjectives ending with *-uto* take the ending *-uta* when describing feminine nouns.

Formed Word	English Equivalent	Related to	English Equivalent
absoluto[1]	absolute	absolver[2]	to absolve, acquit
astuto	astute	*(Lat.)* astutus	shrewd; discerning
el atributo	attribute	atribuir	to attribute

Formed Word	English Equivalent	Related to	English Equivalent
bruto[3]	brutish; coarse; beastly; gross	(Lat.) brutus	dull; insensible
el bruto	brute; beast	(Lat.) brutus	dull; insensible
convóluto	(bot.) convolute; convoluted	(Lat.) convolvere	to roll around
diminuto	diminutive	disminuir	to diminish, lessen
disoluto	dissolute; debauched	disolver	to dissolve, break up
la disputa[4]	dispute	disputar	to dispute, argue (over)
enjuto[5]	dry	enjutar	(build.) to dry
hirsuto	hirsute	(Lat.) hirsutus	hairy
impoluto	unpolluted; spotless	(Lat.) in + polluere	not + to pollute
insoluto	unpaid; insolvent	(Lat.) in + solvere	not + to free from restriction
el instituto	institute	instituir	to institute, establish
involuto	(bot.) involute	(Lat.) involvere	to roll in, envelop
irresoluto	irresolute; unwavering	(Lat.) in + resolvere	not + to loosen
(el) minuto	minute	(Lat.) minutus	small
poluto	polluted; soiled	(Lat.) polluere	to pollute
la prostituta	prostitute	prostituir	to prostitute
resoluto	resolute	(Lat.) resolvere	to loosen, relax
el sustituto	substitute	sustituir	to substitute, replace

Formed Word	English Equivalent	Related to	English Equivalent
el tributo	tribute; tax	tributar	to pay (as tribute or tax)
la voluta	volute; spiral ring	*(Lat.)* volvere	to roll

[1] *(mil.)* licencia absoluta = discharge
[2] absolver de una obligación = to release from an obligation
[3] beneficio bruto = gross profit; peso bruto = gross weight
[4] sin disputa = beyond dispute
[5] a pie enjuto = without getting one's feet wet; without toil

-zuelo; -zuela

Meaning: diminutive
English equivalent: none
Found in: nouns

The endings *-zuela* and *-zuelo* indicate smallness of the root noun. At times this smallness can be deprecative, e.g., *el pintorzuelo* (wretched painter), which is derived from *el pintor* (painter); however, usually it means small in the physical sense, e.g., *la cabezuela* (small head), from *la cabeza* (head). This pair of suffixes has sister suffixes, *-uelo* and *-uela,* which are similar in function. Nouns ending in *-zuelo* are masculine; those ending with *-zuela* are feminine. Note Venezuela's charming derivation.

Formed Word	English Equivalent	Related to	English Equivalent
el actorzuelo	wretched actor; ham	el actor	actor; performer
la bestezuela	small beast; creature	la bestia[1]	beast
la cabezuela	small head	la cabeza	head
el cabezuelo	dolt; "blockhead"	la cabeza[2]	head
el cantorzuelo	wretched singer	el cantor	singer; songbird
la cazuela	casserole	el cazo	pot; saucepan
el cedazuelo	small sieve	el cedazo	sieve
el corpezuelo	small body; carcass	el cuerpo[3]	body
la chozuela	miserable little hovel	la choza	hut; hovel
el escritorzuelo	miserable writer; hack	el escritor	writer
la fontezuela	small fountain	la fontana	fountain

Formed Word	English Equivalent	Related to	English Equivalent
el garbanzuelo	small chick-pea	el garbanzo	chick-pea
el herrezuelo	scrap of iron	el hierro[4]	iron
el ladronzuelo	petty thief; pickpocket	el ladrón[5]	thief
la lanzuela	small lance	la lanza[6]	lance
la lengüezuela	small tongue	la lengua[7]	tongue
la mujerzuela	*(coll.)* prostitute	la mujer	woman
el ovezuelo	small egg	*(arch.)* la ova	egg (shape)
la piecezuela	little piece	la pieza[8]	piece; fragment; part
el pintorzuelo	wretched painter	el pintor[9]	painter
el pobrezuelo	poor little wretched person	el pobre	poor person
el pontezuelo	small bridge	el puente	bridge
la pozuela	pond; puddle	el pozo[10]	well; pit
la puertezuela	small door	la puerta[11]	door
el puertezuelo	small port	el puerto[12]	port; harbor; haven
el reyezuelo	princeling; petty ruler	el rey[13]	king; ruler
la rodezuela	tiny wheel	la rueda[14]	wheel
las tenazuelas	tweezers	la tenaza	pincer; nipper; claw
Venezuela	Venezuela; "little Venice"	Venecia	Venice
el ventrezuelo	small belly	el vientre	abdomen; belly
la viejezuela	little old woman	la vieja	old woman
el viejezuelo	little old man	el viejo	old man

[1]bestia de carga = beast of burden
[2]cabeza de chorlito = scatterbrain
[3]cuerpo y alma = heart and soul
[4]hierro colado *or* fundido = cast-iron
[5]ladrón de corazones = lady-killer
[6]lanza en ristre = ready for action

[7]ligero *or* suelto de lengua = free with one's tongue; outspoken
[8]pieza de recambio *or* repuesto = spare part
[9]pintor de brocha gorda = housepainter
[10]pozo negro = cesspool
[11]a puerta cerrada = behind closed doors
[12]puerto franco = free port
[13]el día de Reyes = Epiphany; Twelfth Night
[14]rueda de andar = treadmill; rueda de presos = police line-up

INDEX

NOUNS

ADJECTIVES

VERBS

ADVERB